IMAGES
of America

CANDLEWOOD LAKE

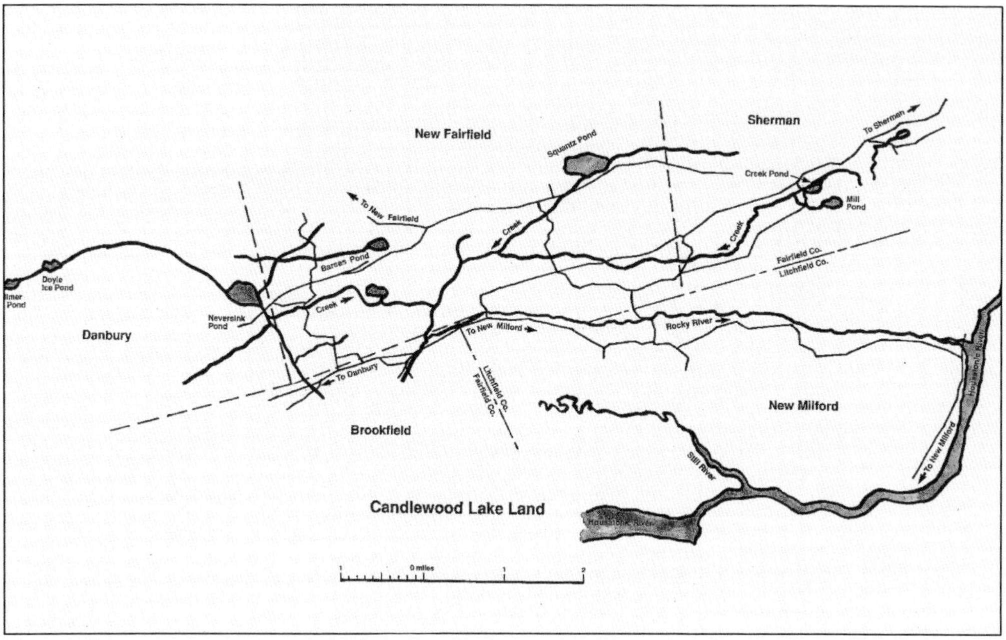

Shown here is an outline of the area before Candlewood Lake was created. The five Connecticut towns that were affected were Brookfield, Danbury, New Fairfield, New Milford, and Sherman.

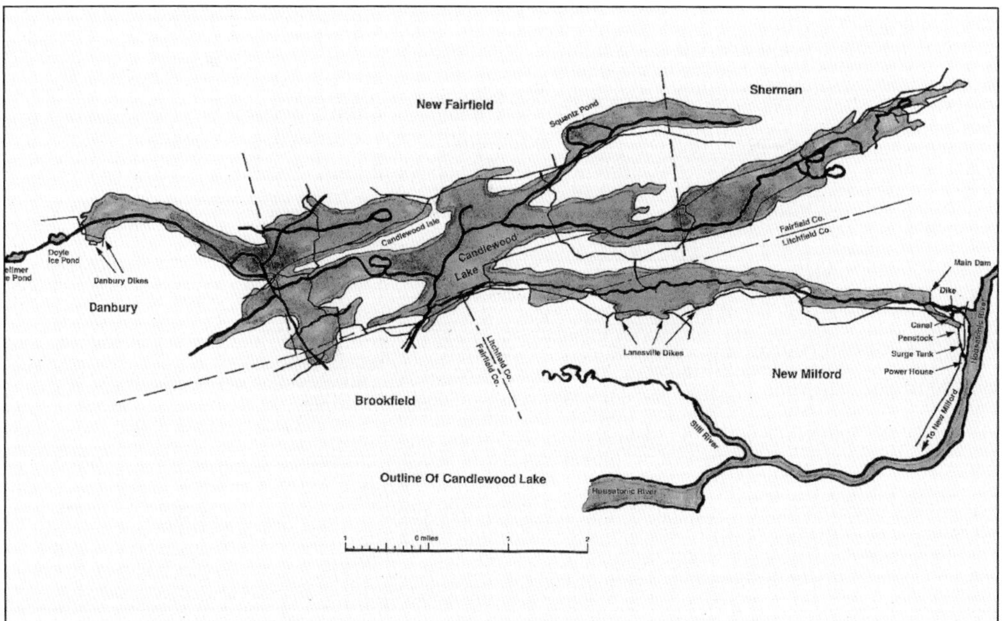

Shown here is the same area after the flooding of what is now Candlewood Lake—the largest lake in Connecticut.

IMAGES
of America

CANDLEWOOD LAKE

Susan Murphy and Gary Smolen

ARCADIA
PUBLISHING

ISBN 978-0-7385-3602-6

Published by Arcadia Publishing
Charleston, South Carolina

Printed in the United States of America

Library of Congress Catalog Card Number: 2004103397

For all general information contact Arcadia Publishing at:
Telephone 843-853-2070
Fax 843-853-0044
E-mail sales@arcadiapublishing.com
For customer service and orders:
Toll-Free 1-888-313-2665

Visit us on the Internet at www.arcadiapublishing.com

On the cover: Deer Run Shores in Sherman, Connecticut.

Contents

ACKNOWLEDGMENTS

Collecting photographs to tell the story of Candlewood Lake is difficult only in that there are so many to choose from. In addition, the descriptions and details that accompany the photographs are what bring life to this story. Those who need to be acknowledged in this book for their consistent help with all of the above are: Bob Brown and Marilyn Whittlesey of the Brookfield Historical Society and Museum; Gloria Thorne of the Sherman Historical Society; Brigid Guertin of the Danbury Museum; Pamela Edwards of the New Milford Historical Society; Carol Ballard of the New Fairfield Historical Society; as well as Bob Gates and Rosemary Plue of Northeast Generation Services Company; and Alton P. Davis Jr., an engineering consultant.

Among the photographs that were lent to us for inclusion in this book are the many original construction photographs from Northeast Generation Company. Other generous contributors include: Len Copicoetto, Bradley Fisher, Peter Bertolami, Raymond Kelley, Teresa Fiamengo, Bruce Byers, John Furlong, Russell Kaye, David Mullen, Jaime Ferris, John B. Gordon, Margaret Laakkonen, Priscilla Eller, and Larry Marsicano and Brian Wood of the Candlewood Lake Authority.

INTRODUCTION

Imagine sitting in a rocking chair on the front porch of a farmhouse in a small valley in western Connecticut during the late spring of 1926. The conversation drifts from the tobacco crops that have been sown to how a mill is operating on the Rocky River, and finally to the fishing in nearby Neversink Pond.

Now imagine a group of businessmen at the same time, sitting in a boardroom discussing the next venture to help their young electric company grow. They see the flooding of a valley and the construction of a new powerplant, the first of its kind in America.

On July 15, 1926, these two worlds collided, as that is when the board of directors of a young Connecticut Light and Power Company approved the construction of the Rocky River powerplant and the necessary creation of Candlewood Lake to fuel it. The idea was to build a new electric plant powered by water, but with a twist that was untested on this scale in America. Instead of building this hydroelectric plant in just the conventional way by damming a river and capturing the power of water as it flowed downhill, this one was to have a unique difference. It would also pump water uphill and store this water for use at a more desirable time. Although it consumed more power in the pumping process, this engineer's dream had merit because with the growth of the new steam-powered electric plants, there would be cheap excess electricity as consumer demand fluctuated, and this would make this plant profitable and useful. These pumps were also necessary because the natural drainage behind the dams was not great enough and could not fill or maintain the lake level by Mother Nature alone.

So with an army of 50 surveyors and a team of lawyers to facilitate the purchase of some 6,000 acres of land in five towns, the project was quickly under way. Some of the land that needed to be purchased had been held in the same families since before the American Revolution, while some had been held for much shorter periods. Regardless, the utility holding the power of eminent domain loomed in the background, and the group started to purchase the land at "fair, pre-lake prices," which equalled \$2,356 for 53 acres, \$3,000 for 34 acres, \$100 for 3.5 acres, and so on.

Construction began almost immediately, and at times more than 1,000 men labored to conquer the many tasks that lay ahead. Some 4,500 acres of trees needed to be cut and burned in massive bonfires reminiscent of Native American campfires that once burned here during the previous centuries. Six cemeteries needed to be relocated. Thirty-five families that once called this valley home needed to move. Several cottages owned by seasonal residents, near the five natural ponds in the valley, needed to be sold. Thirty-one miles of road were abandoned, and another nine and a quarter miles of road needed to be built. In total, about one mile of dams and dikes had to be built at seven locations to build up the lower-lying valleys, with the main dam measuring 952 feet long and 100 feet high. In order to facilitate this workforce, a temporary construction village was built to provide housing, a mess hall, and even supporting shops such as a barbershop, a store, and a bank.

At the same time, the powerhouse, water inlet structure, and water pipe (or penstock) needed to be built as necessary structures for the cause. Inside this powerhouse, there was one large conventional hydroelectric unit, two pumps, and the required equipment to support these machines. The pumps are 8,100 horsepower, and at the time of installation, they were the largest in the world.

Candlewood Lake became the largest lake in Connecticut. It has a surface area of over 8.5 square miles (some 5,500 acres), is almost 11 miles long, and is 2 miles wide at its widest point. It has over 60 miles of shoreline, is about 85 feet deep at its deepest point (averages about 30 feet deep), and contains about 46 billion gallons of water. Water can be pumped from the Housatonic River to Candlewood Lake with the two pumps at a rate of over 3,700 gallons per second. If this process is reversed, and all three units are used to generate electricity, water will flow into the Housatonic River at a rate of over 15,500 gallons per second.

In a little over one and a half years, the project was complete enough to start pumping water. On February 25, 1928, the first water from the Housatonic River was pumped uphill some 225 feet into the new lake. On September 29, 1928, 26 months after construction began, the water reached an elevation of 429 feet, and the project was considered complete. The cost was some $6.5 million.

This project also represents a truly great engineering accomplishment. Although not well known, the American Society of Mechanical Engineers and the American Society of Civil Engineers both recognize this project as a major accomplishment in history, and they have independently honored this project with their respective awards of historical engineering significance. This places the Rocky River and Candlewood Lake Project amongst such notable company as the Empire State Building, Golden Gate Bridge, and select others around the country.

We celebrate the 75-year history of Rocky River and Candlewood Lake with this book. It is a great pictorial history of an industrial dream that forever changed the personality of western Connecticut and especially the five towns that border Candlewood Lake. If we return to our rocking chair, the discussion now is less likely to be about crops or mills, but very well could be about fishing. However, discussion about Neversink Pond is very unlikely. With the construction of Candlewood Lake, that pond was sunk.

One

GENERATING POWER

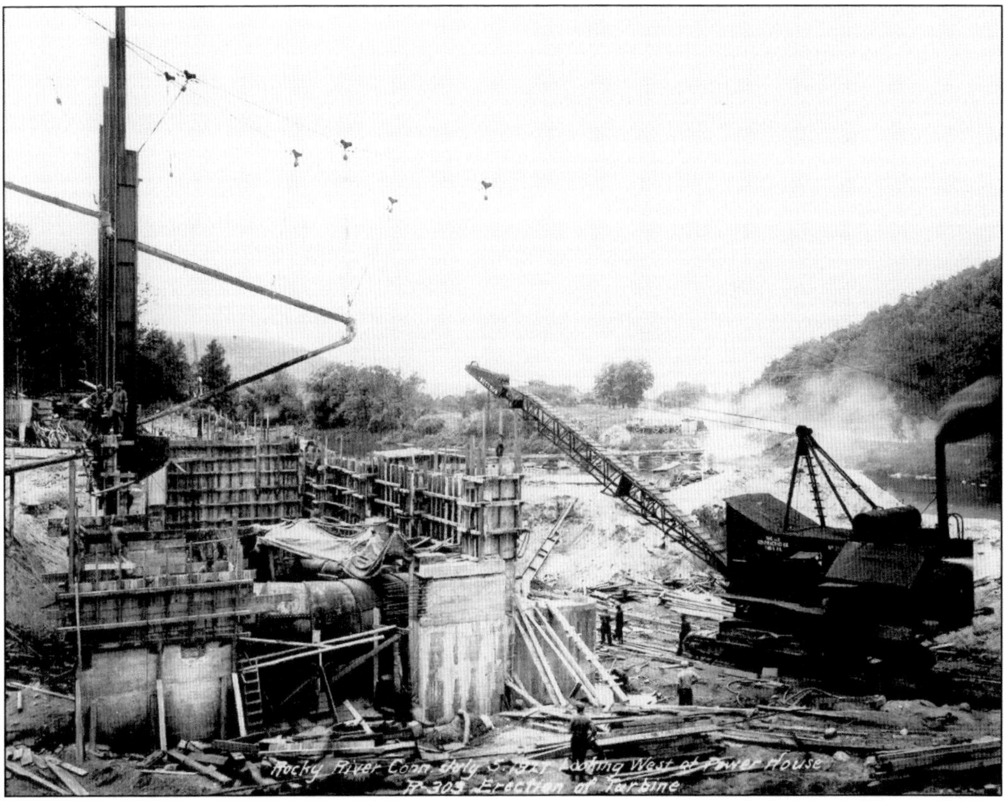

In this view upstream, one of the earliest photographs of the Rocky River powerhouse—taken on July 5, 1927—shows the foundation and the steel water conduit for the turbine.

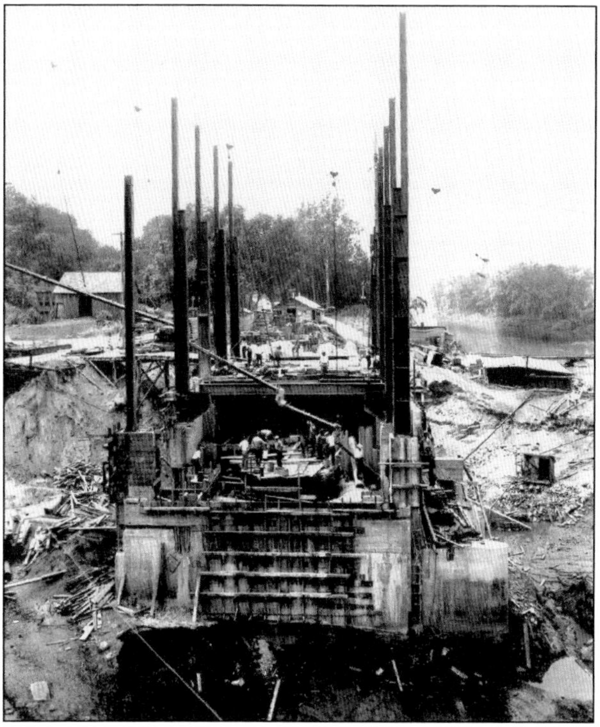

This July 15, 1927 photograph shows the foundation closed in and steel columns for the powerhouse in place.

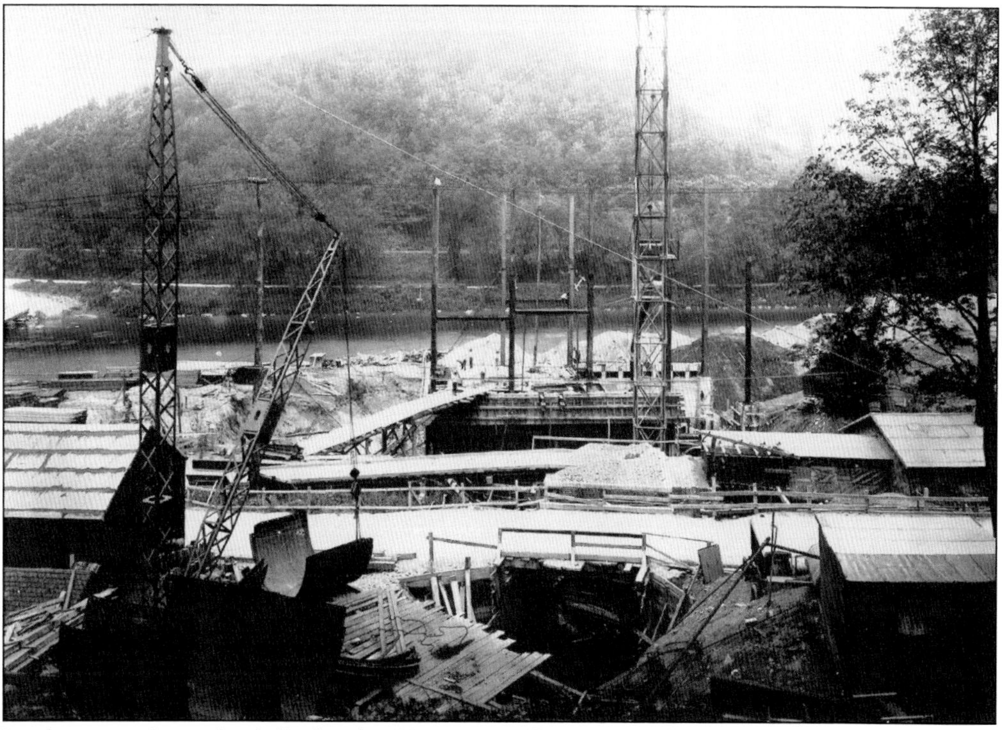

In this view from the hillside, the Housatonic River is visible in the background, and a temporary bridge for Route 7 can also be seen. Note the rolled pieces of steel that later became the pipe or penstock.

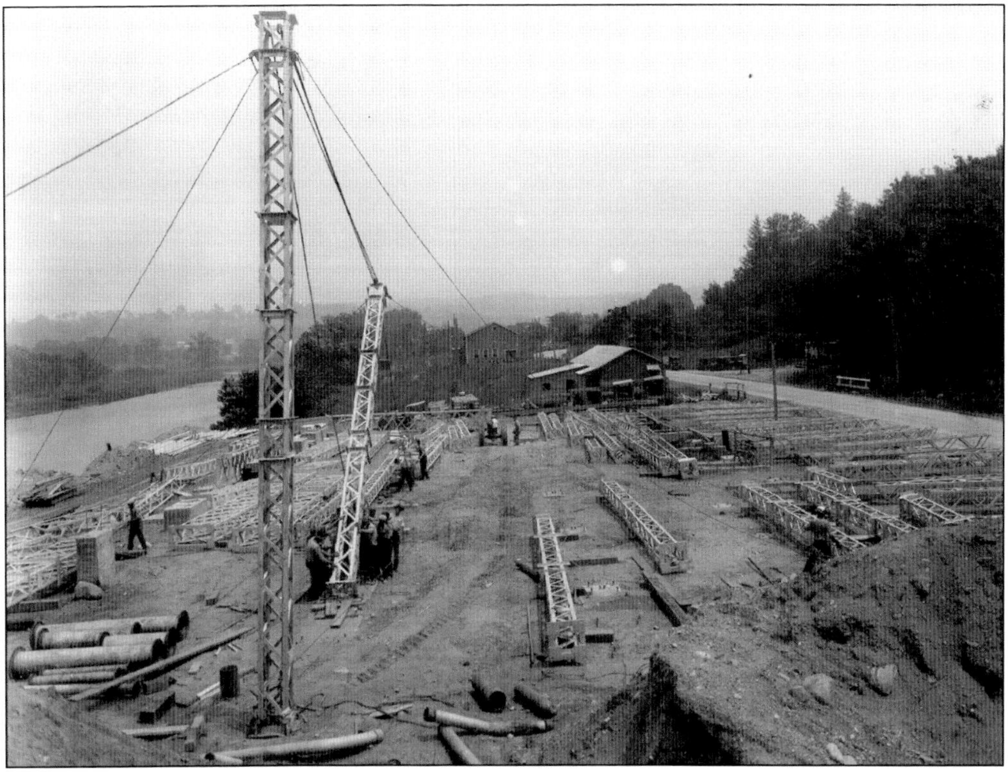

The early phases of the construction of the electrical switchyard are seen in this photograph taken July 15, 1927.

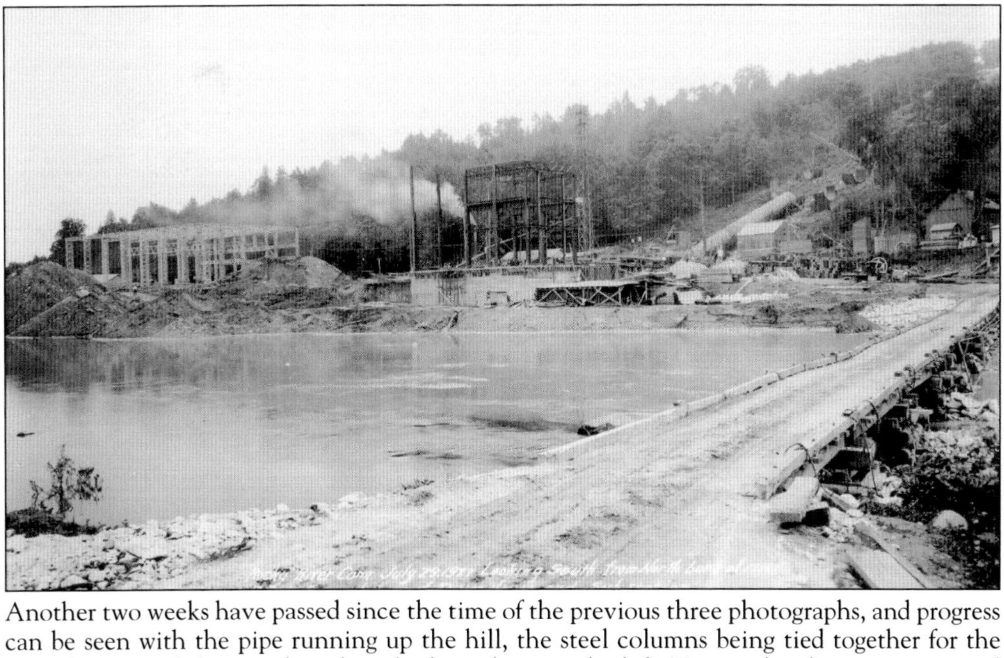

Another two weeks have passed since the time of the previous three photographs, and progress can be seen with the pipe running up the hill, the steel columns being tied together for the powerhouse, and the switchyard steel taking shape to the left. Notice also the temporary road that crosses the Housatonic River.

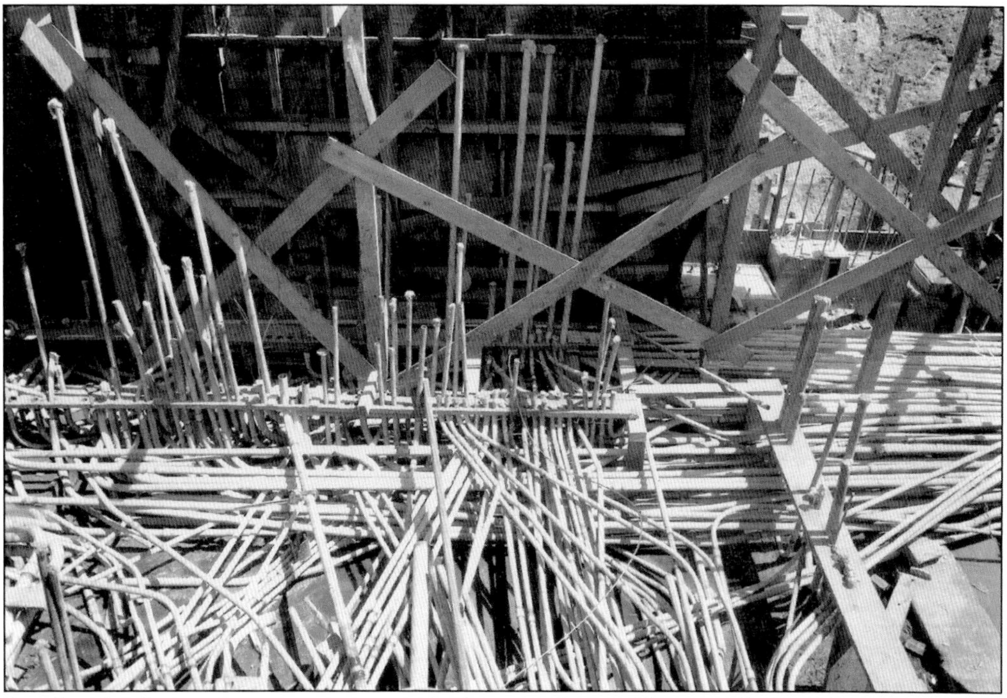

Conduit for electrical wiring is seen inside the powerhouse. Photographed on August 15, 1927, much of this framework is buried in concrete today.

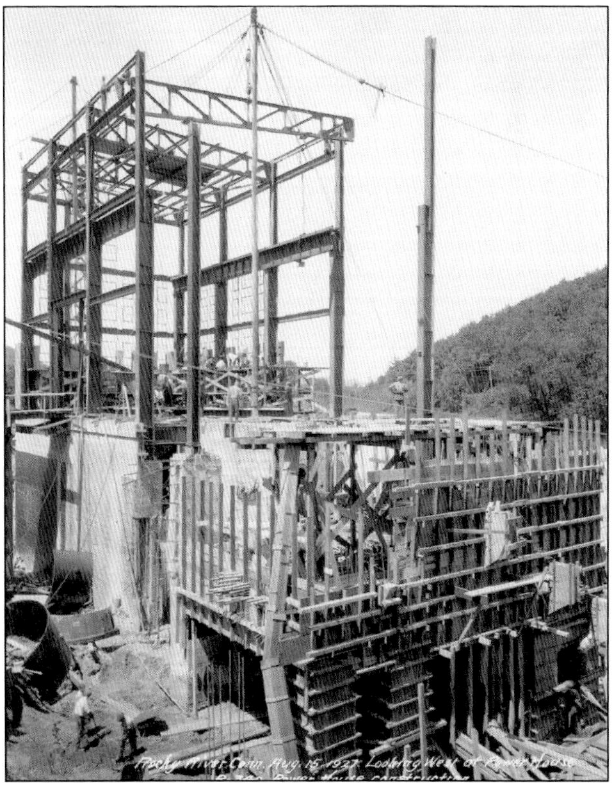

This photograph looks upstream at the powerhouse from Route 7.

The switchyard is seen to the left in this photograph, which looks downstream at the powerhouse from the riverbank, back toward Route 7.

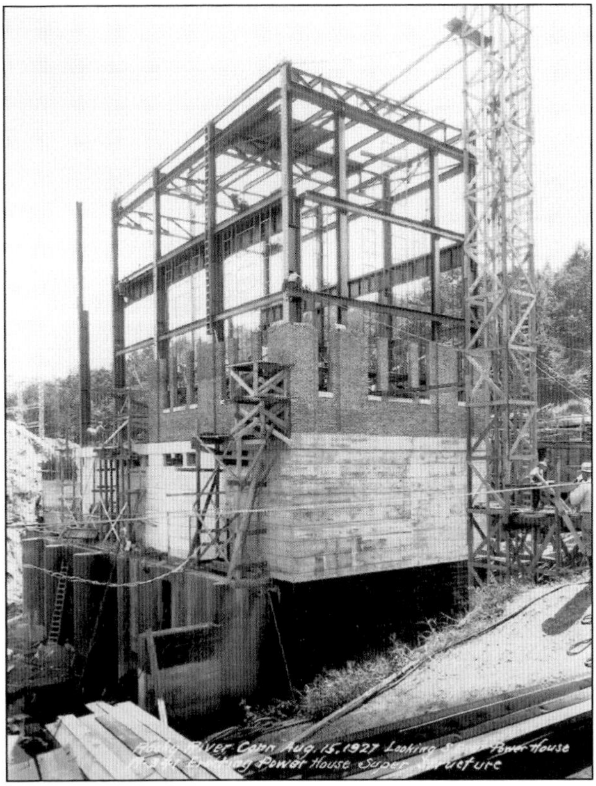

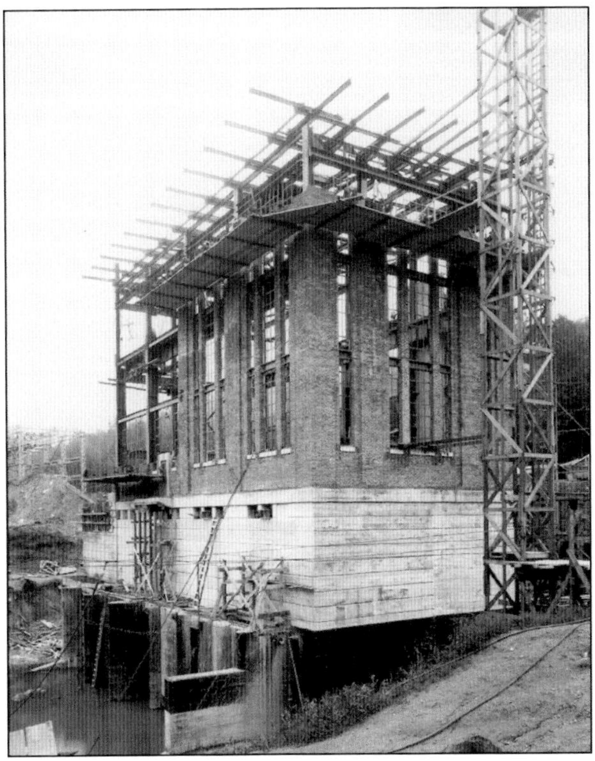

Dated September 1, 1927, this photograph was taken from the same spot as the previous one, with two more weeks of construction completed. By this time, the brick walls are starting to take form.

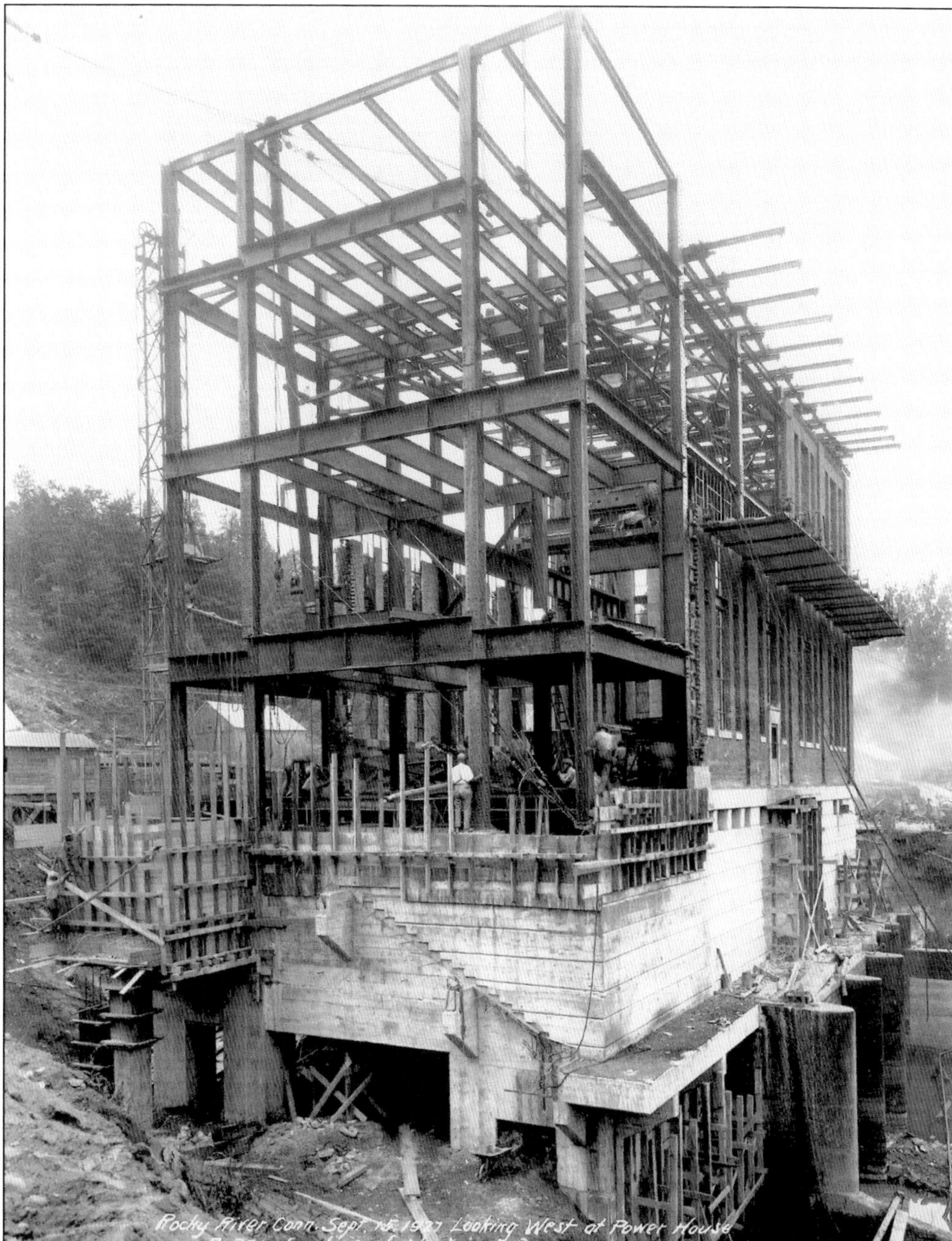

Looking upstream from the switchyard riverbank, this photograph from September 15, 1927, shows that most of the powerhouse steel is in place. Today, the Housatonic River is to the lower right of this site.

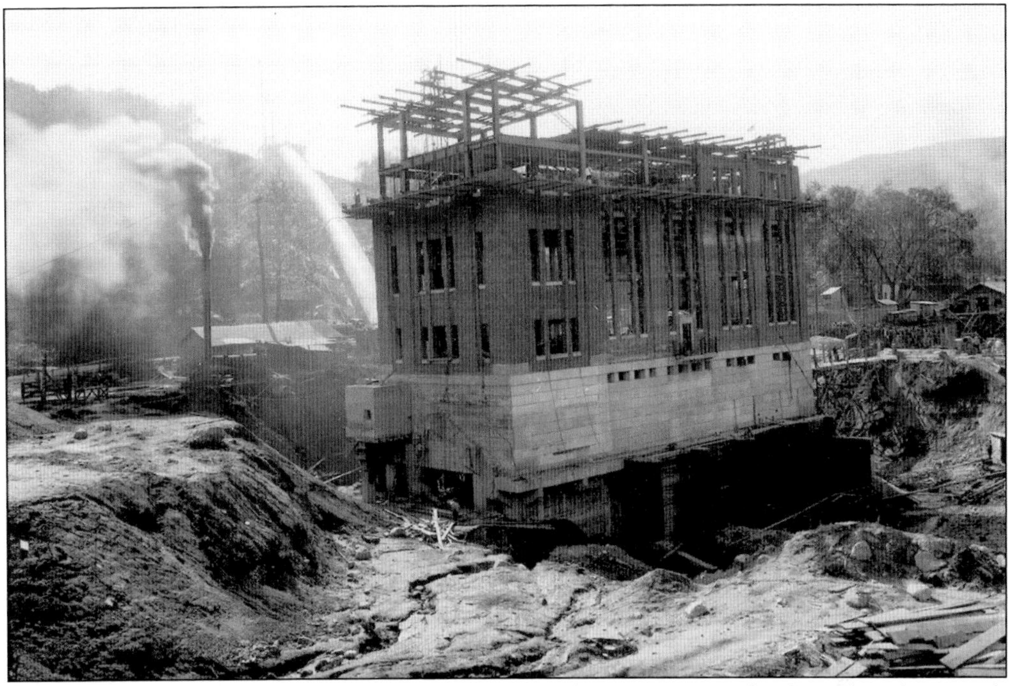

The nearly completed powerhouse is seen from the downstream riverbank in this photograph taken October 5, 1927. Note the pipe or penstock that runs up the hill to the foundation for the future surge tank.

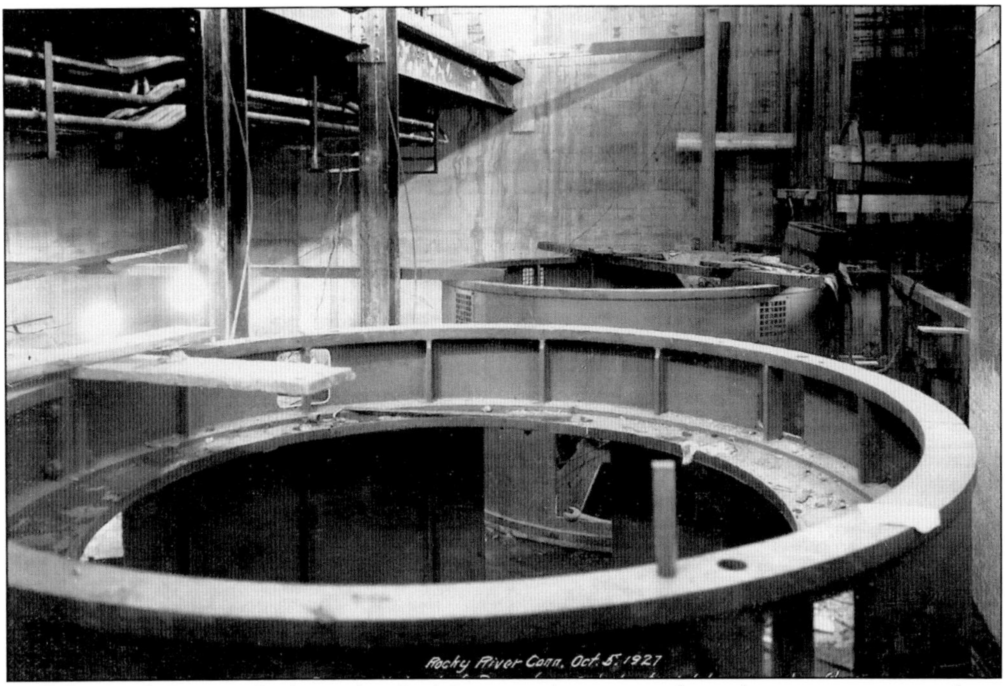

The two steel rings in the lower level of the powerhouse are where the two pumps were later installed to pump water from the Housatonic River into Candlewood Lake. At the time of installation, they were the largest pumps in the world.

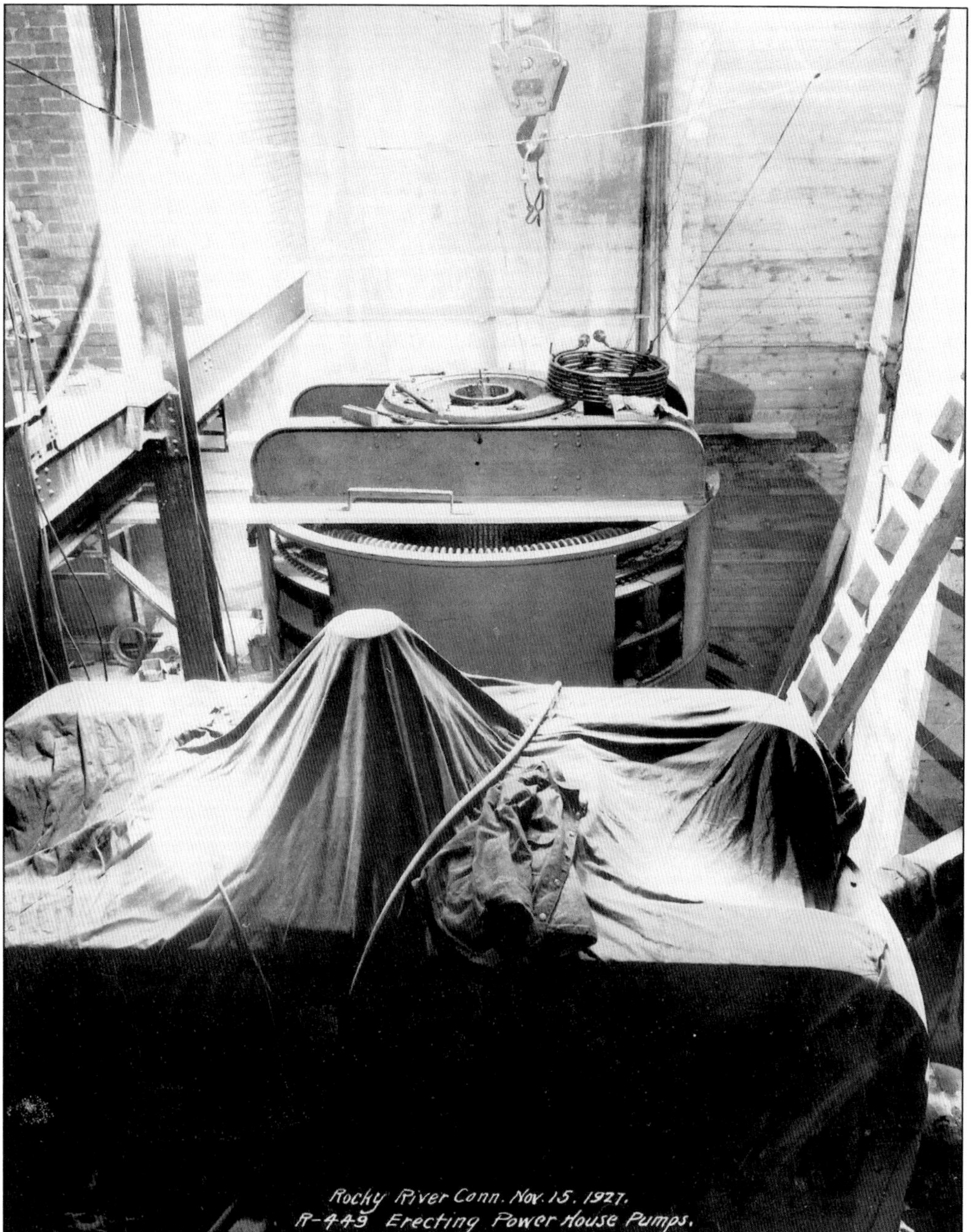

Subsequent to the preceding photograph, and jumping forward in time to November 15, 1927, this image shows the two pumps in an almost-finished state, with the electric motor portions in place.

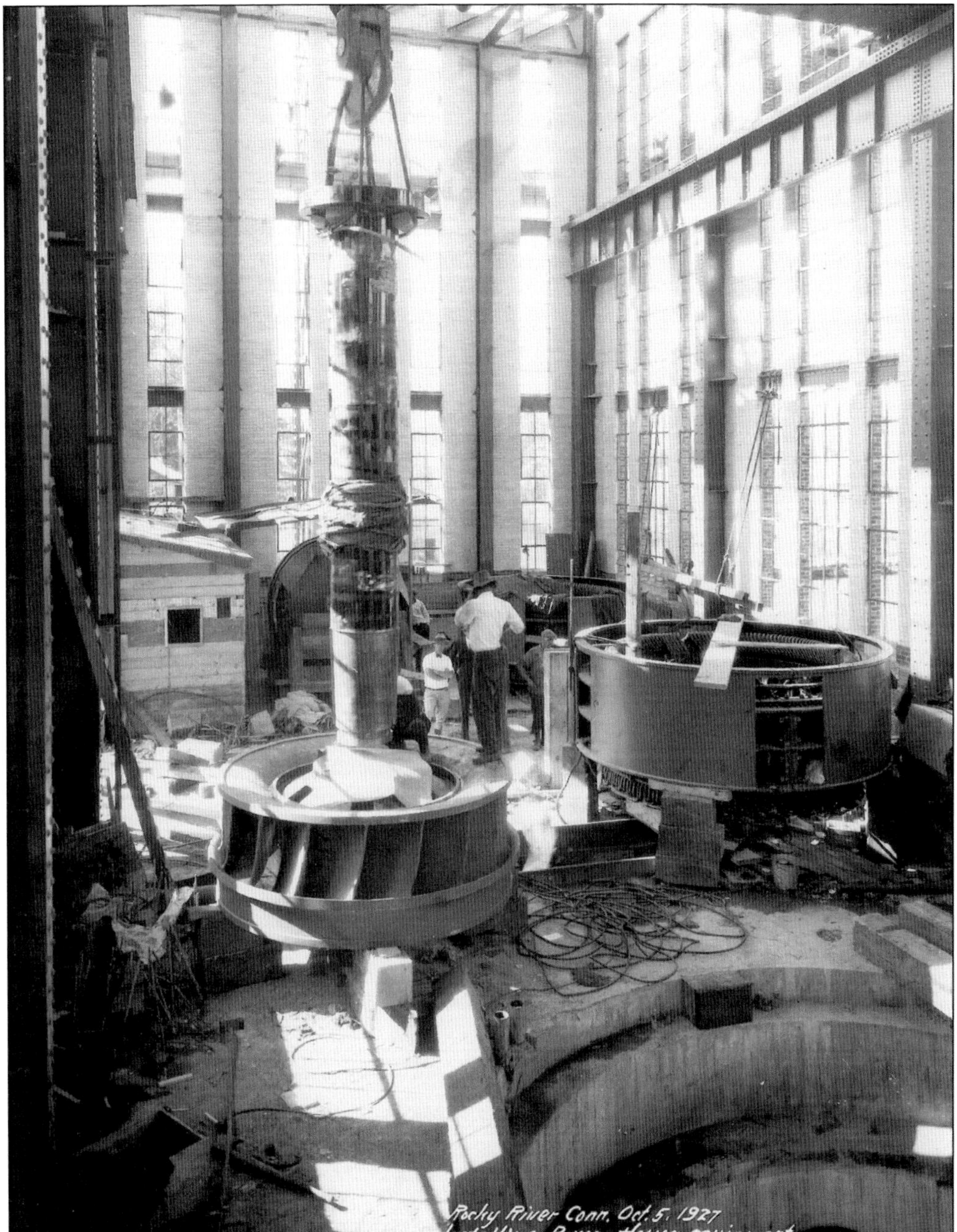

This October 1927 photograph shows some of the miscellaneous equipment that was not yet installed. Note the people standing on top of the waterwheel for the main generator. To make electricity, water enters through the side of the wheel and exits out the bottom, forcing the shaft to spin in the process. The ring on the right is the outside of the electrical motor for one of the pumps.

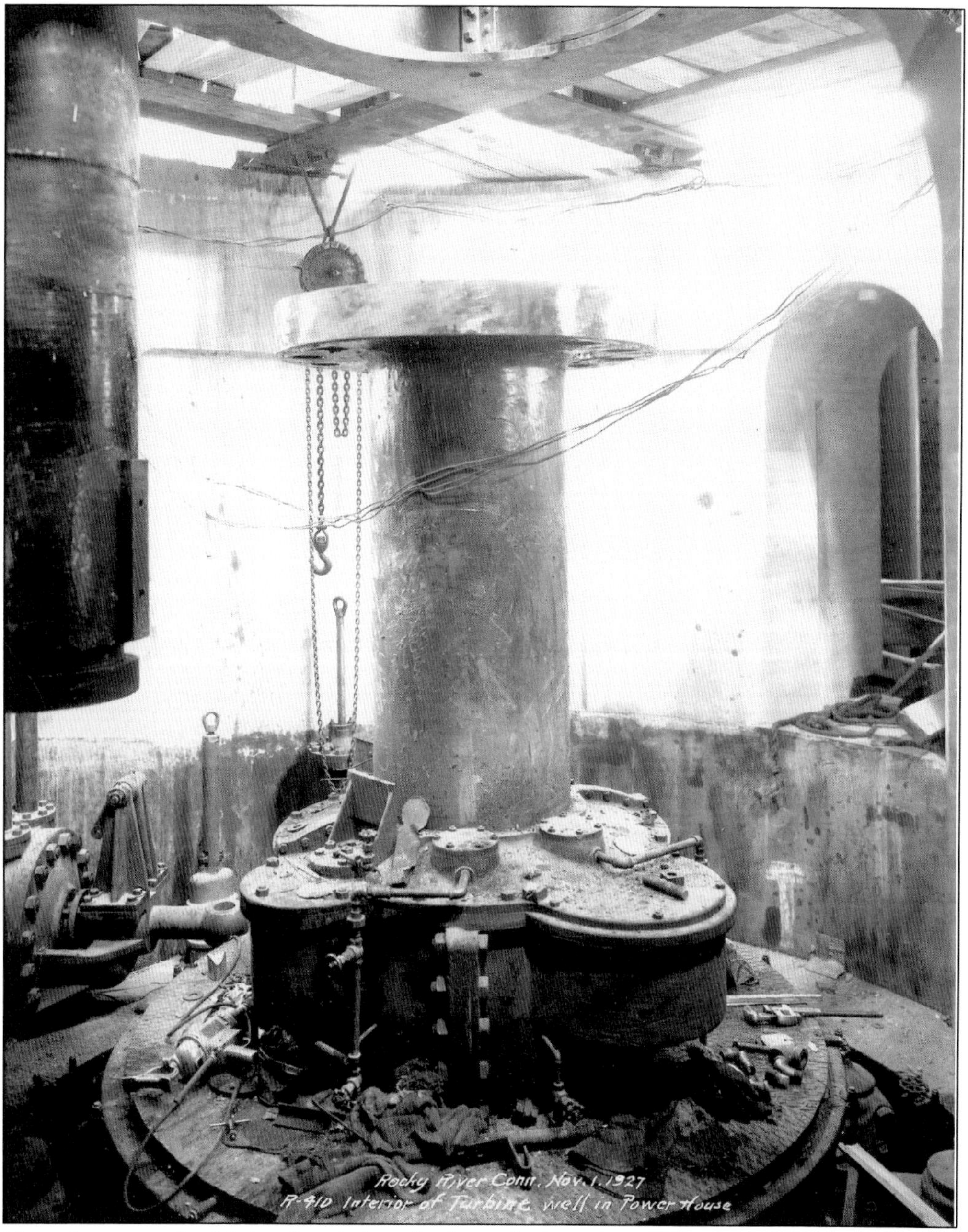

Here, the waterwheel is in place below the large shaft in the middle, and when assembly was finished, water would pass below these pieces. The electrical portion of the unit was later installed above this level and connected to the main shaft.

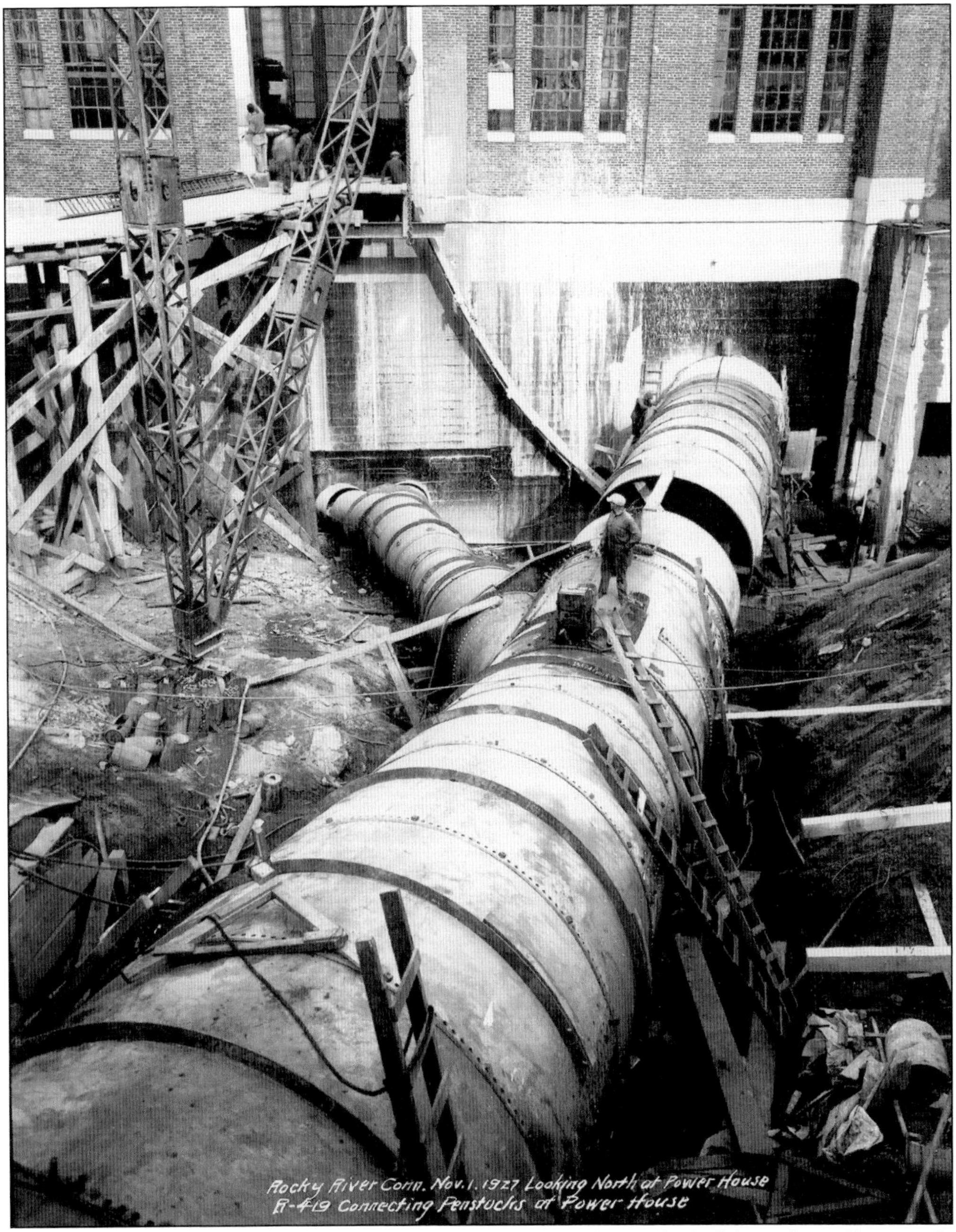

Shown here is the place where the single pipe that runs down the hill branches off to supply water to both the two pumps on the left and the main generator. This area is now buried under Route 7 and the parking lot.

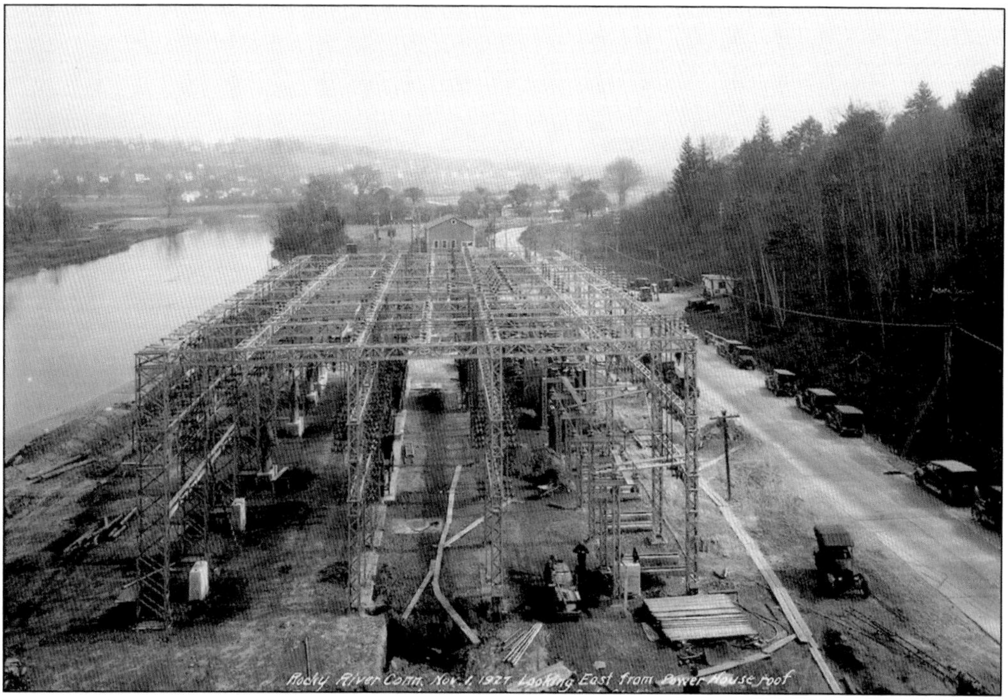

Taken on November 1, 1927, this photograph shows the switchyard as construction continues to make progress. Note the vehicles parked on the side of Route 7.

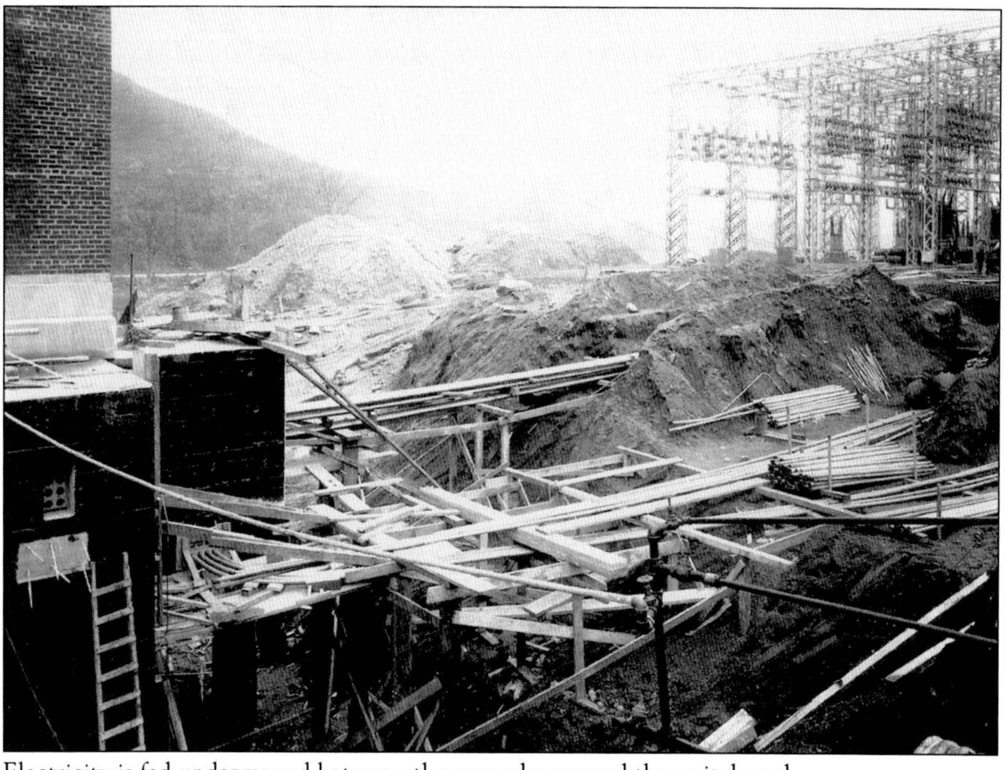

Electricity is fed underground between the powerhouse and the switchyard.

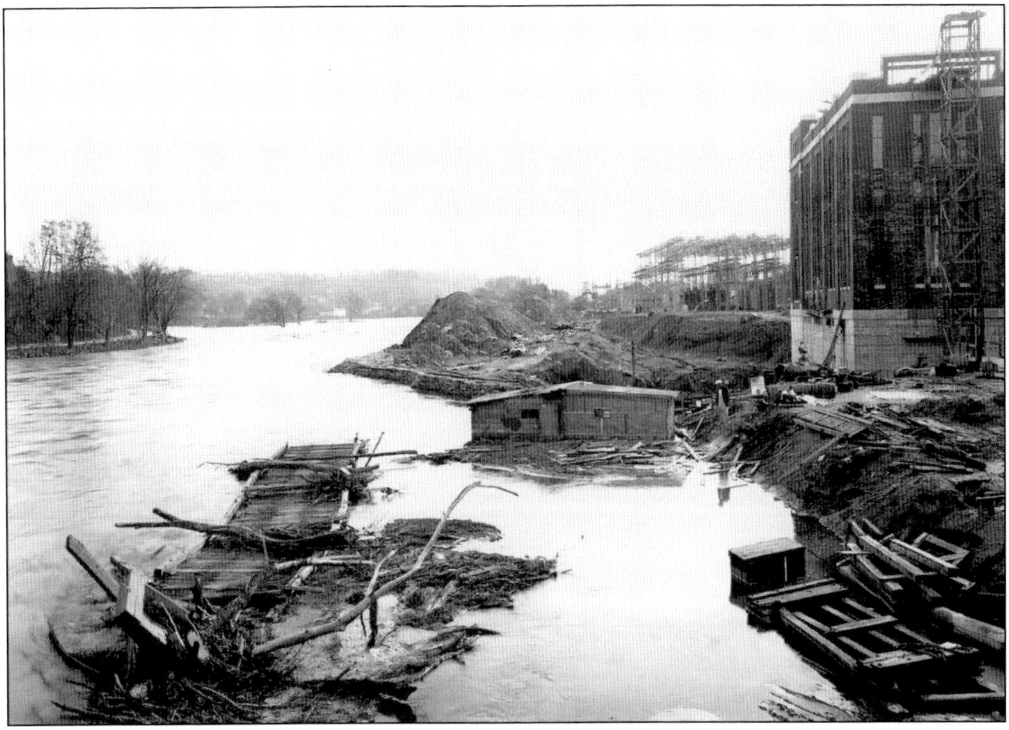

Whenever one works near water, there is a risk. Seen here are the flood challenges that took place on November 5, 1927.

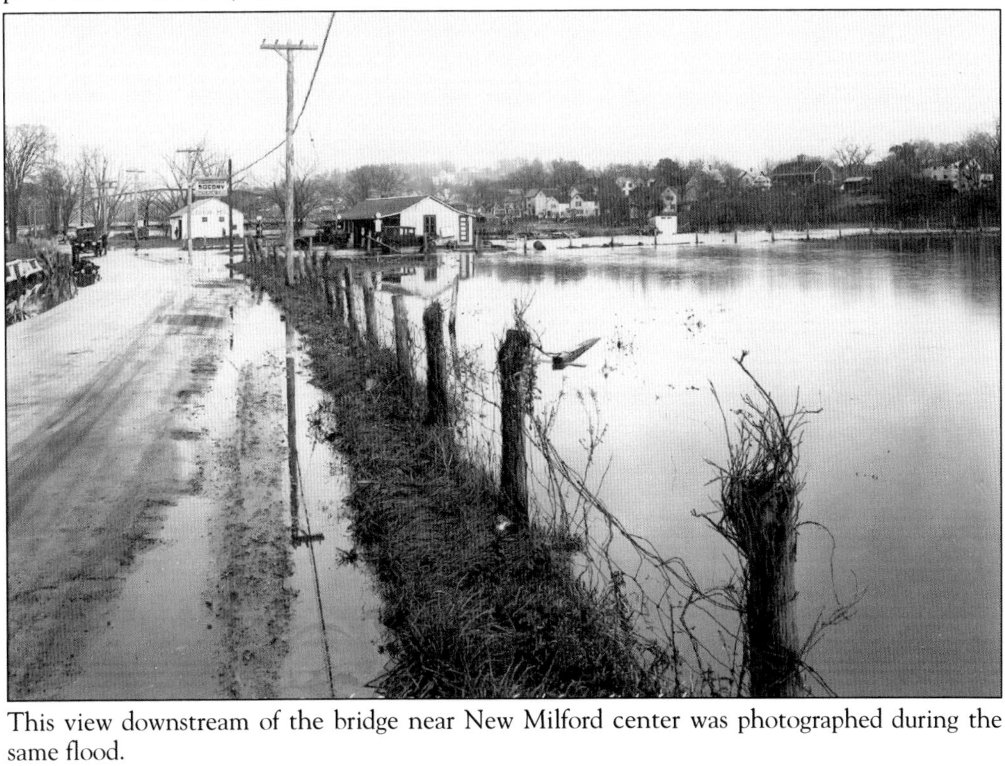

This view downstream of the bridge near New Milford center was photographed during the same flood.

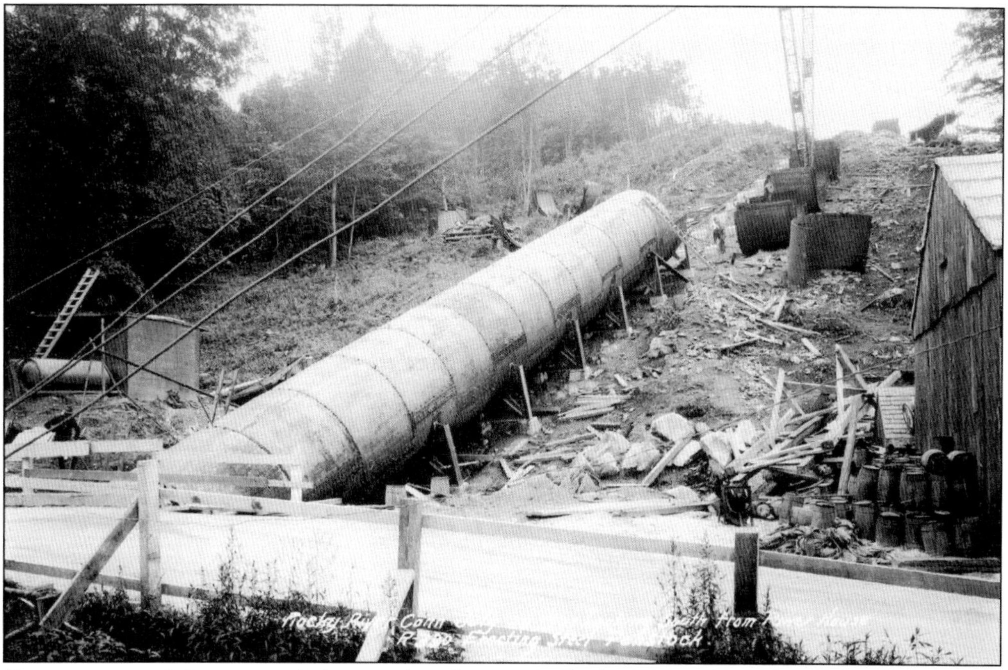

Construction of the penstock (or pipe) is shown, at the location where the pipe emerges from under Route 7 and extends up the hill opposite the powerhouse. The curved sections of steel on the hillside were assembled by riveting the pieces together.

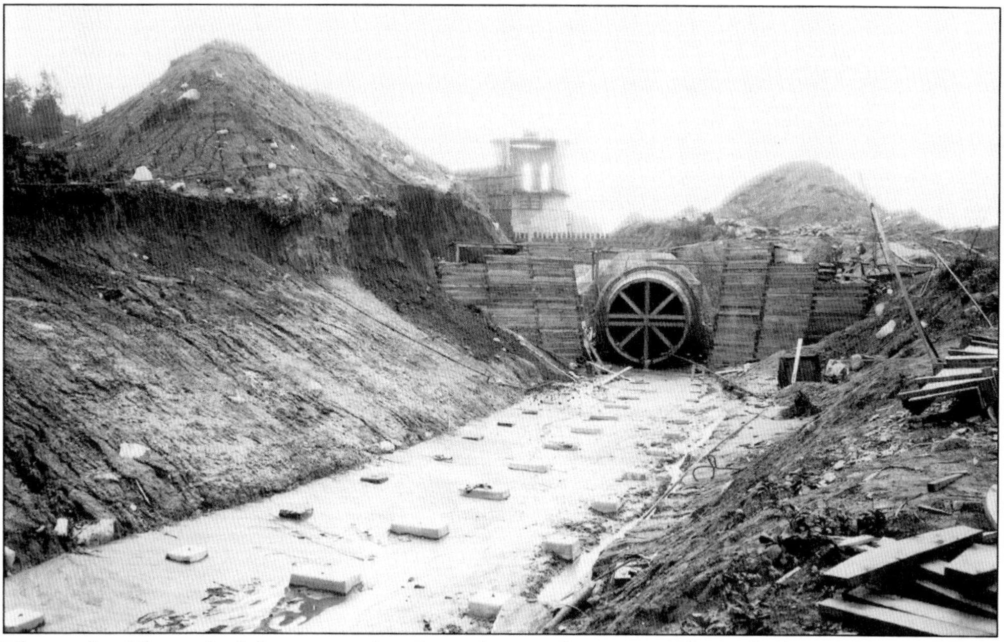

This is the lake end of the penstock, where the pipeline passes through the earthen dike and connects with the intake structure in the lake, which is seen in the background. Moving from the back of the picture to the front, after the penstock passes through the dike, the construction of the pipe changes from concrete to wood, and the pipeline is ultimately supported by the concrete pads seen in the foreground.

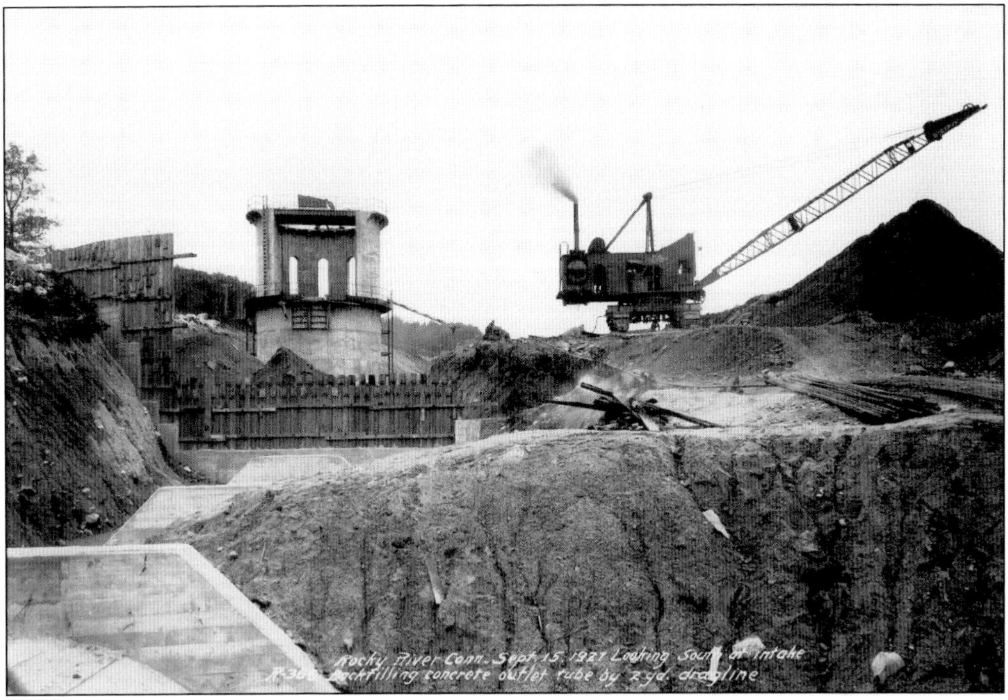

This is a better view of the penstock (or pipe) as it is being buried inside the earthen dike, as well as the intake structure in the lake.

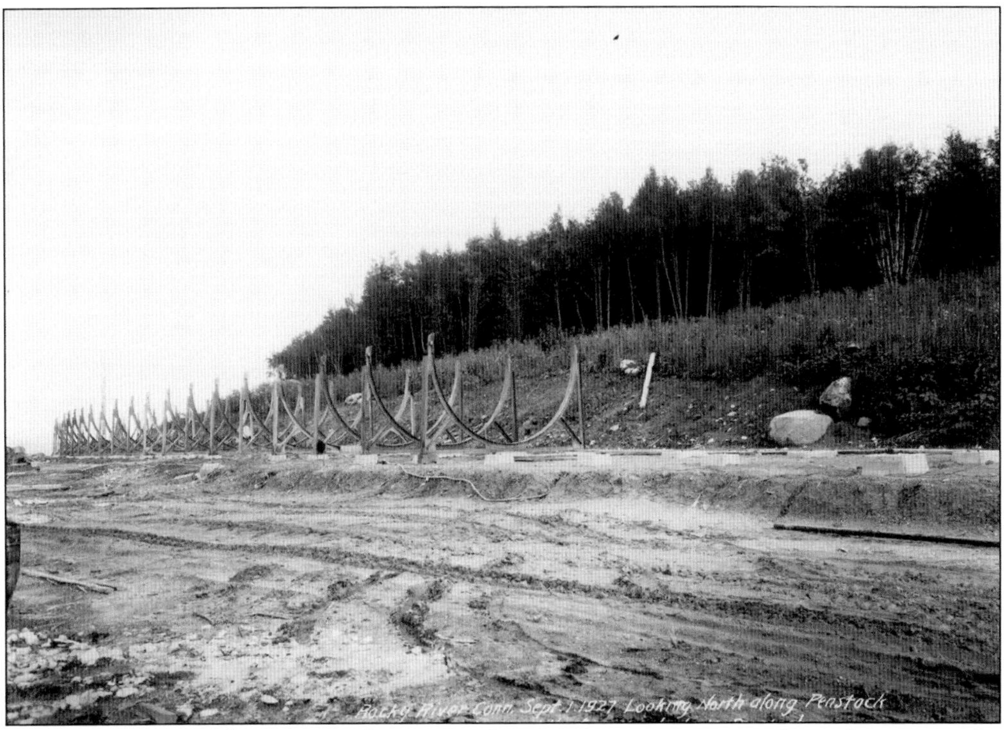

Here, the steel saddles are in place atop the supporting concrete, where they await the placement of the wooden penstock pieces.

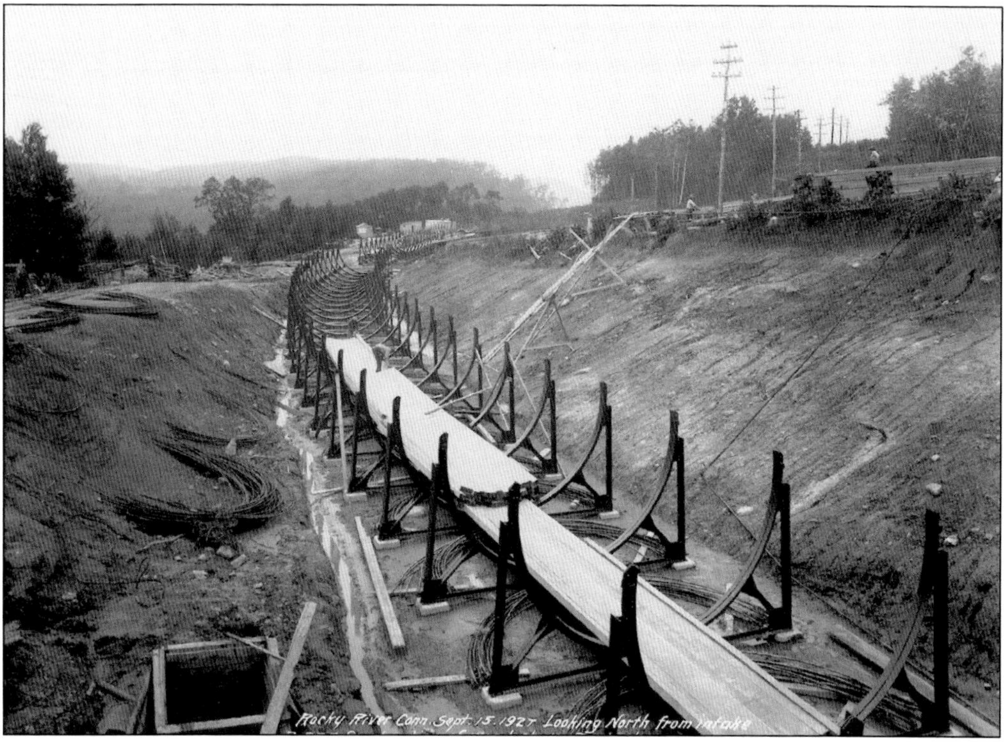

Some of the wooden pieces are in place to begin forming a wooden pipe that measures 15 feet in diameter.

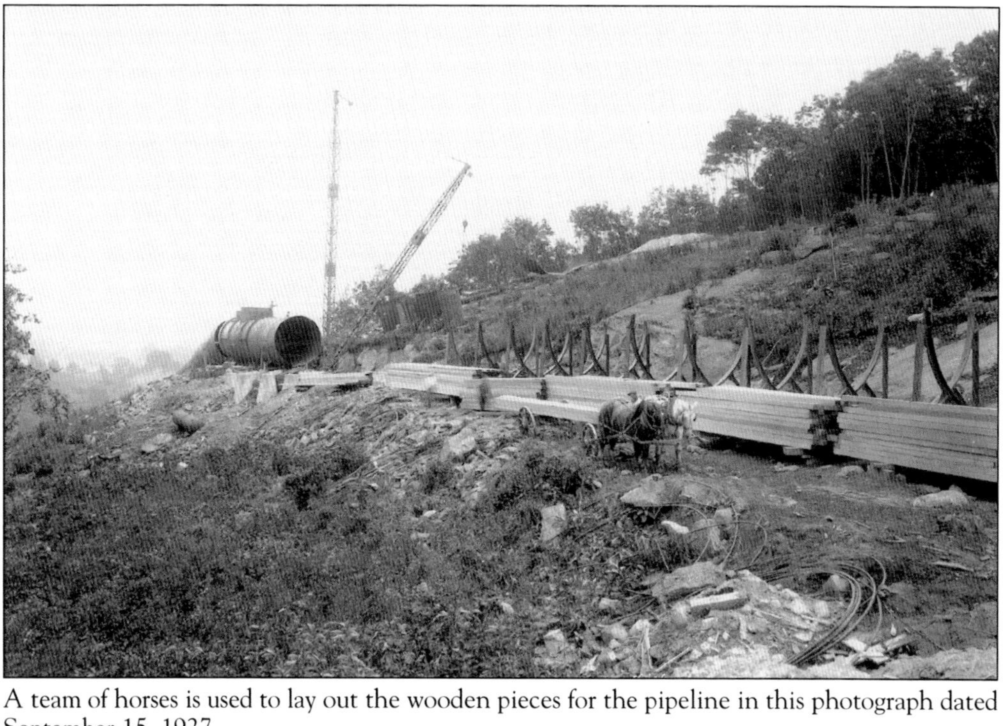

A team of horses is used to lay out the wooden pieces for the pipeline in this photograph dated September 15, 1927.

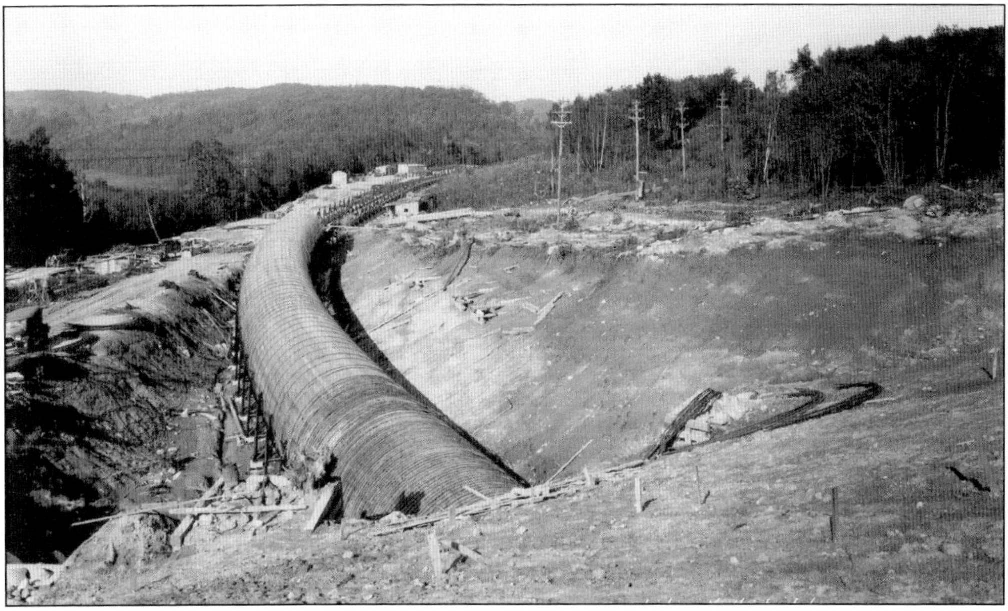

This October 5, 1927 view shows the partially completed wooden penstock where it exits Candlewood Lake, as well as the steel hoops that wrap around the pipe for added strength.

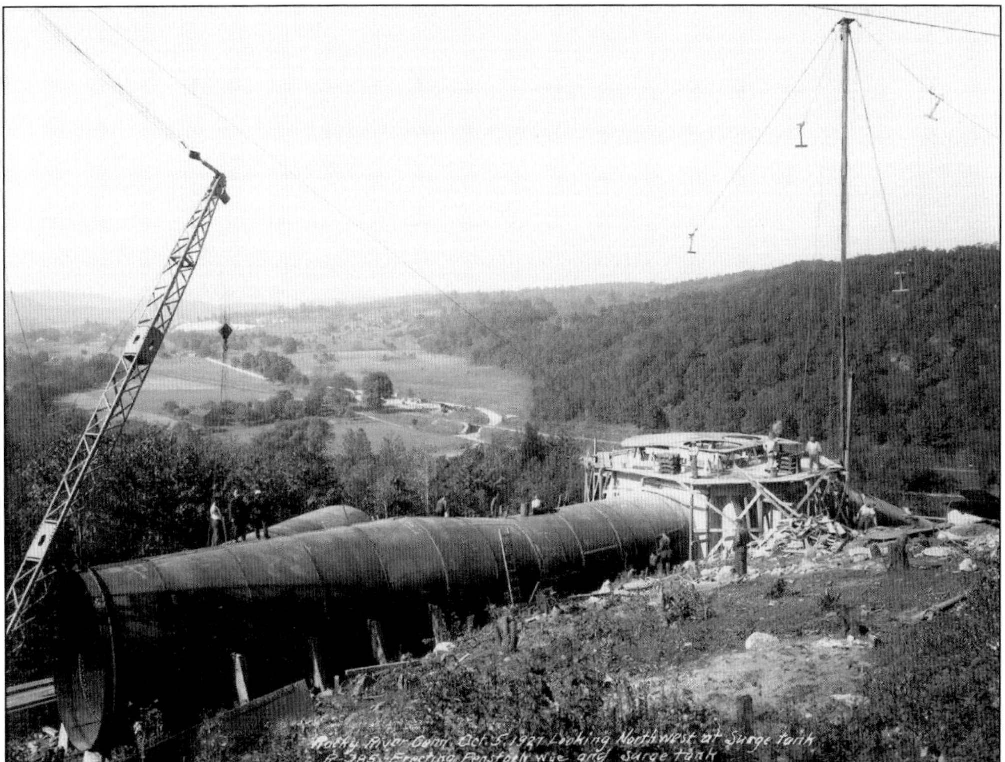

Before the penstock heads down the hill to the powerhouse, the pipe construction changes from wood to steel. The penstock is made of steel where it extends up from the surge tank, the foundation of which is in place here.

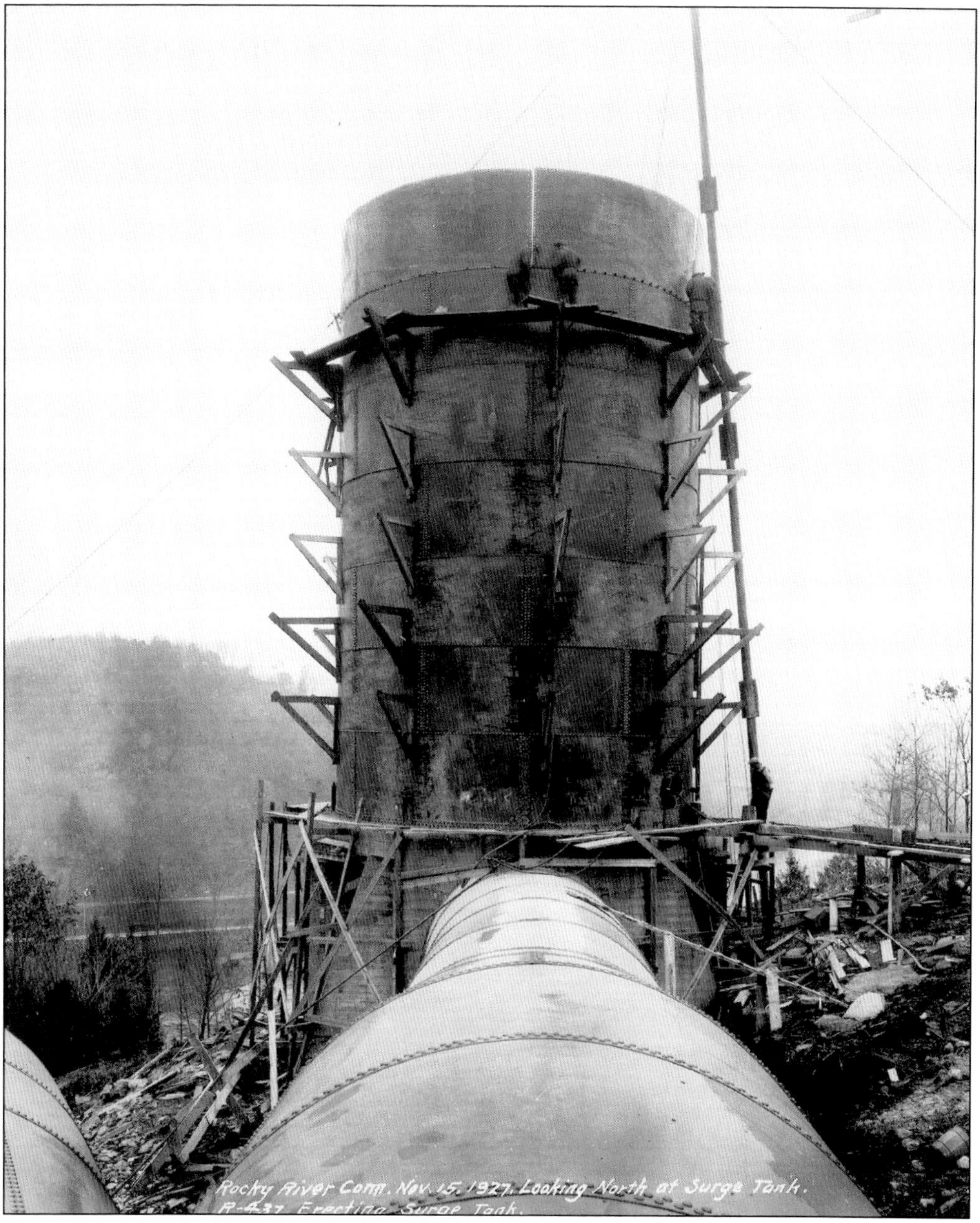

The surge tank, which can be seen from Route 7, is partially complete in this photograph dated November 15, 1927. If the generating equipment shuts down rapidly, a water surge or "water hammer"–type pressure can result. The purpose of this surge tank is to minimize the damaging effects of these pressure surges.

Two

Creating the Lake

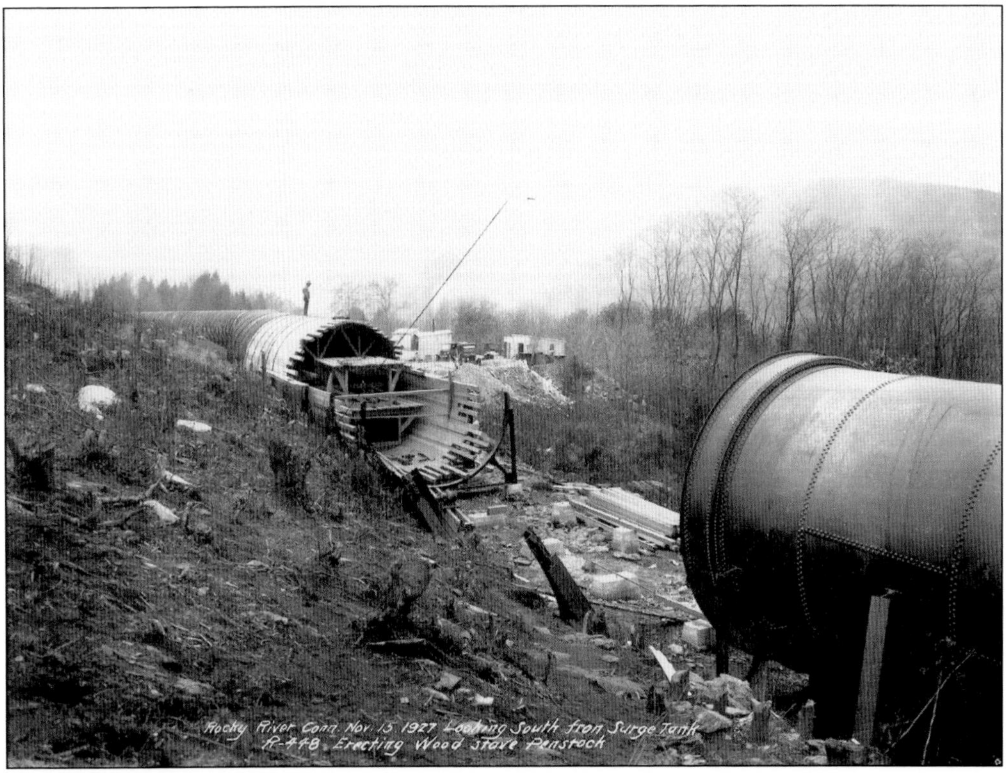

This photograph provides a view of how a wooden penstock is made. The penstock is shown here just before it joins the steel section that is upstream of the surge tank.

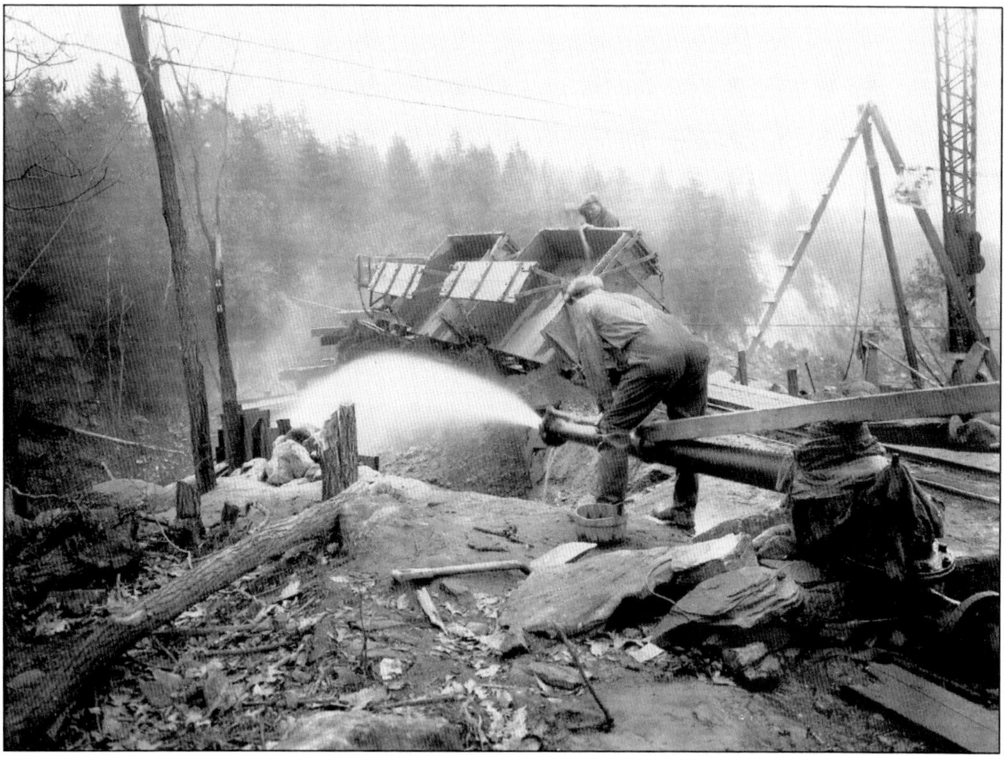

The use of water to move soil into place is called sluicing. This was the primary method used to build most of the earthen dams and dikes that were necessary to create Candlewood Lake.

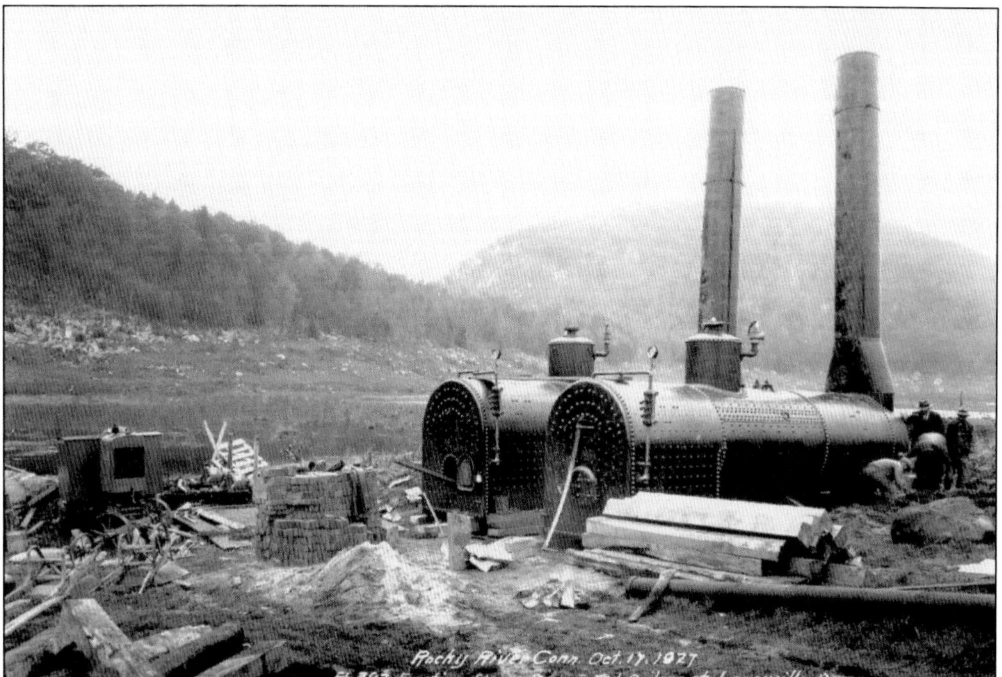

These pumps, which were needed to move the water, were powered by steam.

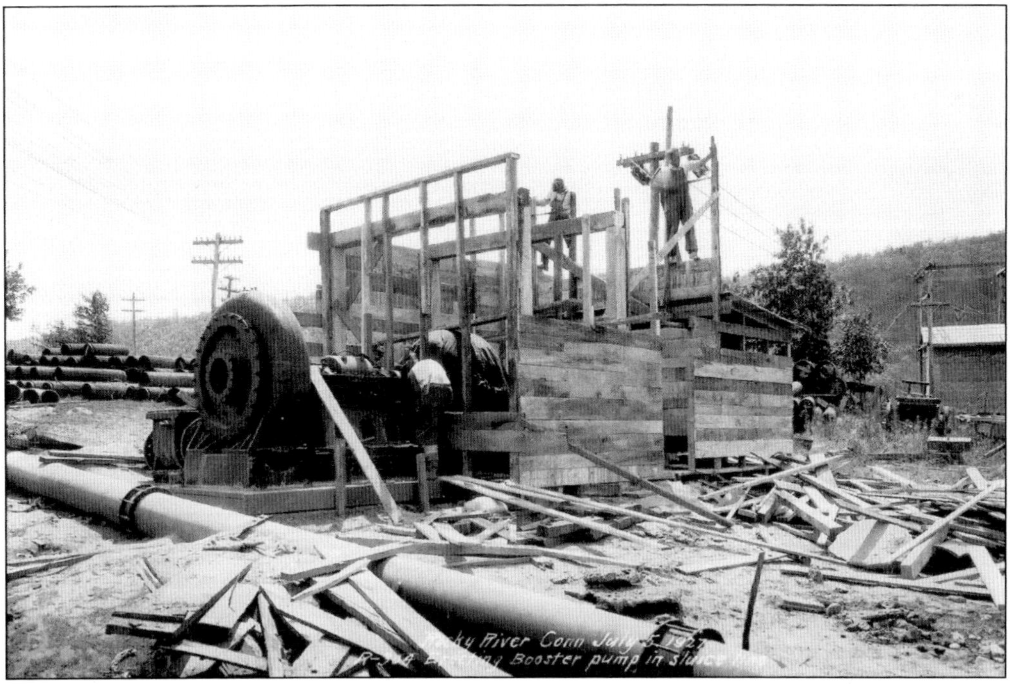

At times, a booster pump was needed to provide additional lift up onto the dam or dike.

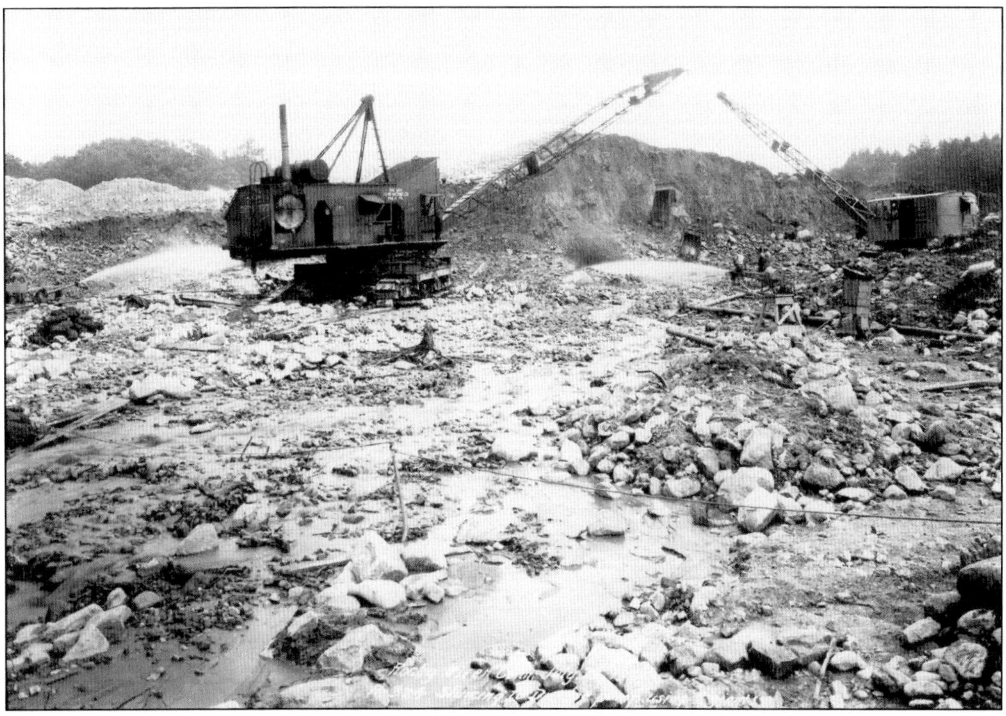

In the sluicing process, cranes initially remove a mix of soil and rocks from where the canal or lake is being created. This mixture of soil and rock is placed near water jets, which act to wash out the fine soils. Then the mixture of fine soil and water is moved to where the dam is wanted.

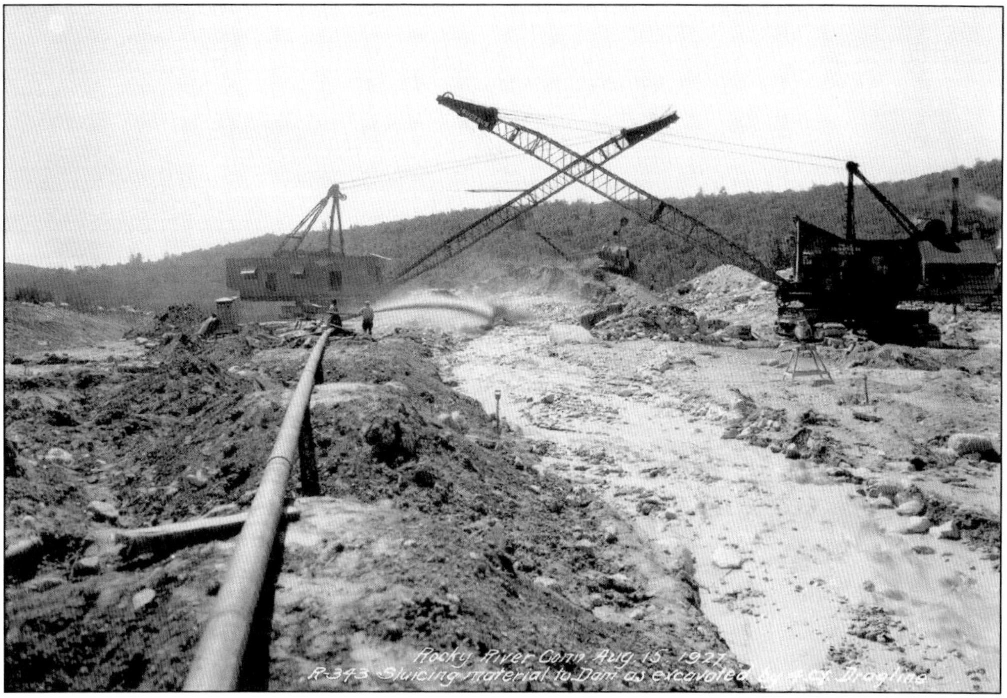

The finer soil material is placed near the center of the dam and serves the purpose of resisting the internal movement of water, which is desirable for dam stability. The larger material is placed on the outer edges of the dam for sheer weight.

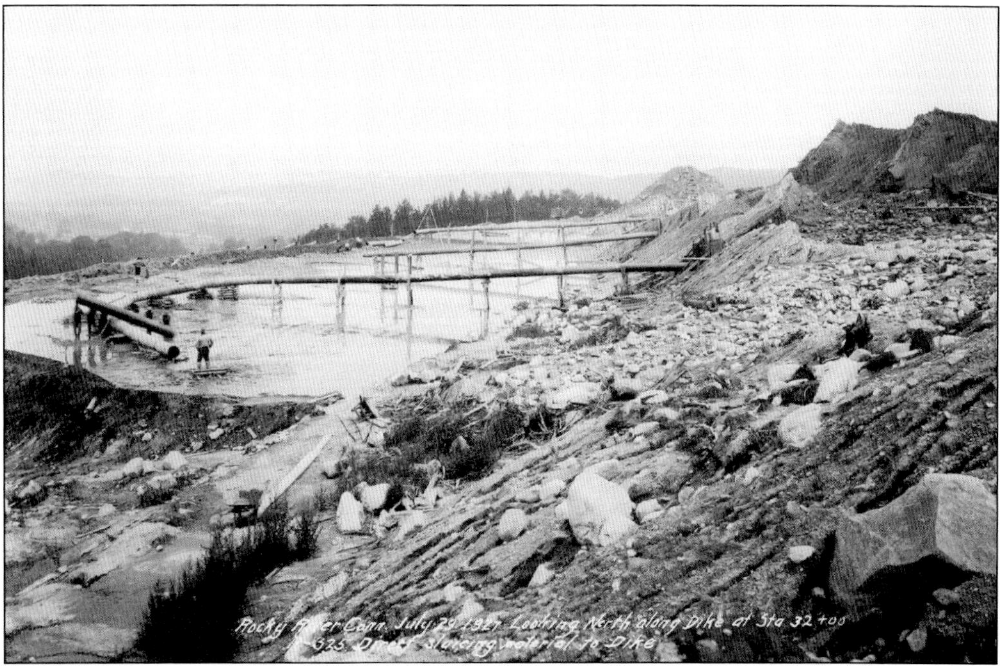

In this view, multiple sluicing lines deliver fine soil to what became the middle of the dam or dike. Here the soil settles, and excess water is drained off. Repeating this process raises the height of the dam.

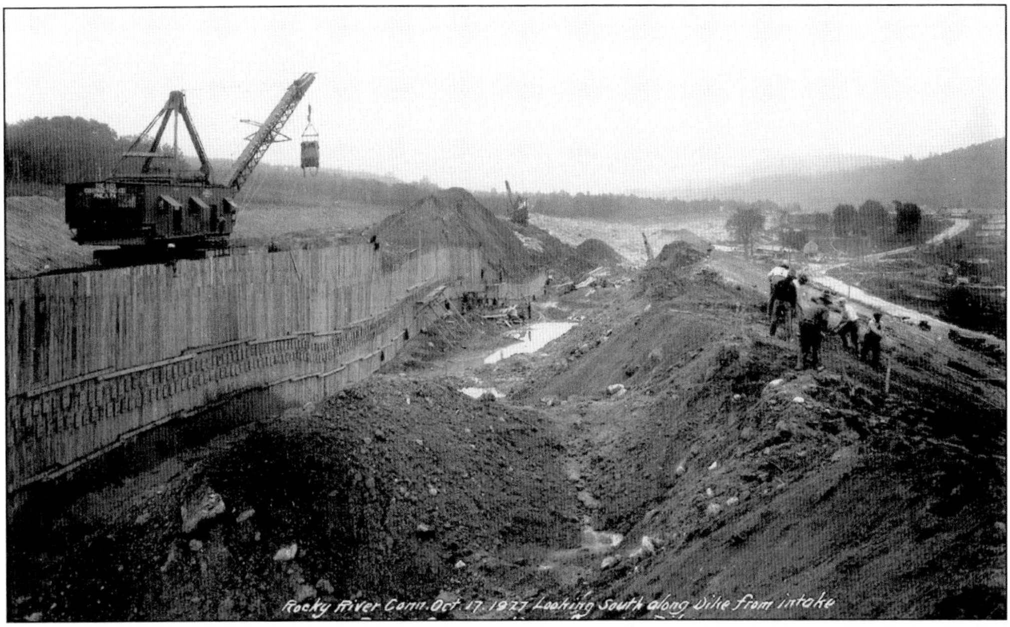

One additional method that was used to prevent water from passing internally through the dams was the construction of wooden core walls from the bottom to the top. These core walls were built for all the earthen dams and dikes to make them more stable.

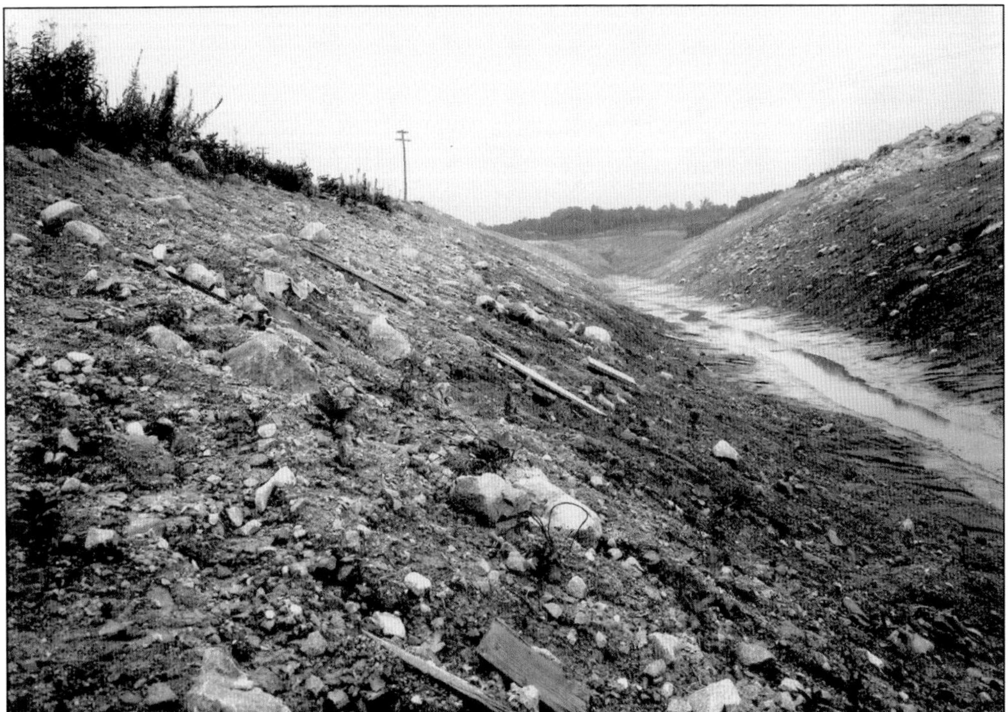

This photograph from September 15, 1927, shows that the canal entrance is taking shape. The area in this view is around the corner from the present New Milford Town Beach. Note the large amount of boulders in the native soil.

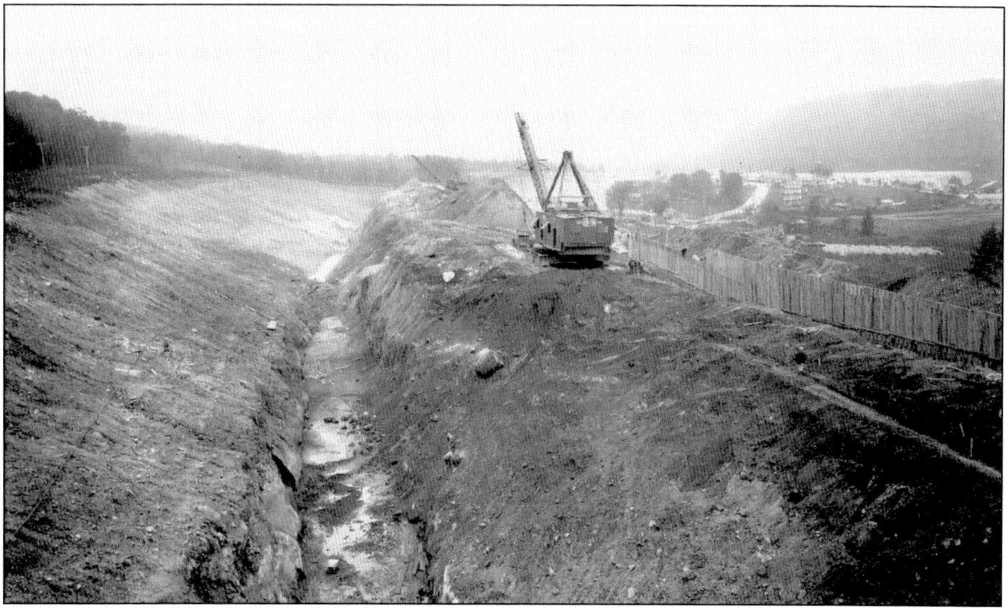

Dated October 17, 1927, this photograph was taken from the intake structure and shows the different phases of the canal's construction. The cranes drag the soil from the left side down into the bottom of the canal, and from there they lift up the soil for sluicing and final placement on the canal dike to the right. The wooden core wall is also visible.

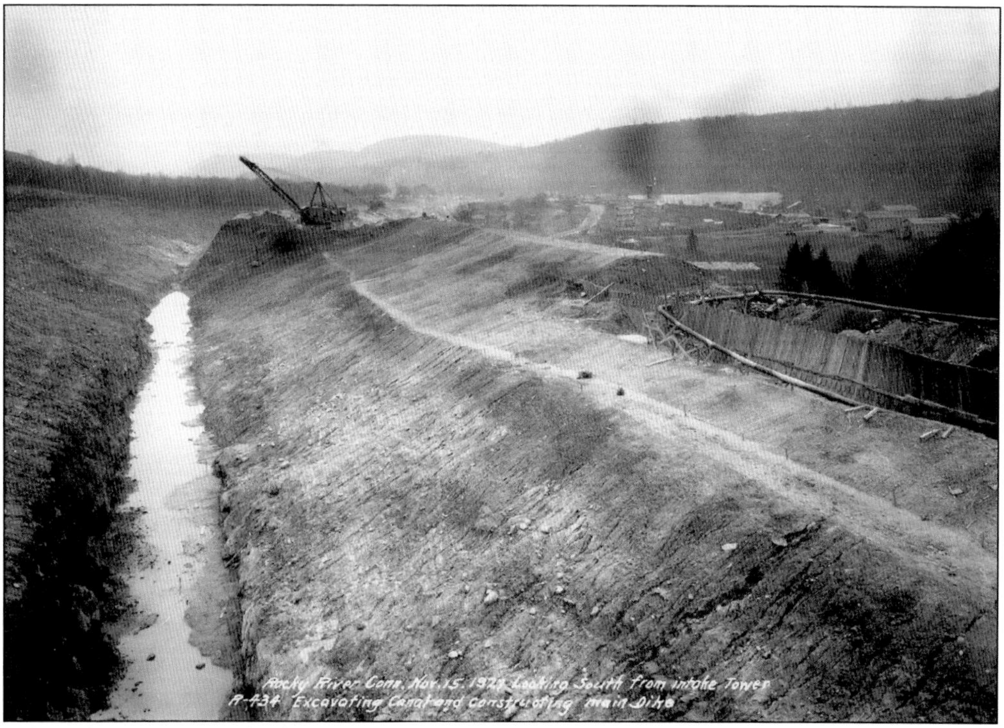

Taken about one month after the previous photograph, this image shows the finished look of the canal dike, with the wooden core wall now buried inside the earthen fill. In the background is the temporary construction village, and the lighter-colored area is the main dam.

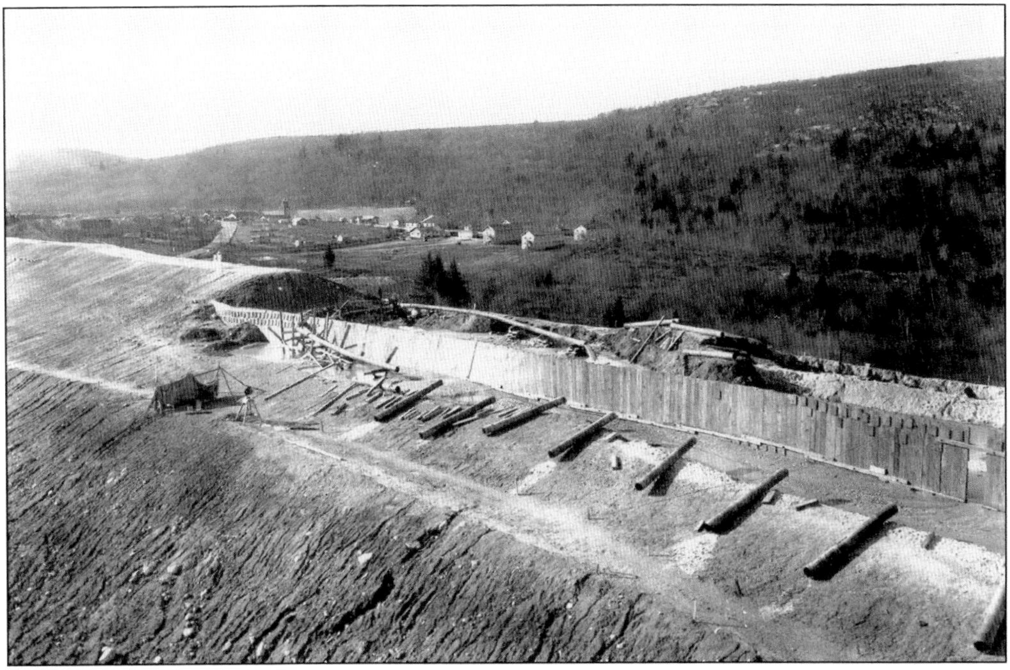

Another two weeks have passed since the previous photograph. The final appearance of the main canal dike is presenting itself. Note sluice pipes that deliver the soil slurry, and the somewhat tipsy core wall that awaits backfilling.

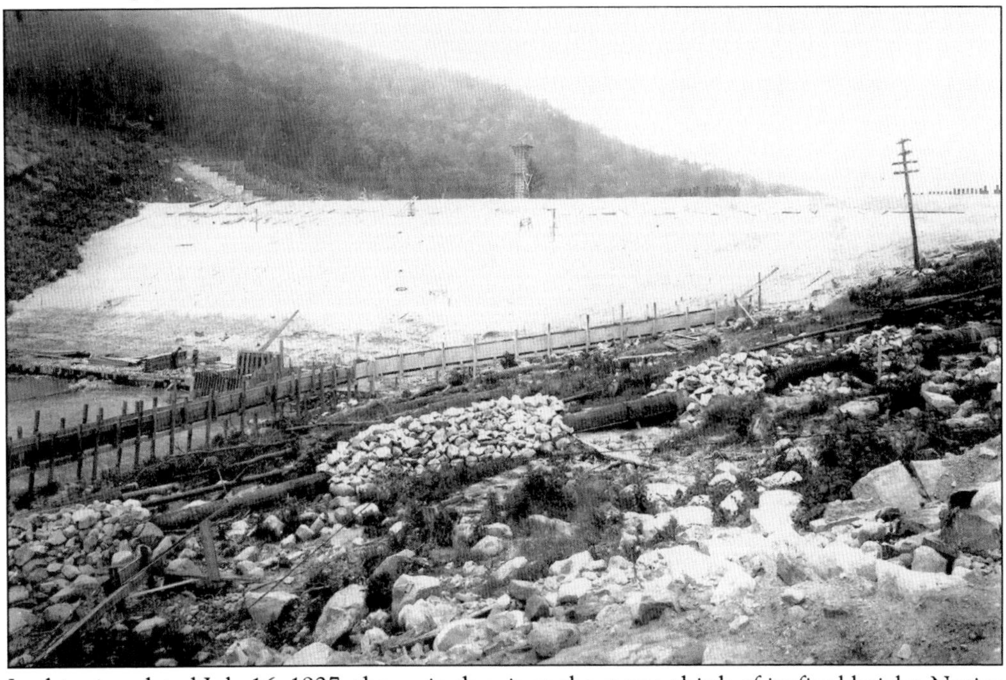

In this view dated July 16, 1927, the main dam is at about two-thirds of its final height. Notice what appear to be steps on the upper left side of the photograph. This is a concrete base upon which the wooden core wall is positioned, and this base is placed on bedrock. This view is from what is today the New Milford Town Beach.

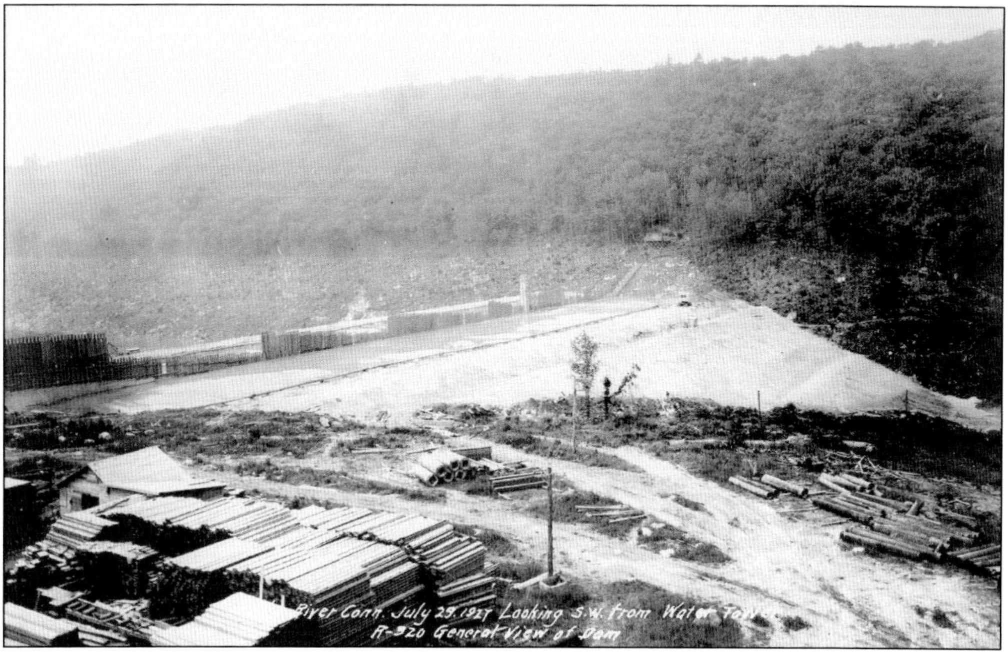

This view looks at the main dam from downstream of where the lake was built. Notice that on the near side of the wooden core wall is a level area of sluiced material that is settling out. The excess water is draining into the tower in the center of this photograph, which was taken on July 29, 1927.

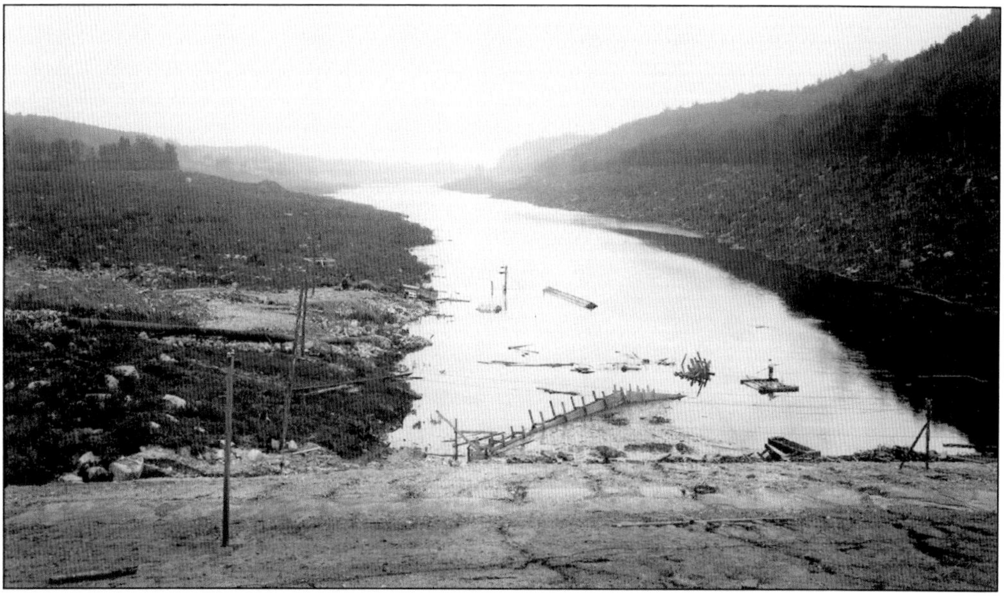

There is a risk when working near water, as can be seen here when a flood occurred during construction. The very peak of the pump house roof can be seen in this photograph taken September 1, 1927. Under normal conditions, when the water level was much lower, this area was where the water came from to facilitate the sluicing operations. The water pipeline is seen on the left side, in the middle of the photograph. To the left is where New Milford Town Beach is located today.

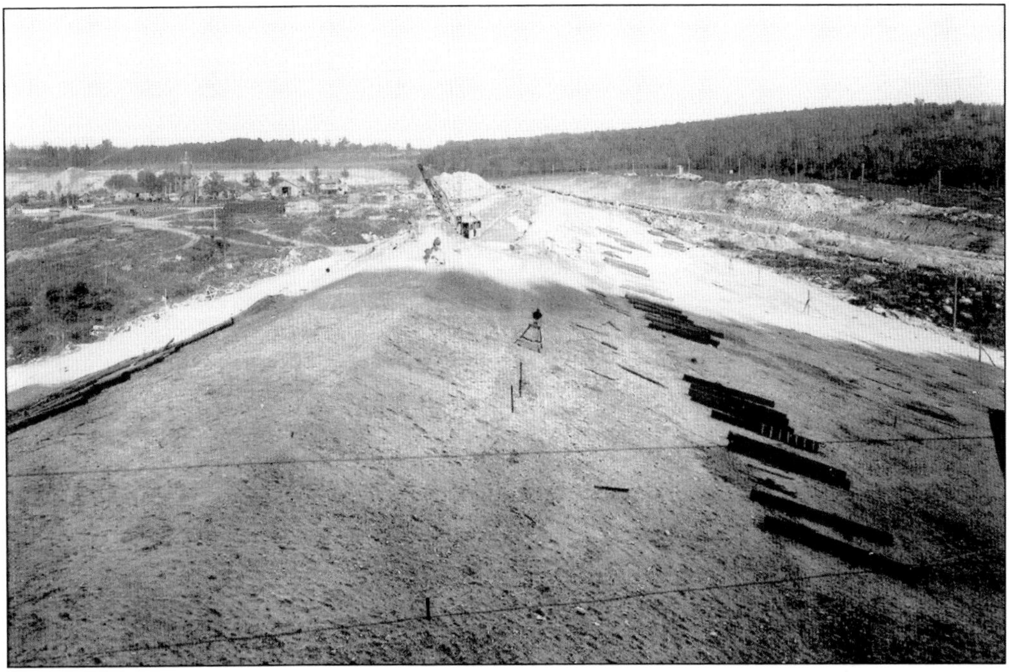

A crane drags and places the last of the material atop the main dam. This view looks toward the entrance to the main canal. The new lake will be built on the right. Notice the water tower and a few of the remaining buildings left over from the construction village on the left.

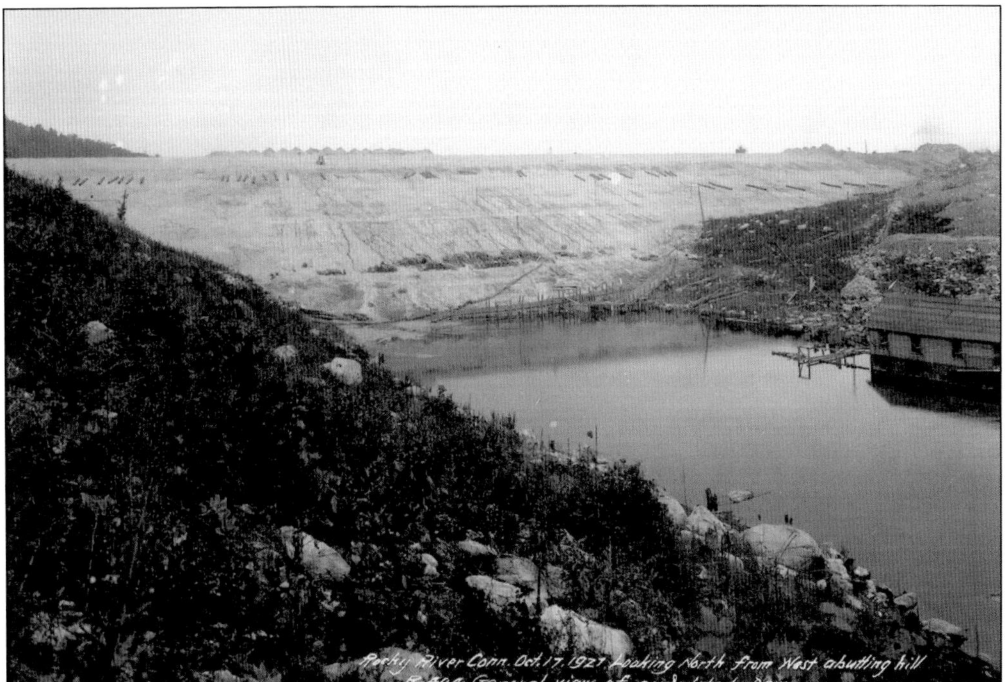

This is the nearly completed main dam as seen from the shore opposite what is now the New Milford Town Beach. This dam filled the Rocky River Valley just upstream of where this river would have joined the Housatonic River, and that is the notable origin of this project's name.

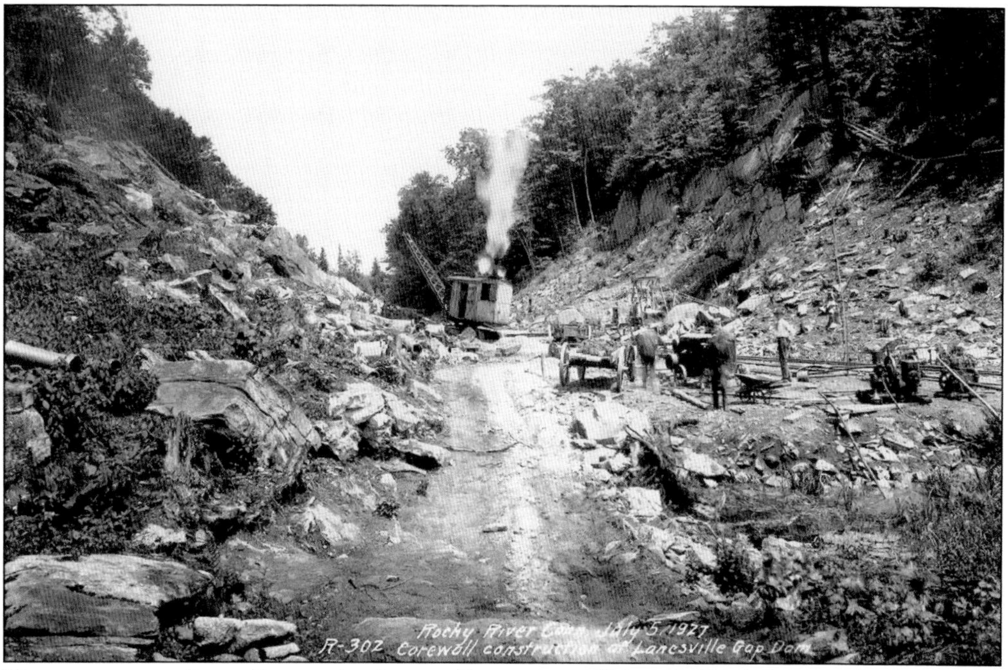

There was a smaller valley in the Lanesville section of New Milford that needed to have a dam built. This photograph, taken on July 5, 1927, shows the valley as it is being prepared for construction of the dam.

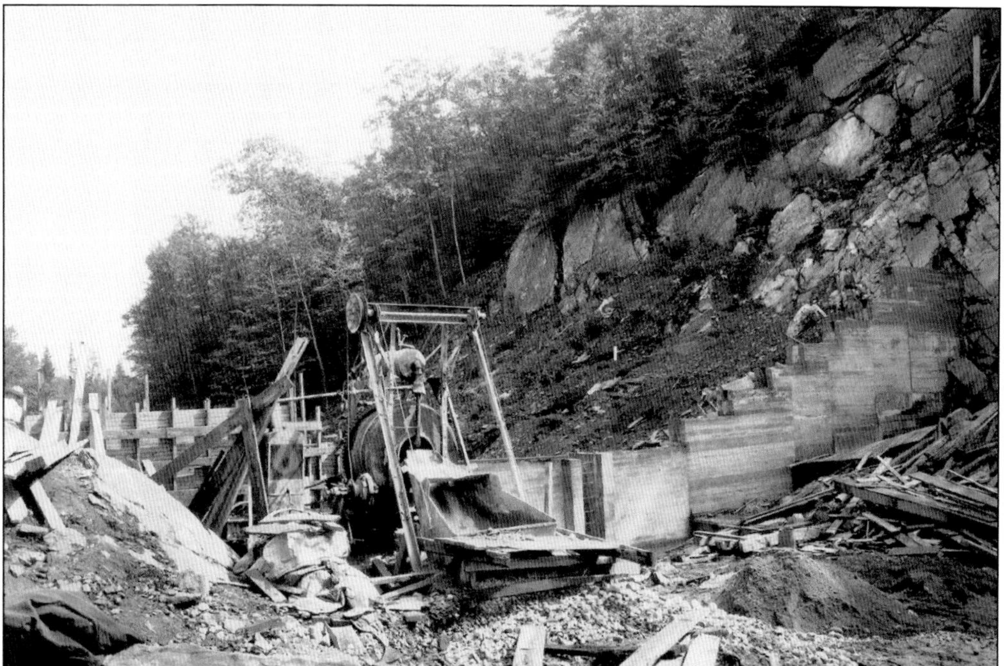

Similar to the other dams, there is a concrete core wall base that was later topped with a wooden core wall to limit water flow through the dam. This is the concrete base as it appeared on August 15, 1927.

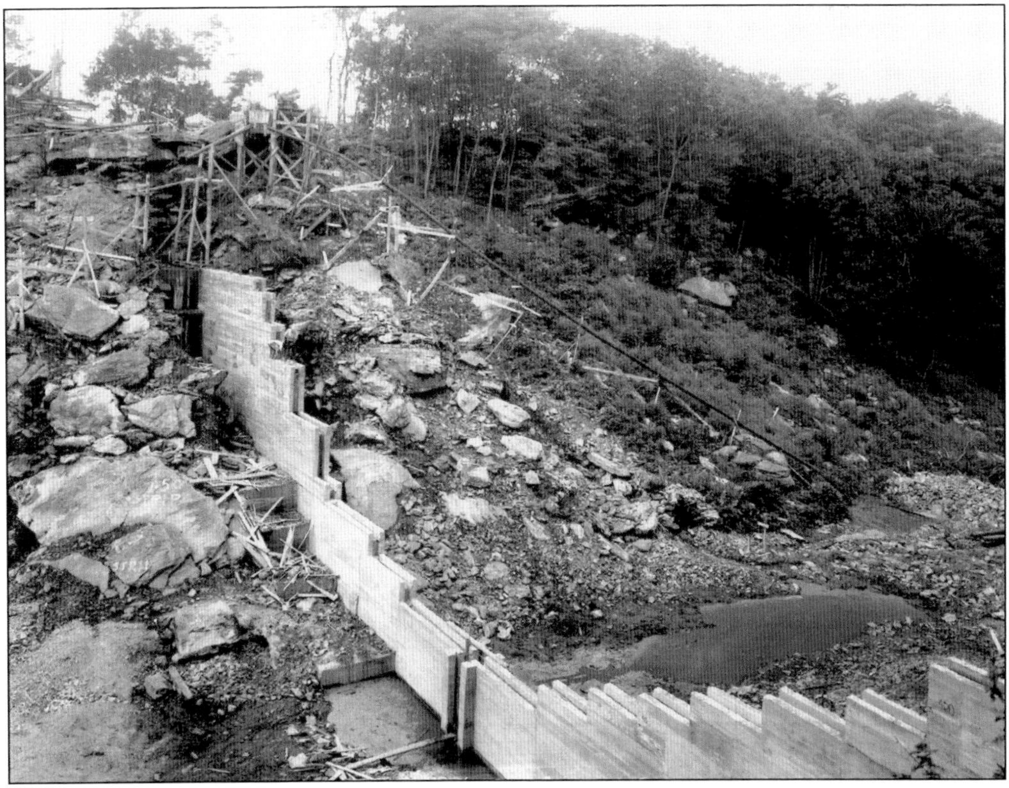

This is another view of the concrete base, seen on September 15, 1927, one month after the previous photograph.

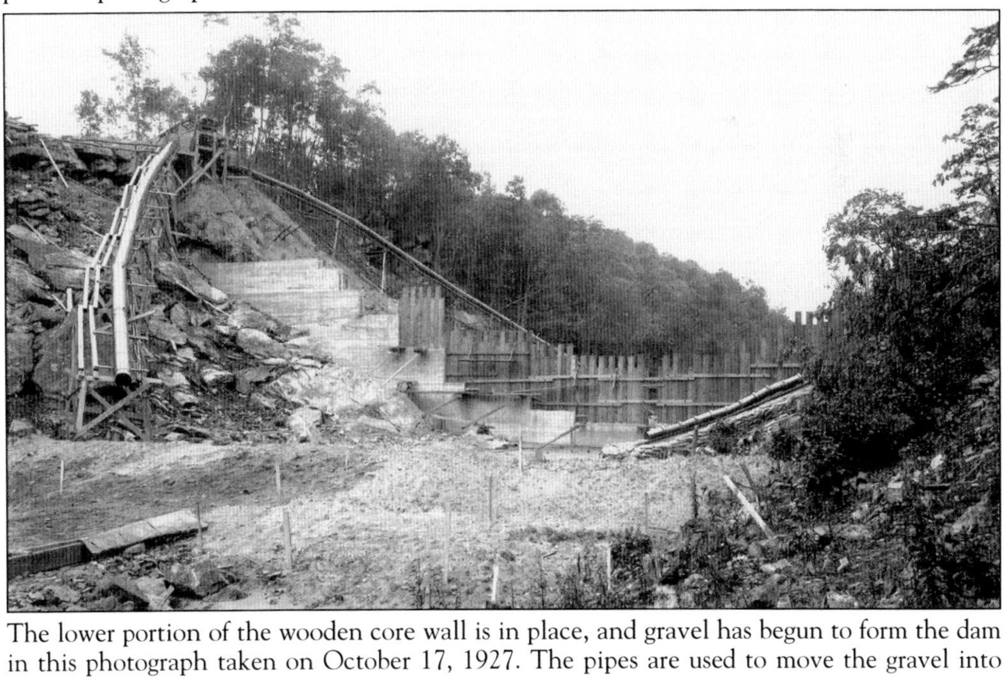

The lower portion of the wooden core wall is in place, and gravel has begun to form the dam in this photograph taken on October 17, 1927. The pipes are used to move the gravel into place using water.

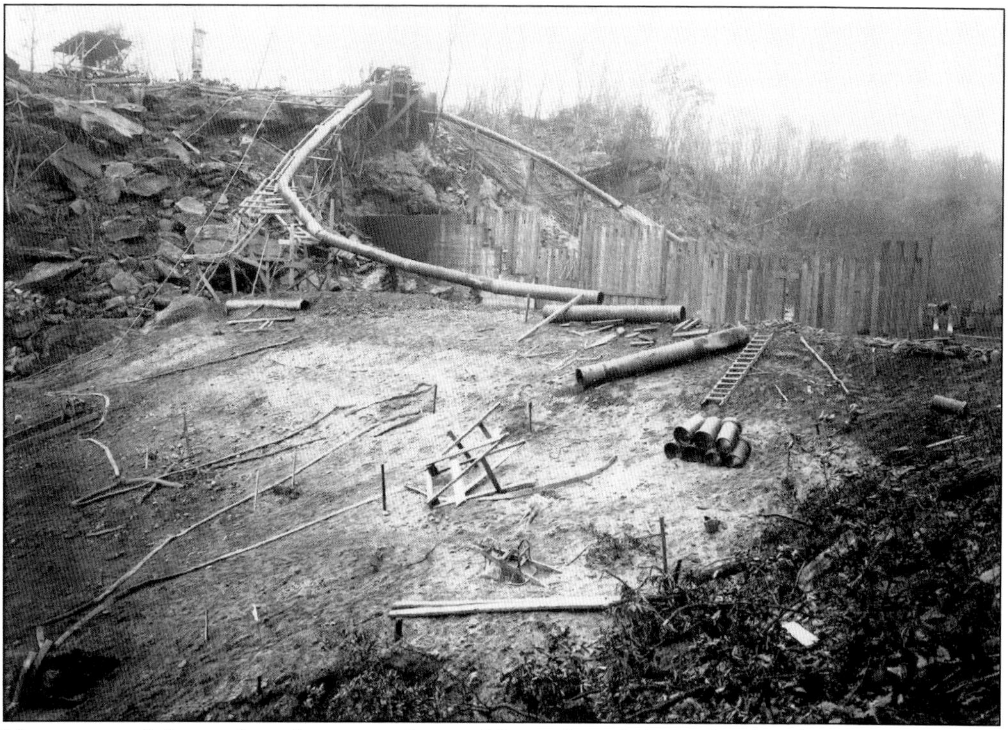

Here, more of the earthen dam is in place in November 1927. Today this dam is found at the far end of Dike Point Recreation Area in New Milford.

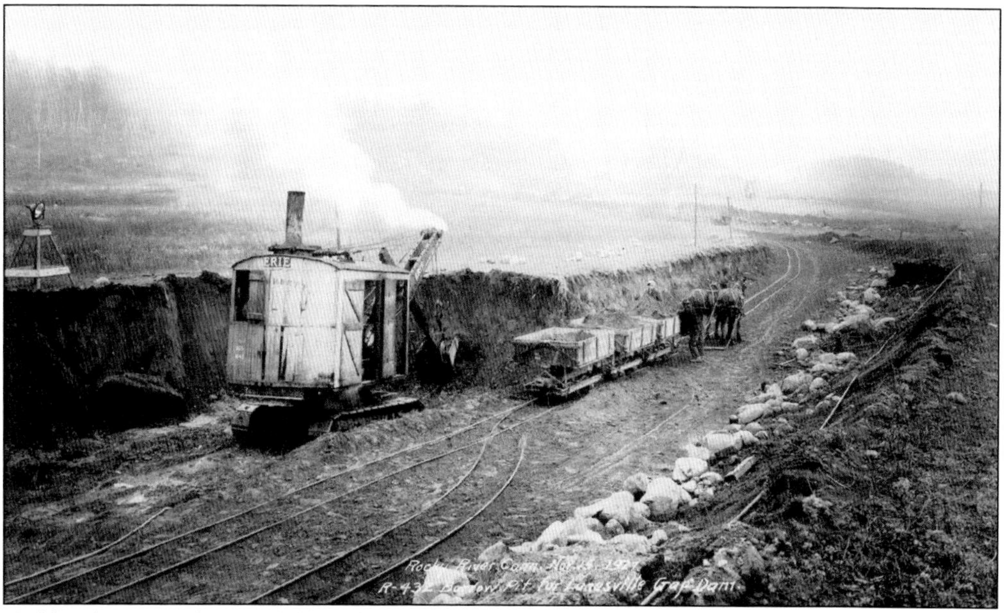

Unlike the main dam and dike, this Lanesville site did not have a natural supply of earthen material next to it for building a dam. Instead, the material had to be dug up and transported from a nearby area. This photograph, taken on November 15, 1927, shows that process. Note the tracks that were placed to facilitate the transport, and the horses that were used to pull the load.

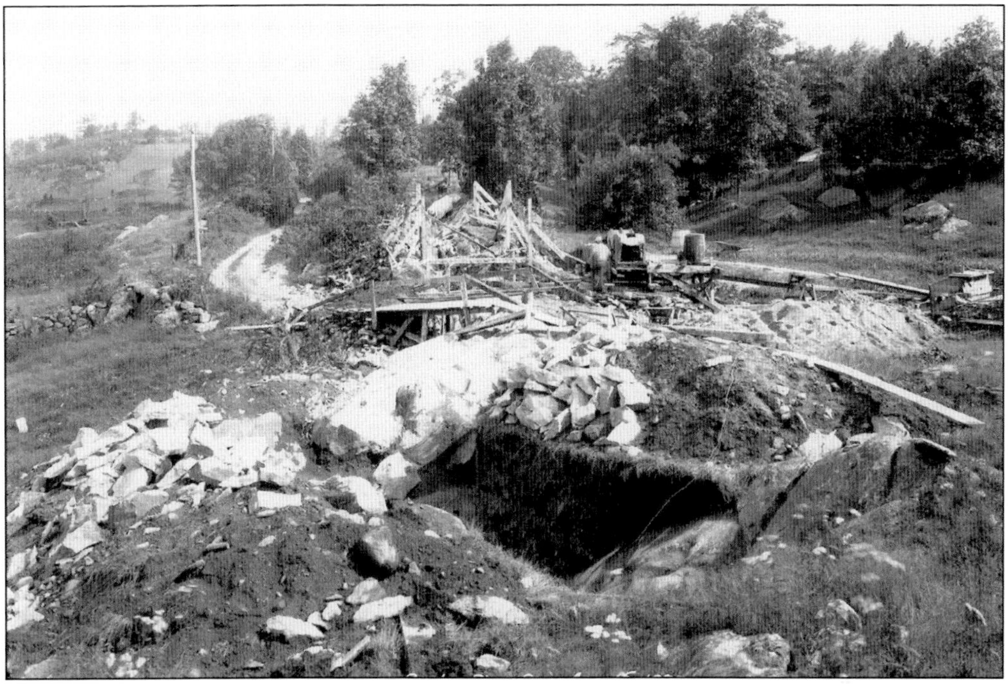

This photograph, dated August 15, 1927, shows the early conditions at a site where a smaller concrete dike was later built in New Milford. Today, the concrete extends between Gerard's Marina and the Dike Point Recreation facility.

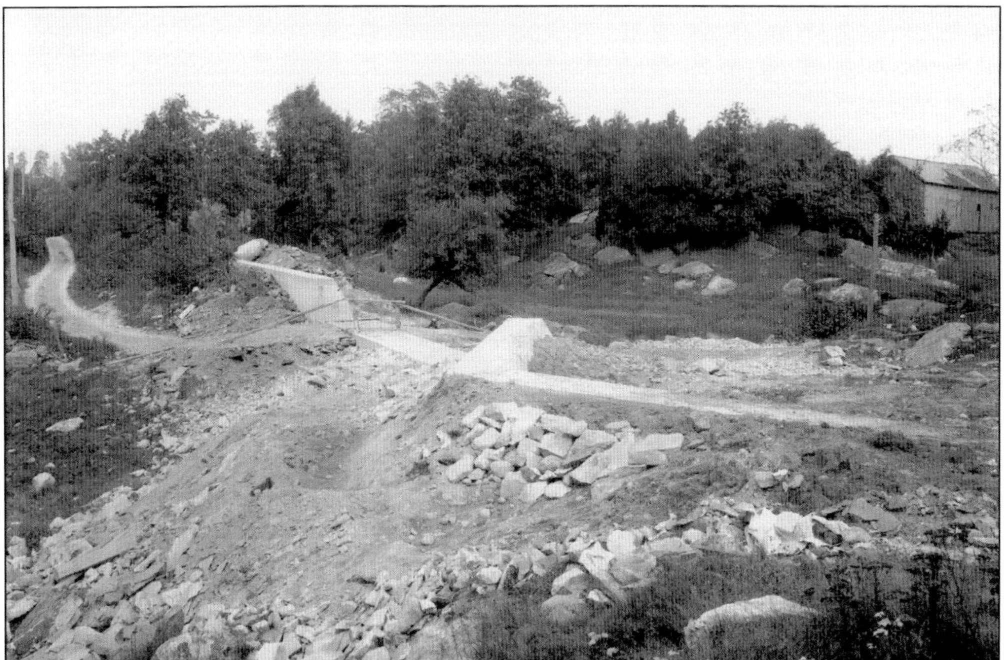

One month later, the New Milford structure is complete. Some 60 years later, concrete was used to raise the lower portion of the dike to its present height as a modification to control all foreseeable floods.

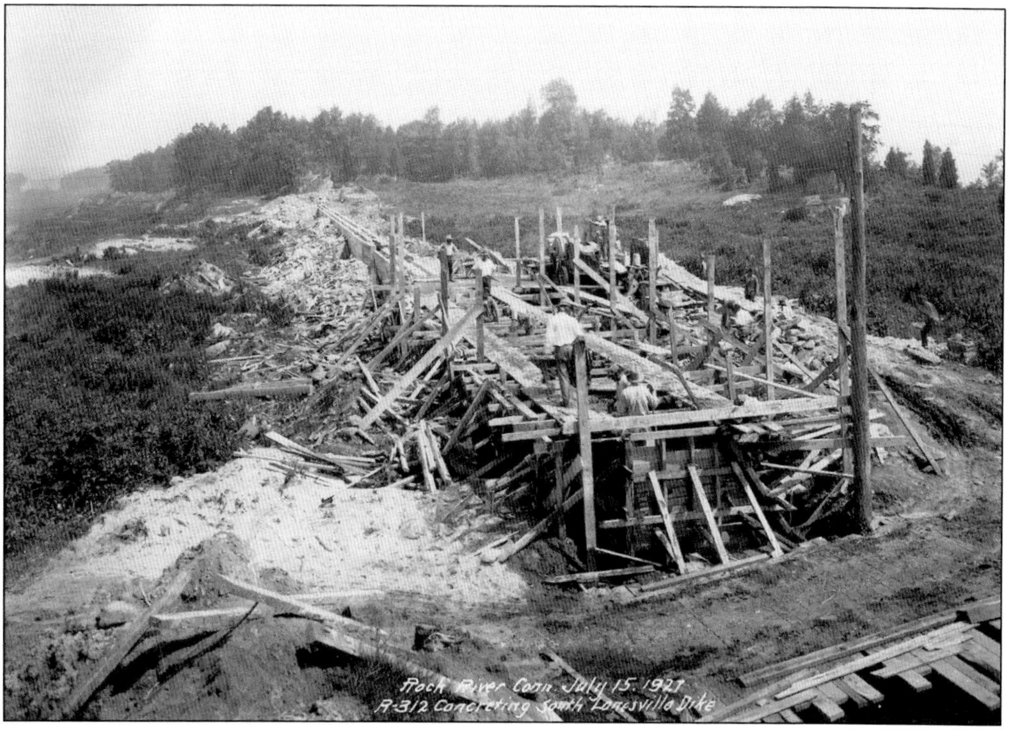

Another smaller dam, similar to the structure seen on the previous page, was needed further south in New Milford. This photograph shows construction in progress on July 15, 1927.

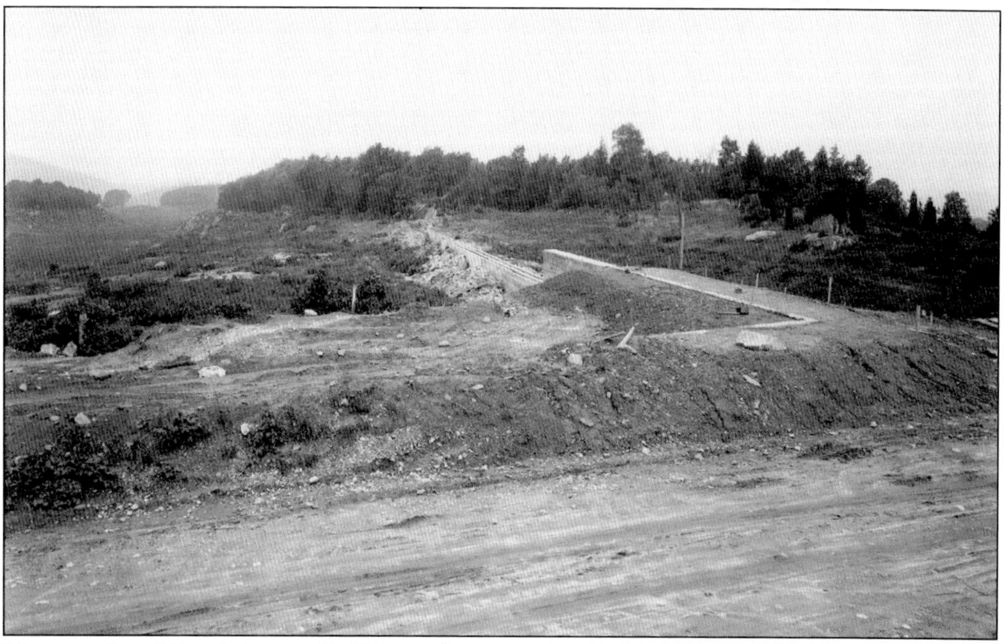

The completed South Lanesville Dike is shown on September 1, 1927. The lower portion was raised with concrete some 60 years after the dike was built. The road in the foreground is now Candlewood Lake Road. Today, the lake is in the area to the upper left of the photograph, and the Candlewood Heights Beach Club graces the shoreline.

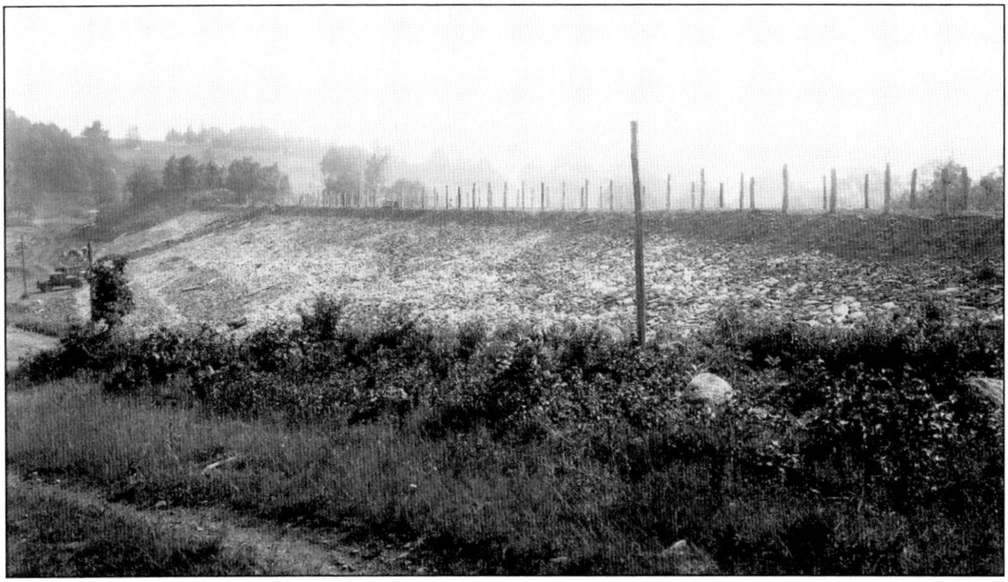

Two more earthen dams were needed in Danbury. This photograph shows the Danbury Main Dam, with Hayestown Road running across the top. This photograph was taken on July 15, 1927, from what is today the Danbury Boat Launch.

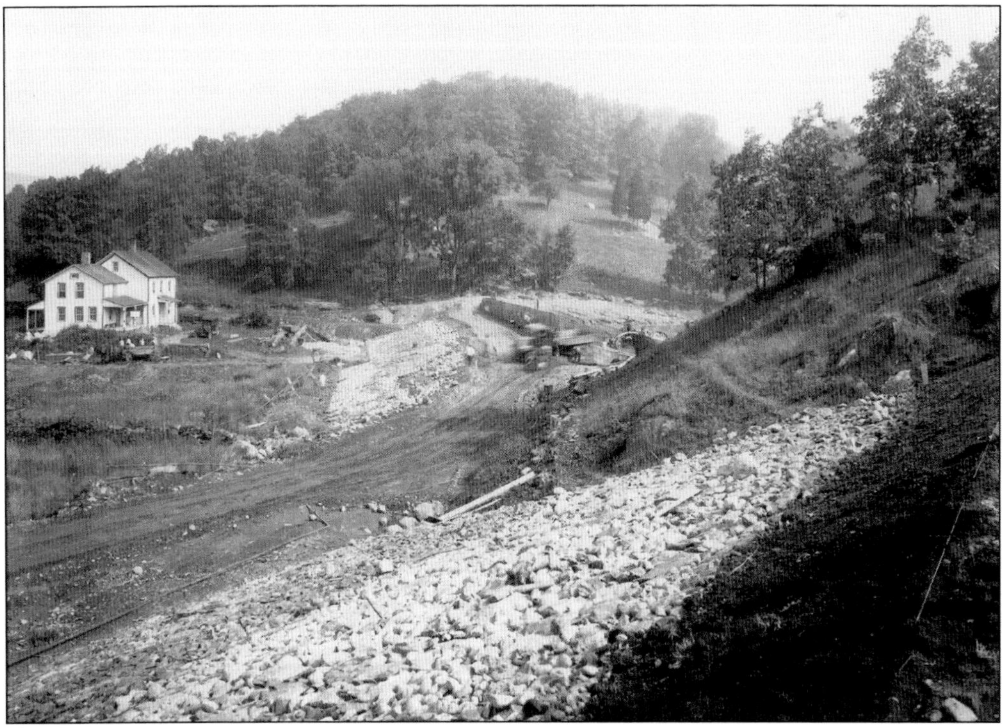

This view from the top of the Danbury main dam looks on the construction of the smaller adjacent Wing Wall Dike. Similar to the other dams, a wooden core wall with concrete foundation is used. However, unlike the other dams, sluicing is not used due to lack of available water. Instead, the fill material is hauled in by truck and compacted, much like today's conventional construction. Note the house that soon found itself in the lake.

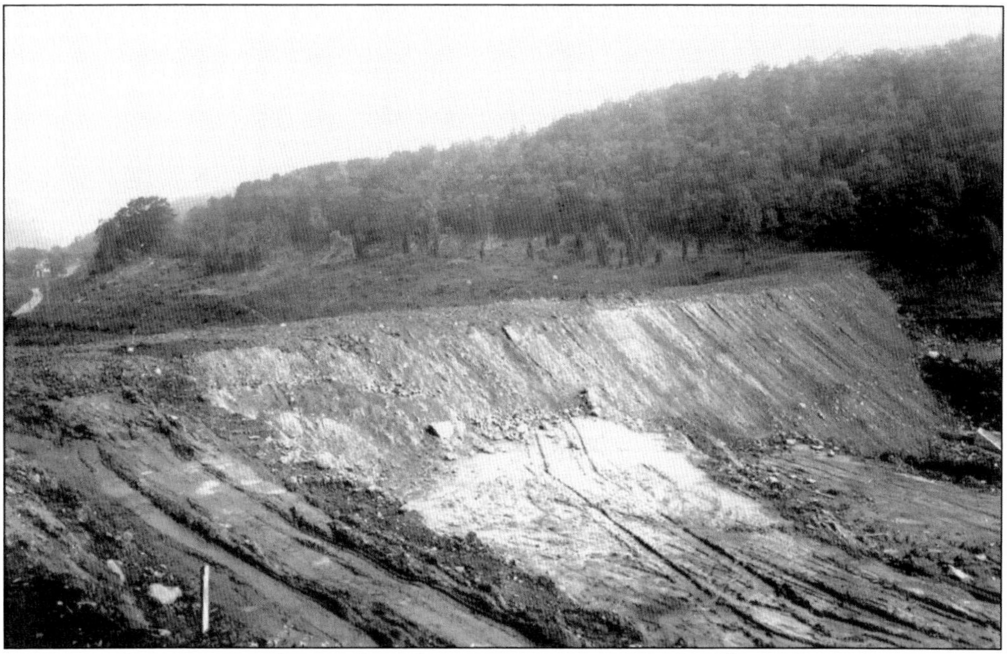

The original Squantz Pond was enlarged to its present size with the filling of Candlewood Lake. The area in this view is now Route 39, which divides the two bodies of water. However, the lake and pond are connected by a pipe that keeps the two water levels at the same elevation.

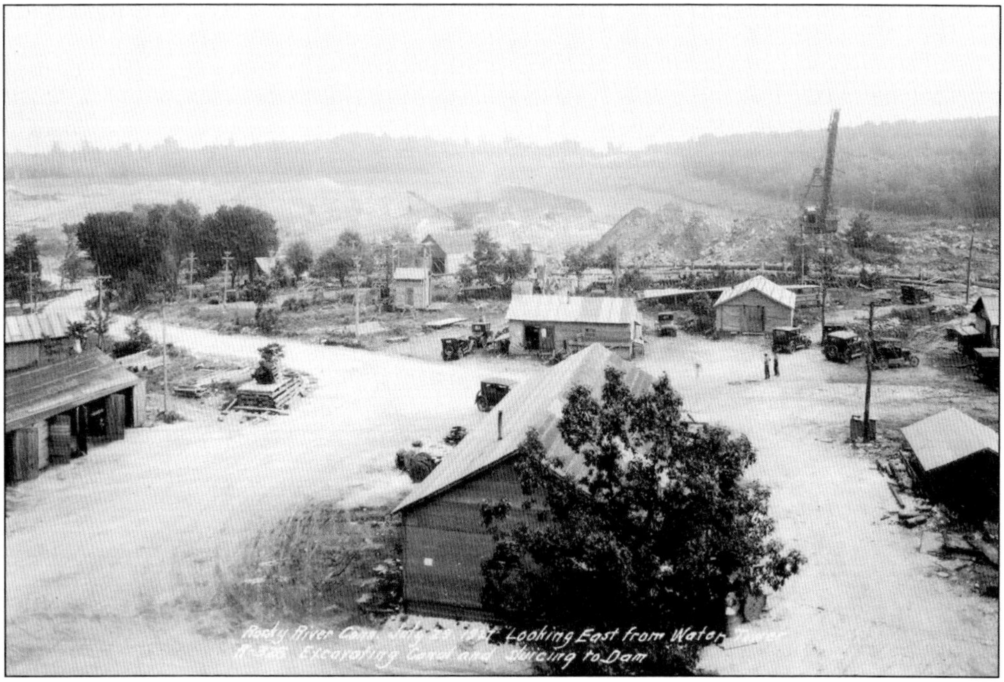

In order to construct the Rocky River powerplant and Candlewood Lake, more than 1,000 men were needed. About 600 of them were fed and housed in a temporary village, called UGI-ville, which is pictured here, near the main dam in New Milford. UGI-ville was named after United Gas Improvement Company of Philadelphia, the firm that was contracted to build the project.

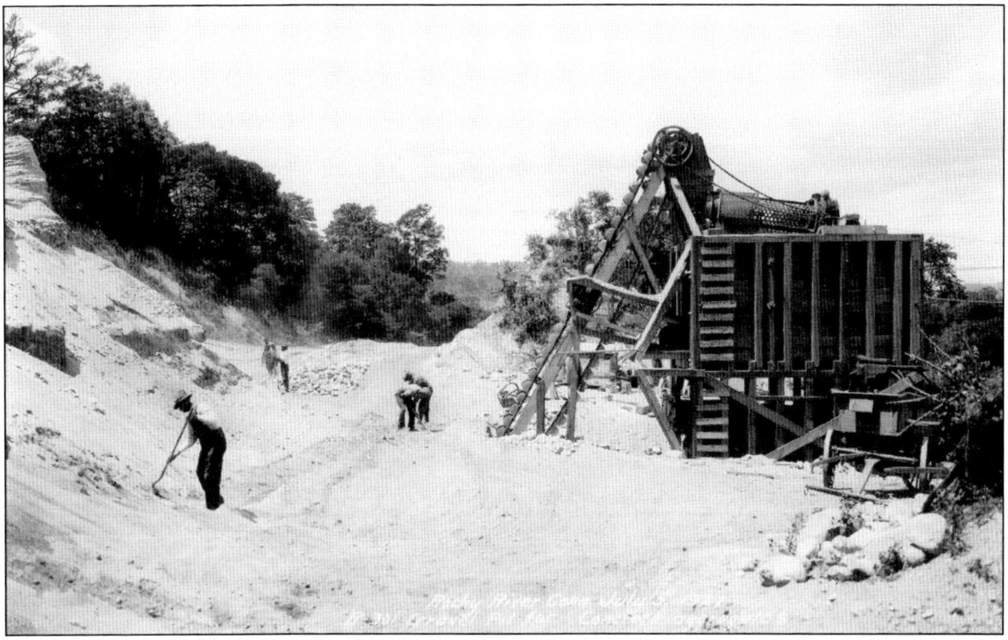

In order to make quality concrete, the correct size of soil and rock is needed. This structure separates the desirable sizes from the undesirable sizes.

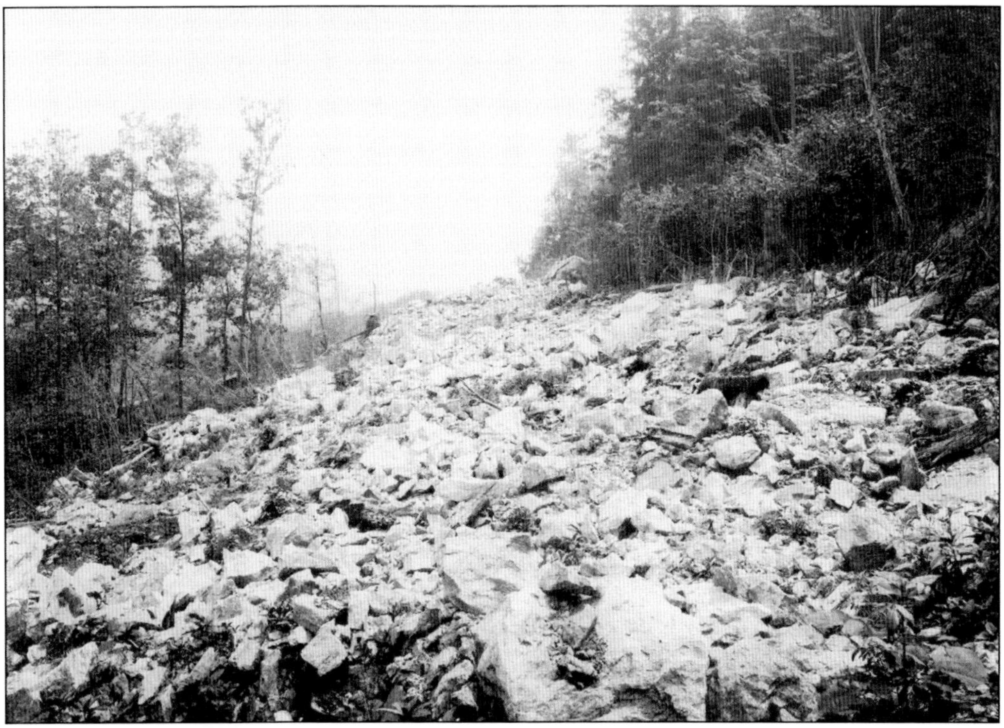

The creation of Candlewood Lake necessitated the flooding of many existing roads, and resulted in the abandonment of some 31 miles of roadway. The project also required the construction of over 9 miles of new roads. This July 29, 1927 photograph shows an area that became Route 39 between Sherman and New Fairfield.

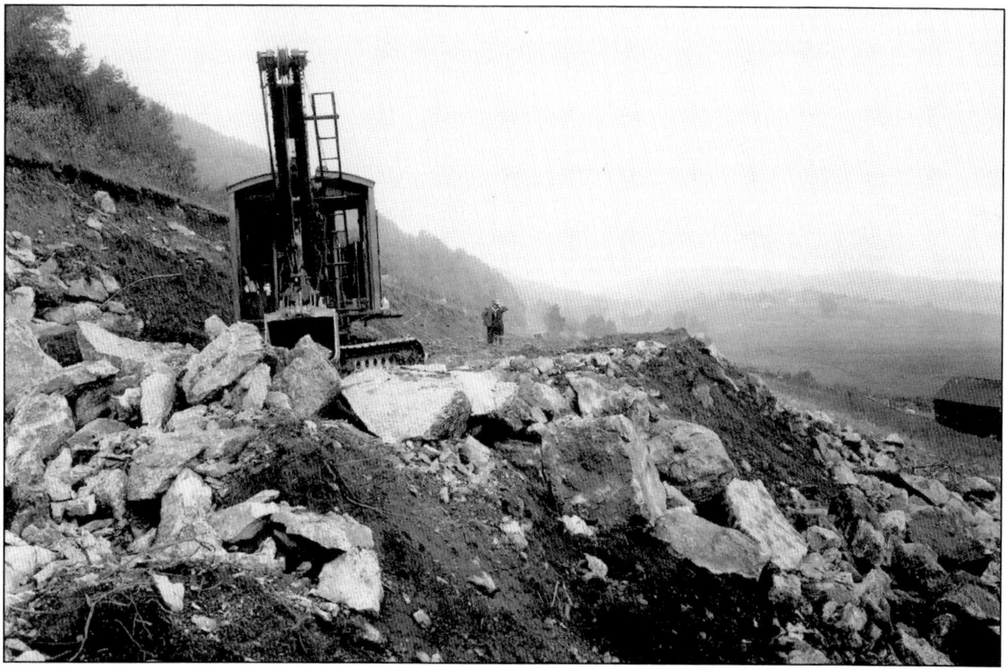

Another photograph of what is now Route 39 shows how mechanized equipment was used to help build the road.

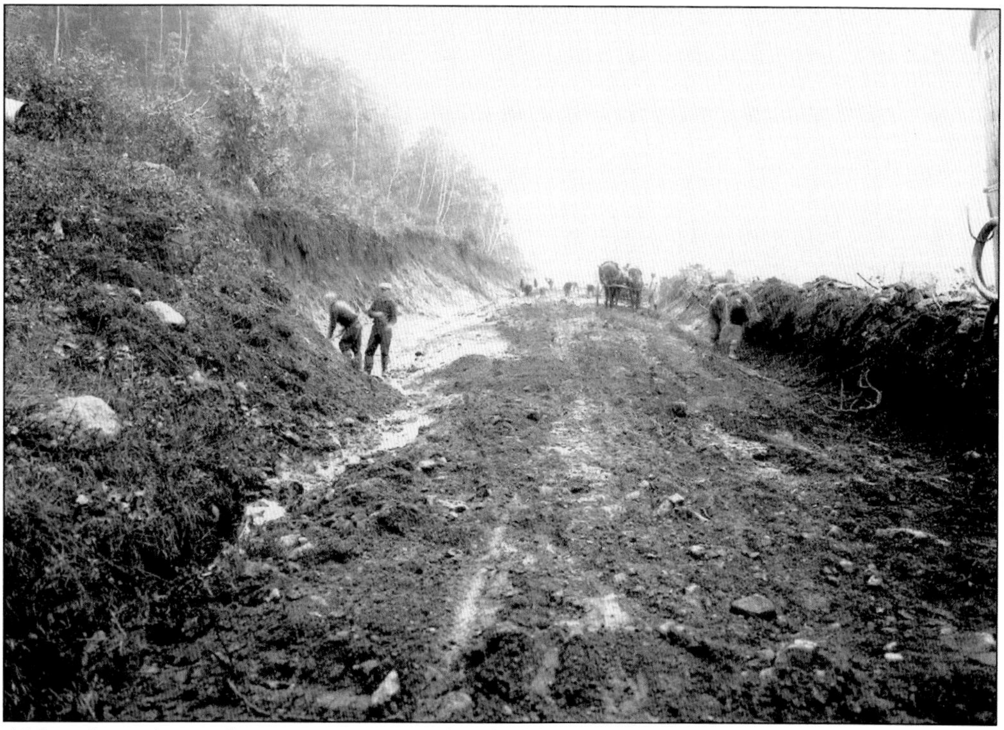

Although mechanized equipment was used in building the roads, so too were the old standbys of hand labor and horses. This is another photograph of what became Route 39 between New Fairfield and Sherman.

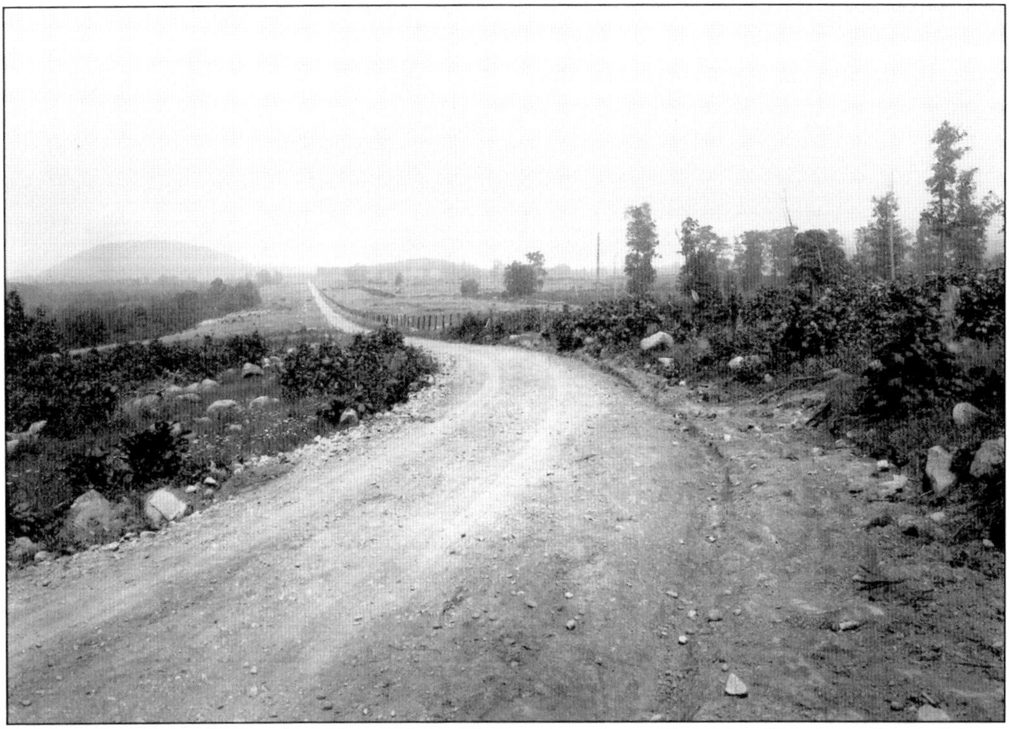

Another road that had to be relocated was the road to Green Pond in Sherman, shown here.

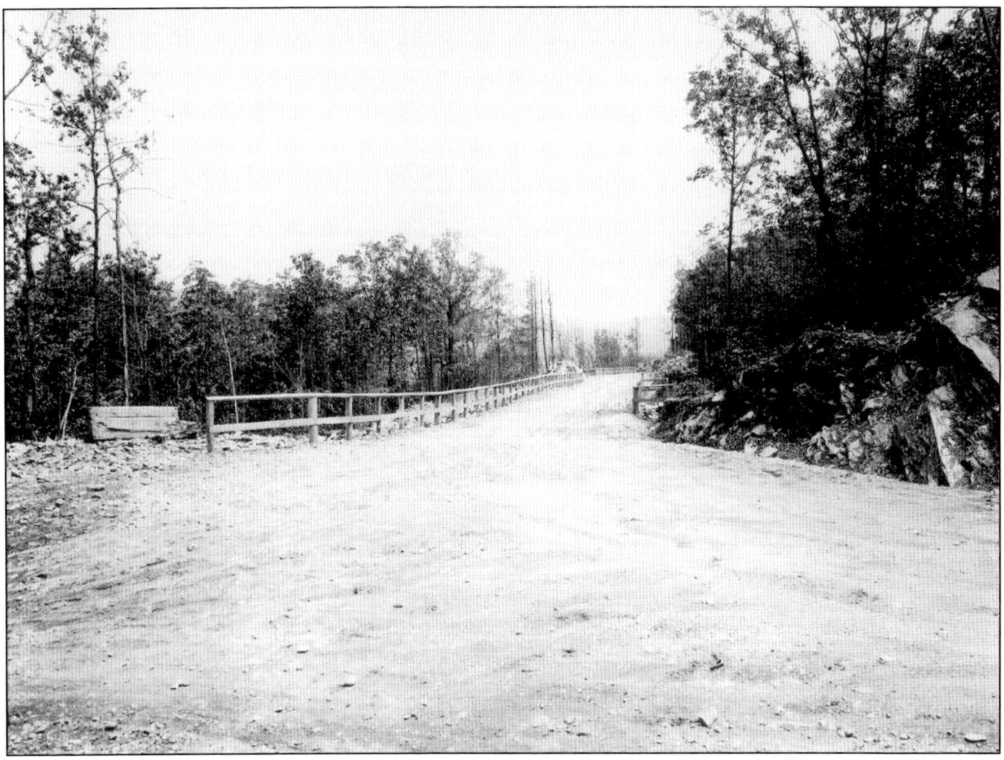

In Danbury, the Stadley Rough Road needed to be relocated.

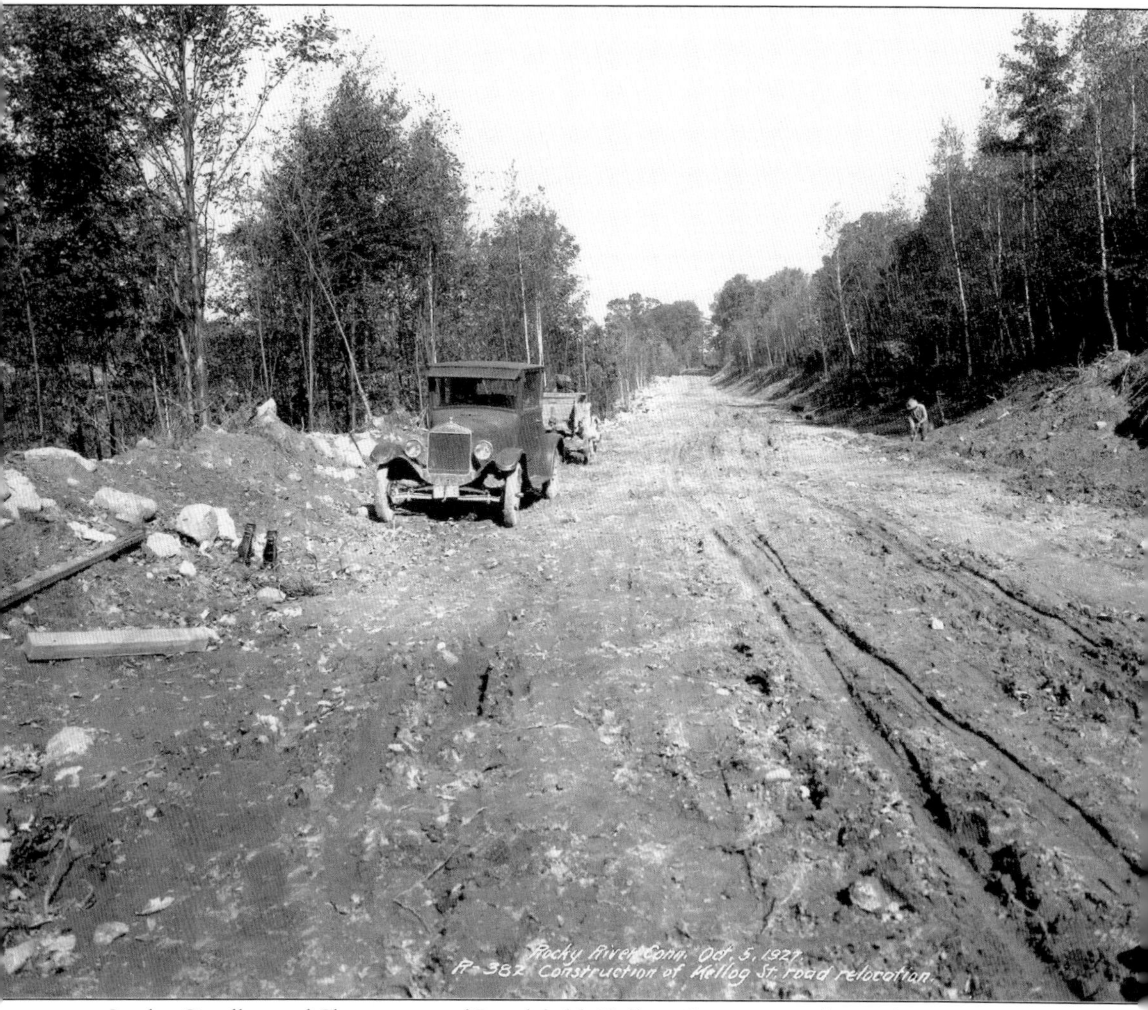

In the Candlewood Shores area of Brookfield, Kellogg Street was relocated.

Three

TOWNS AROUND THE LAKE

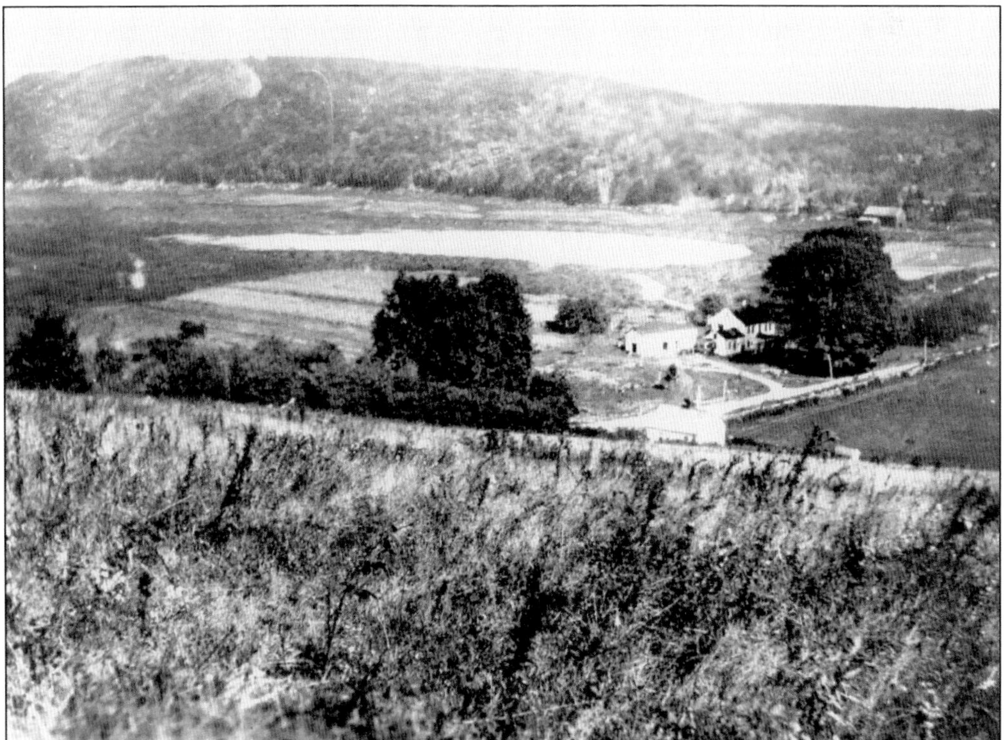

This panoramic view of the valley, looking east in Sherman, depicts the Leach Hollow School and Leach/Constable residence in the middle foreground. Tudor Haviland's barns appear in the background. The body of water is Creek Pond, one of the natural ponds that was flooded by the new lake.

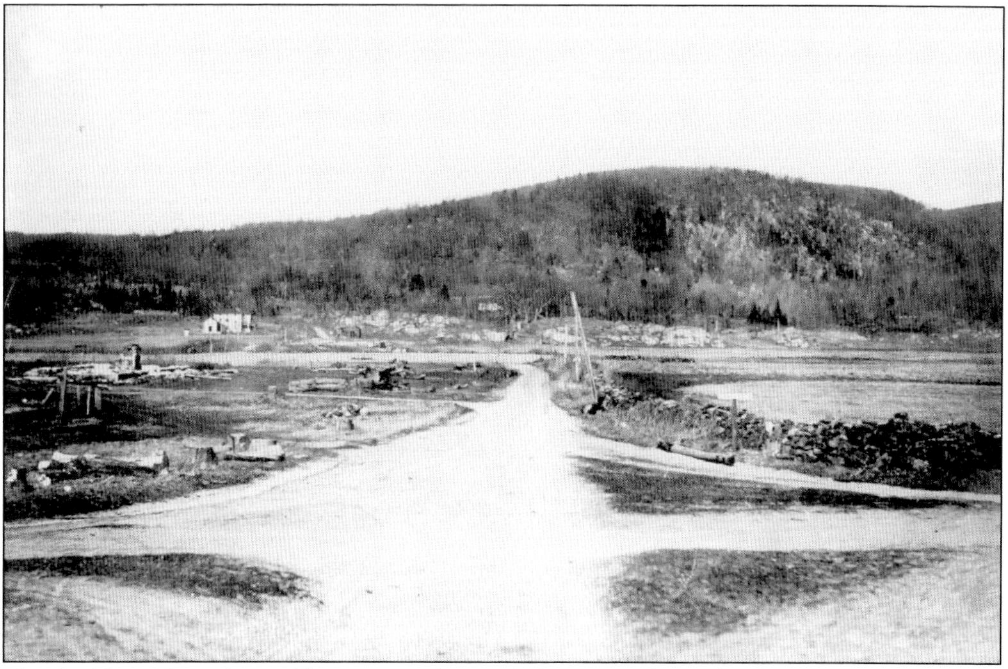

The Redding Turnpike in Sherman is the road that runs along the foreground, intersected by Mill or Mill Pond Road. Only the chimney of the Leach/Constable house remains, as the practice by Connecticut Light and Power Company (CL&P) was to burn down the houses once the homes had been vacated.

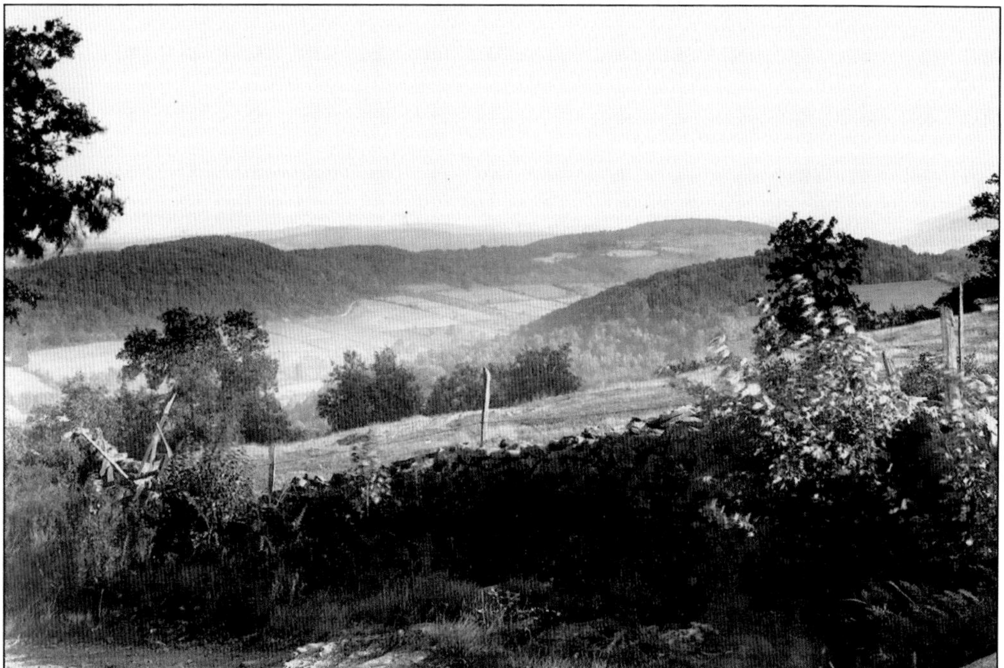

Sherman's Leach Hollow area was a natural valley for flooding in 1926, as this photograph taken from the east ridge of the Theodore Rogers farm shows.

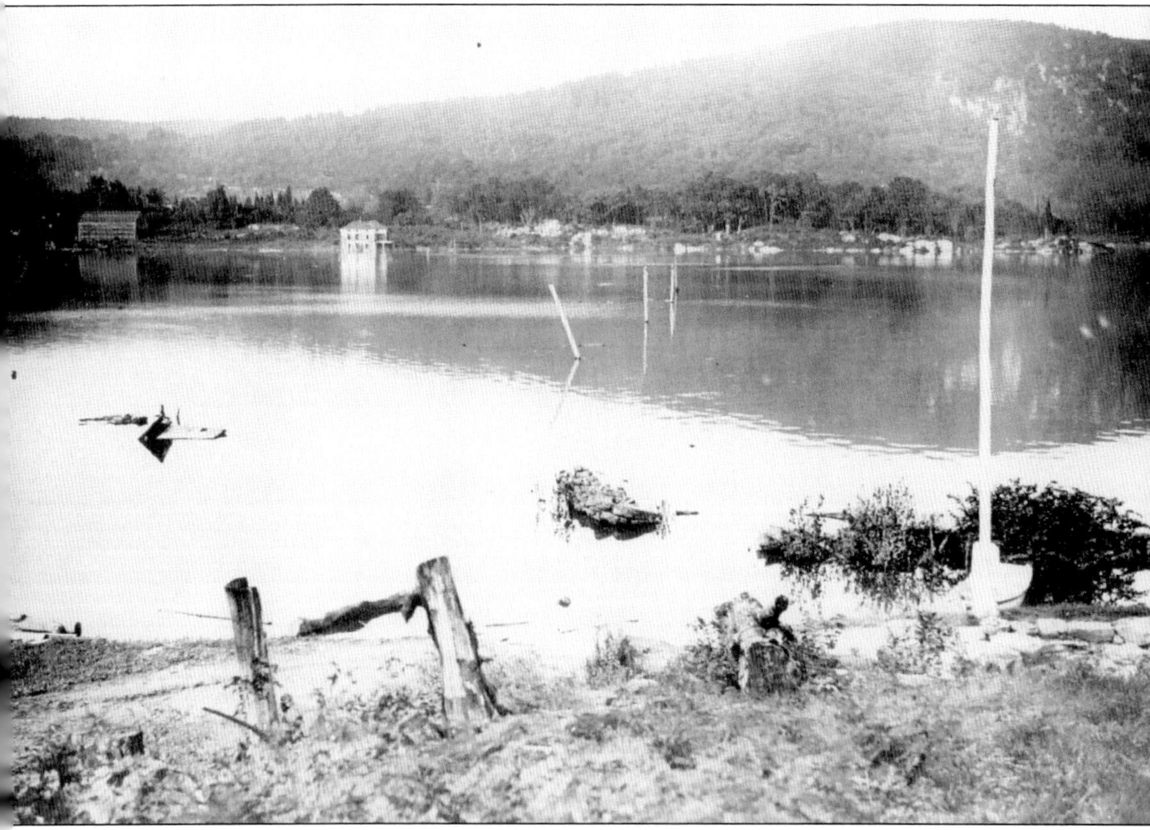

The filling of Candlewood Lake was in progress during the summer of 1928, and it is seen here from the Sherman side of the lake in an area known as the Leach Hollow community. Note that the flooding is well under way and appears to be reaching the Tudor Haviland home on the far shore, which was later flooded over. Also, the telephone poles and the flagpole from the Leach Hollow School are still standing and can be seen on the right.

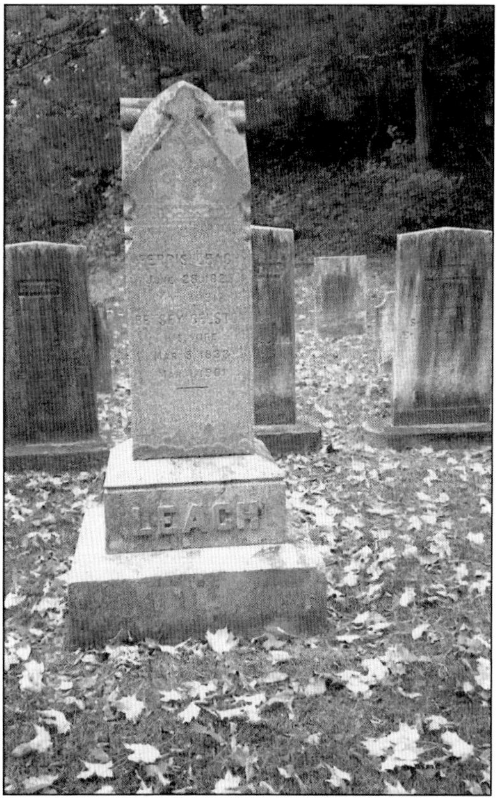

The construction of Candlewood Lake also affected the dead, as small cemeteries and family plots were located within the lake's boundaries. Workers were paid $1 per body to disinter and rebury the remains in other local cemeteries. A small property on Saw Mill Road was purchased by the Sherman Cemetery Association and became the final resting place for many Leach, Hall, and Hoag family members. This is a recent photograph of the Leach family plot in the Saw Mill Cemetery.

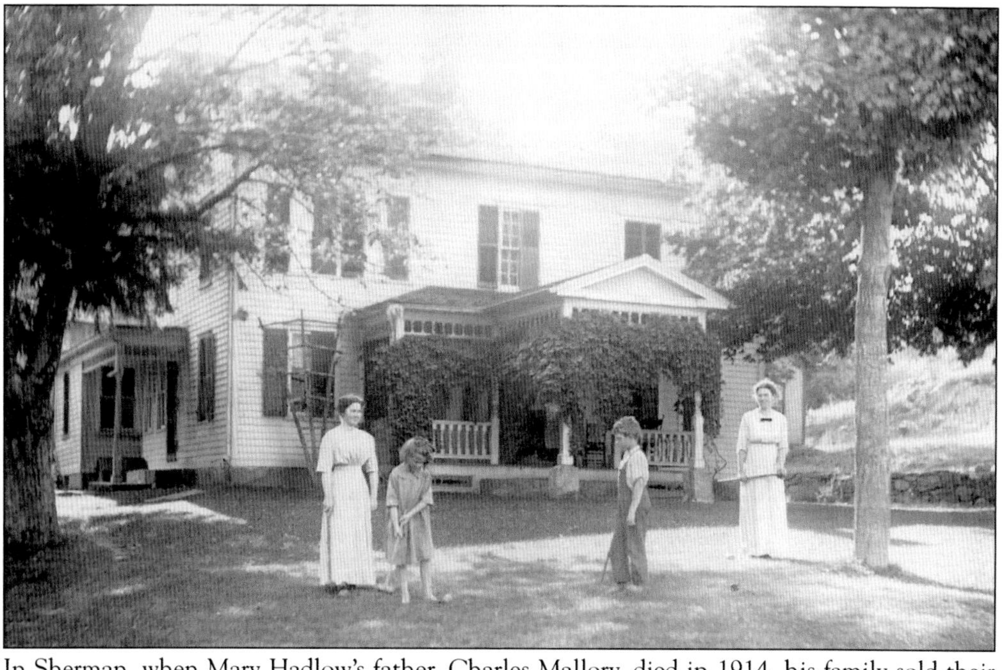

In Sherman, when Mary Hadlow's father, Charles Mallory, died in 1914, his family sold their homestead to Charles and Anna Strid. Due to the home's location, it was probably one of the last houses reached by the rising waters of Candlewood Lake.

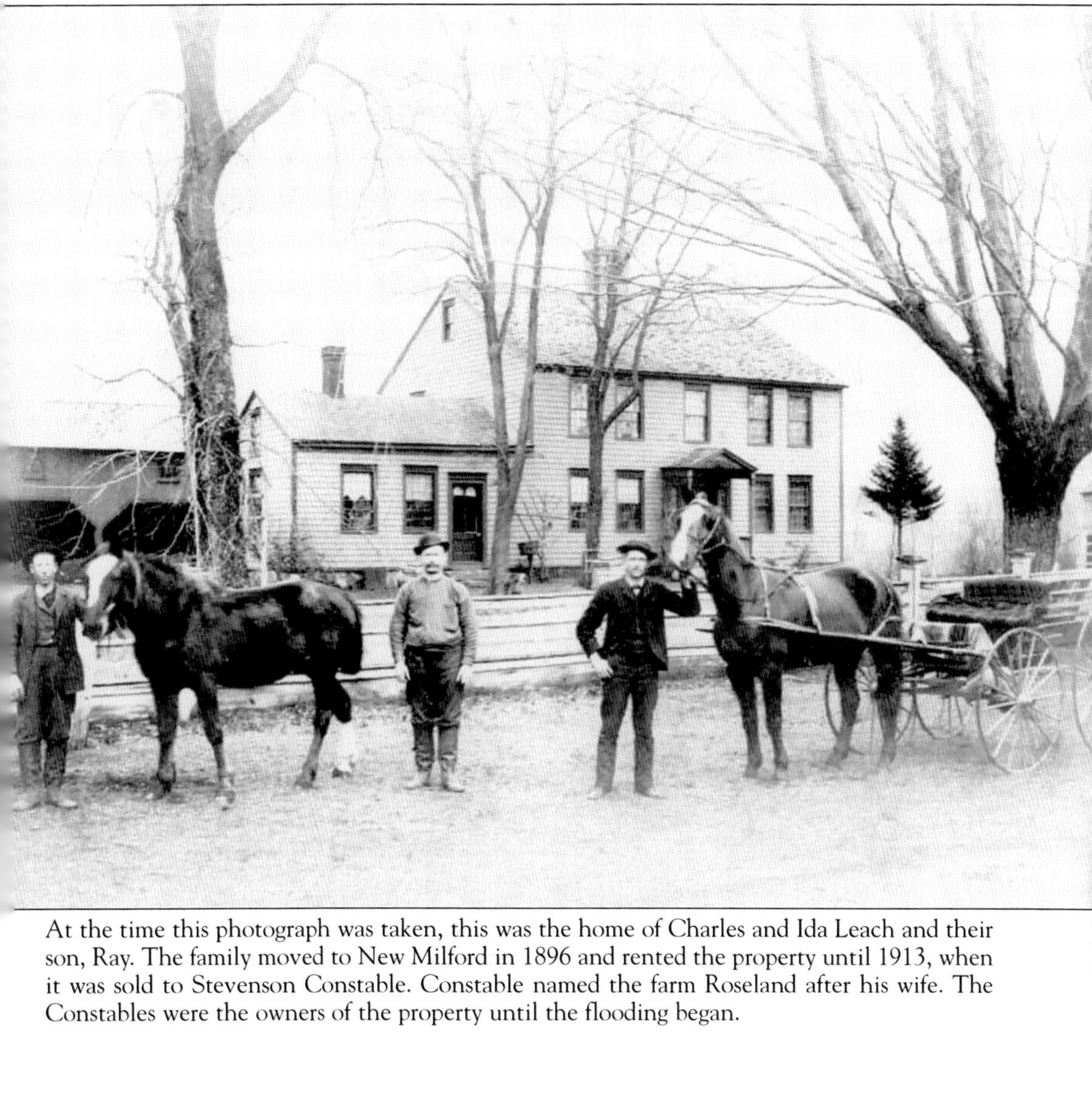

At the time this photograph was taken, this was the home of Charles and Ida Leach and their son, Ray. The family moved to New Milford in 1896 and rented the property until 1913, when it was sold to Stevenson Constable. Constable named the farm Roseland after his wife. The Constables were the owners of the property until the flooding began.

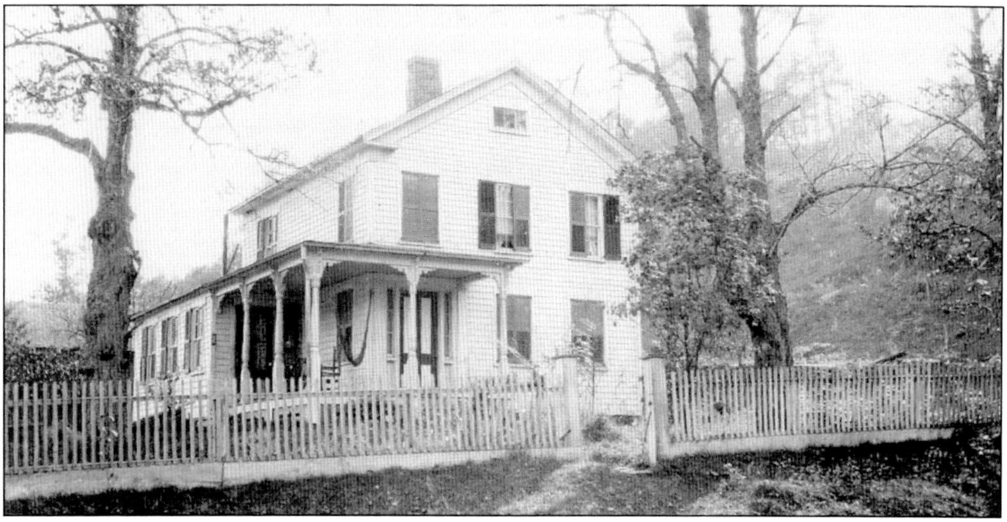

Thomas McGoldrick was the last owner of this house in Sherman before the flooding. It was referred to as the Roswell Place, after its 19th-century owner, Elliott Roswell. In 1926, CL&P began its purchase of properties that were going to be affected by the flooding, paying "pre-lake," fair-market values. The sale prices were not recorded, but Lester Bennett Sr. recalled that his family's 90-acre farm, originally purchased by the Bennetts for $3,500, was sold to CL&P five years later at a $3,000 profit. Since CL&P had been granted eminent domain by the state, land was flooded even if the owners of the property refused to sell. The Atchison brothers were such a case, and the present homeowners in Atchison Cove still pay taxes to the town of Sherman for land now covered by water.

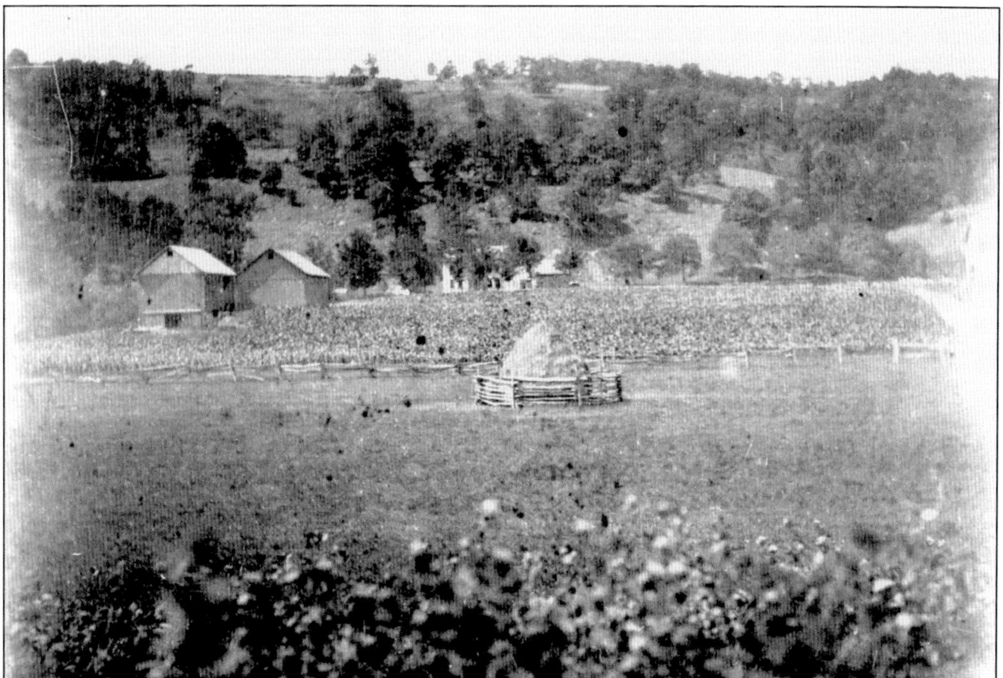

This photograph shows the days of tobacco farming in the valley. This is the Charles Mallory farm in Sherman, in the Leach Hollow section of town.

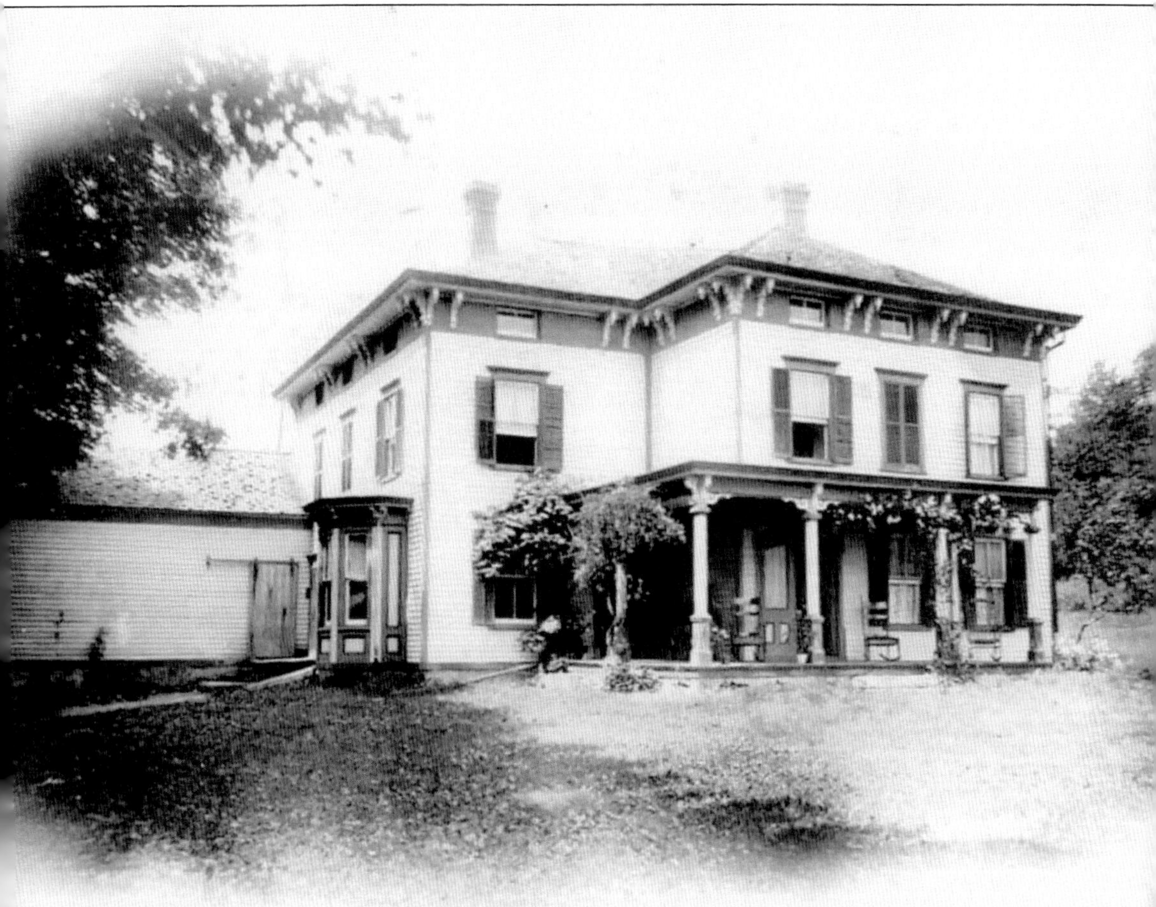

H. Tudor Haviland built this Victorian home in Sherman in the 1880s for his new bride, Florence Briggs. Their daughter, Nettie, and son-in-law, Charles E. Akin, later sold the property to CL&P. Itinerant photographers often took pictures of families posed in front of their residences with their farm workers. By the time construction of Candlewood Lake began, most properties had been transferred to new owners, but were still referred to by the names of the original owners.

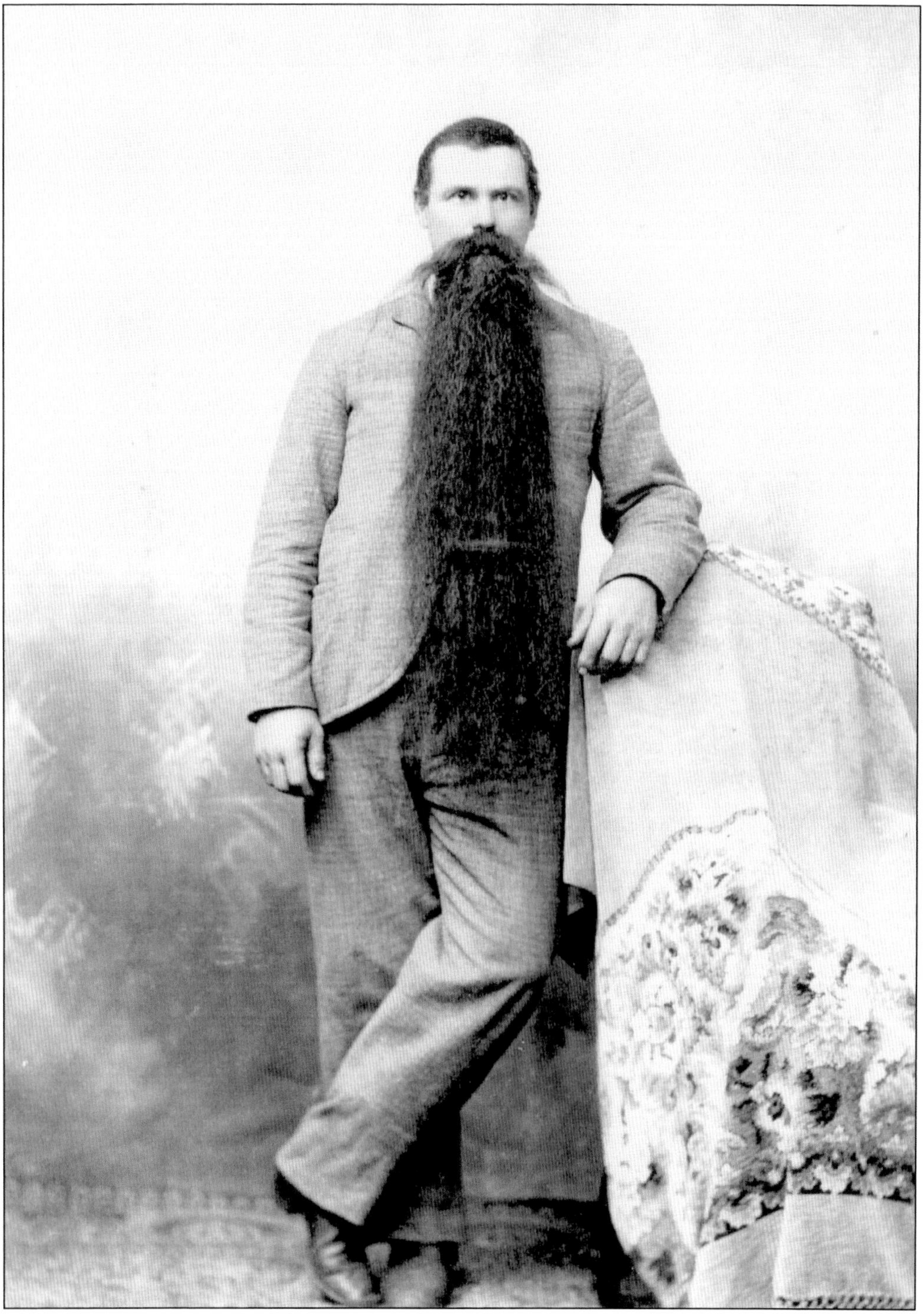

Shown here is H. Tudor Haviland, a prominent Sherman resident. This photograph was likely taken at the beginning of the 20th century.

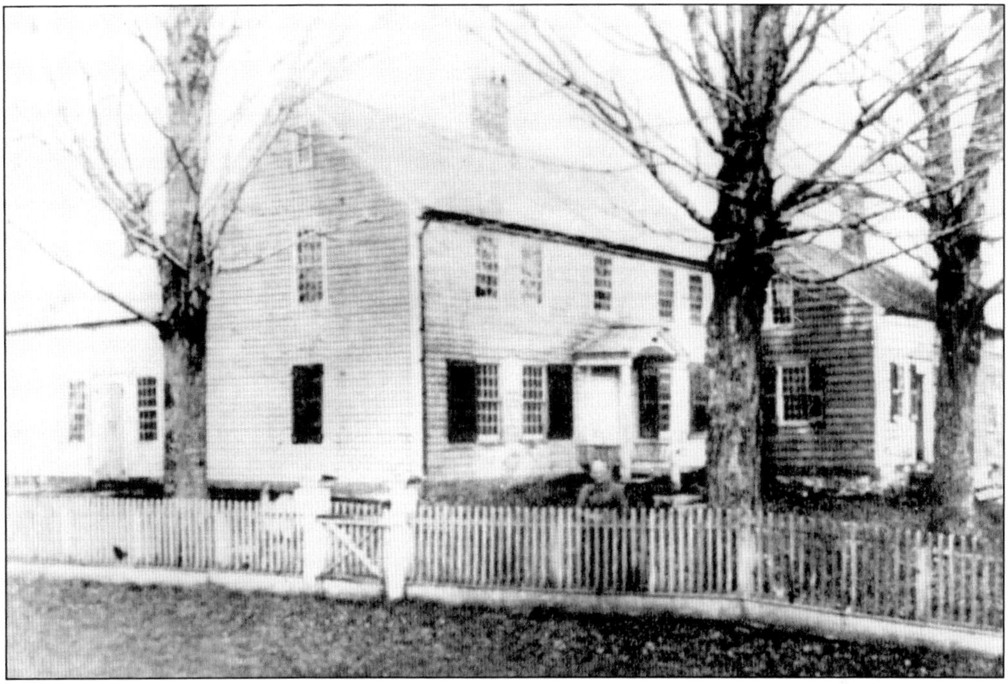

This is the R. P. Brady residence in Sherman. Mr. and Mrs. Brady were the maternal grandparents of H. Tudor Haviland. Mrs. Brady made lovely quilts, which are still with the family in the area.

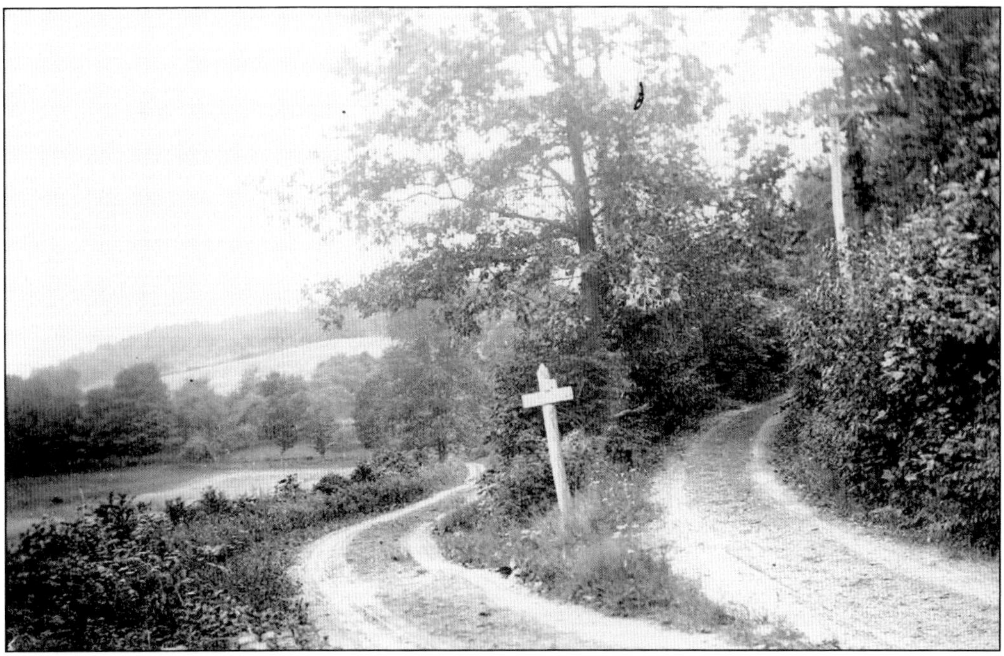

The left fork of the Redding Turnpike approaches Leach Hollow in Sherman from the north. Both the turnpike and the "cat path" on the right are now flooded.

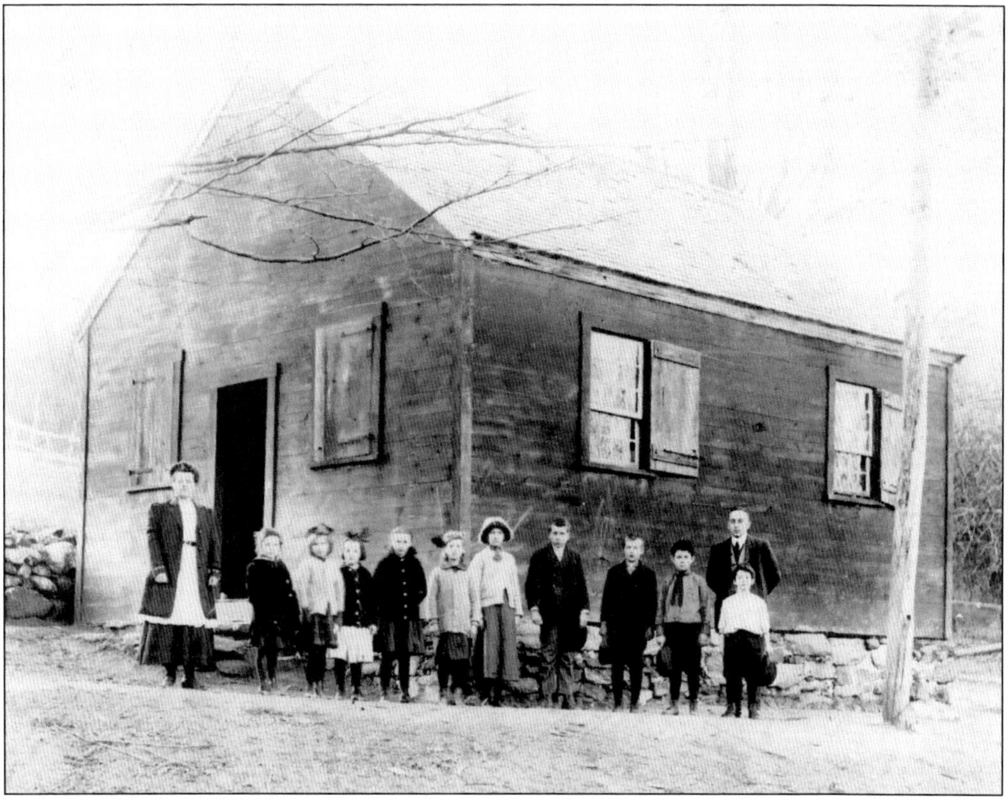

To avoid flooding of the Leach Hollow School in Sherman, the building was relocated near the cat path. The schoolhouse was used as a dwelling, and the Leach Hollow students were transferred to the old Center School.

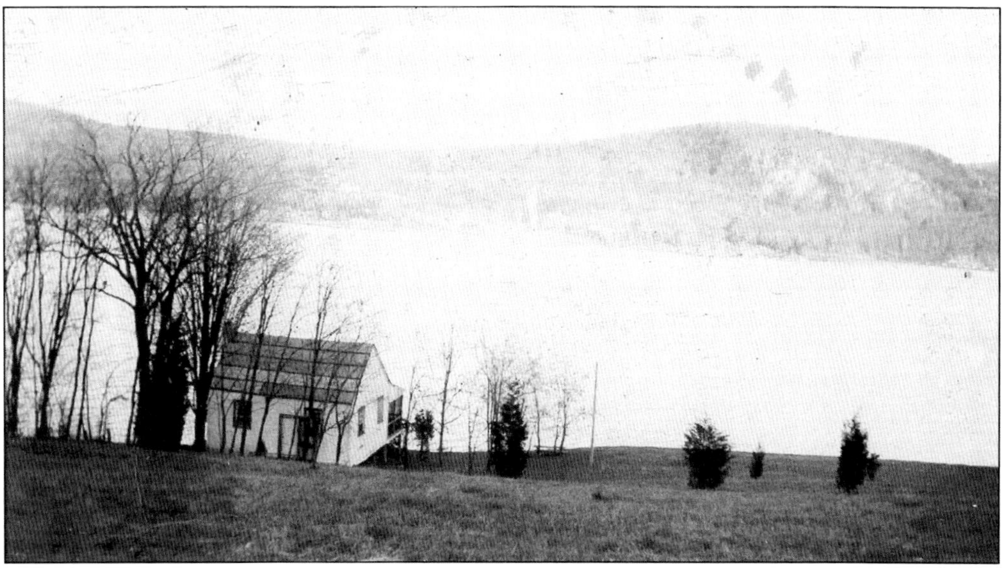

This photograph, taken about 1929, shows the Leach Hollow School, which had been moved up to safer ground to prevent it from being flooded. It was used by the Kelley family of Sherman as a summer camp until 1953, when a new house was built on the same site.

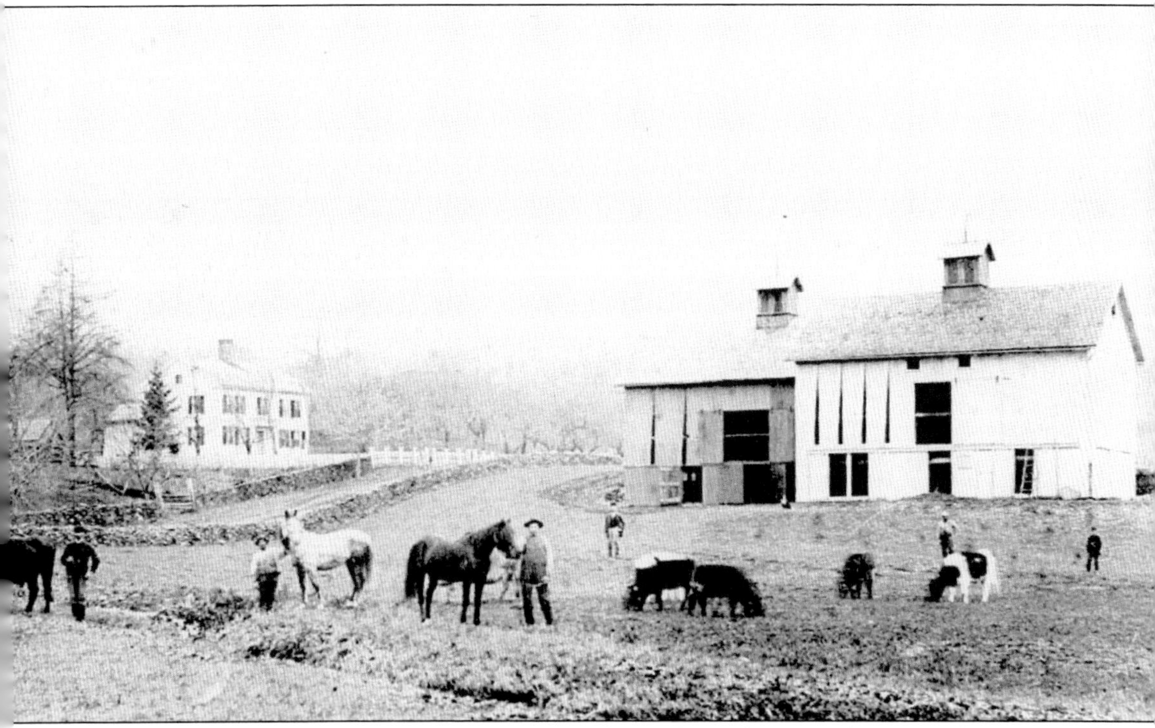

The open slats of the Mallory barns in Sherman indicate that tobacco is drying inside. Once an important cash crop to Sherman's farmers, the price of tobacco dropped almost 50 percent between 1920 and 1930.

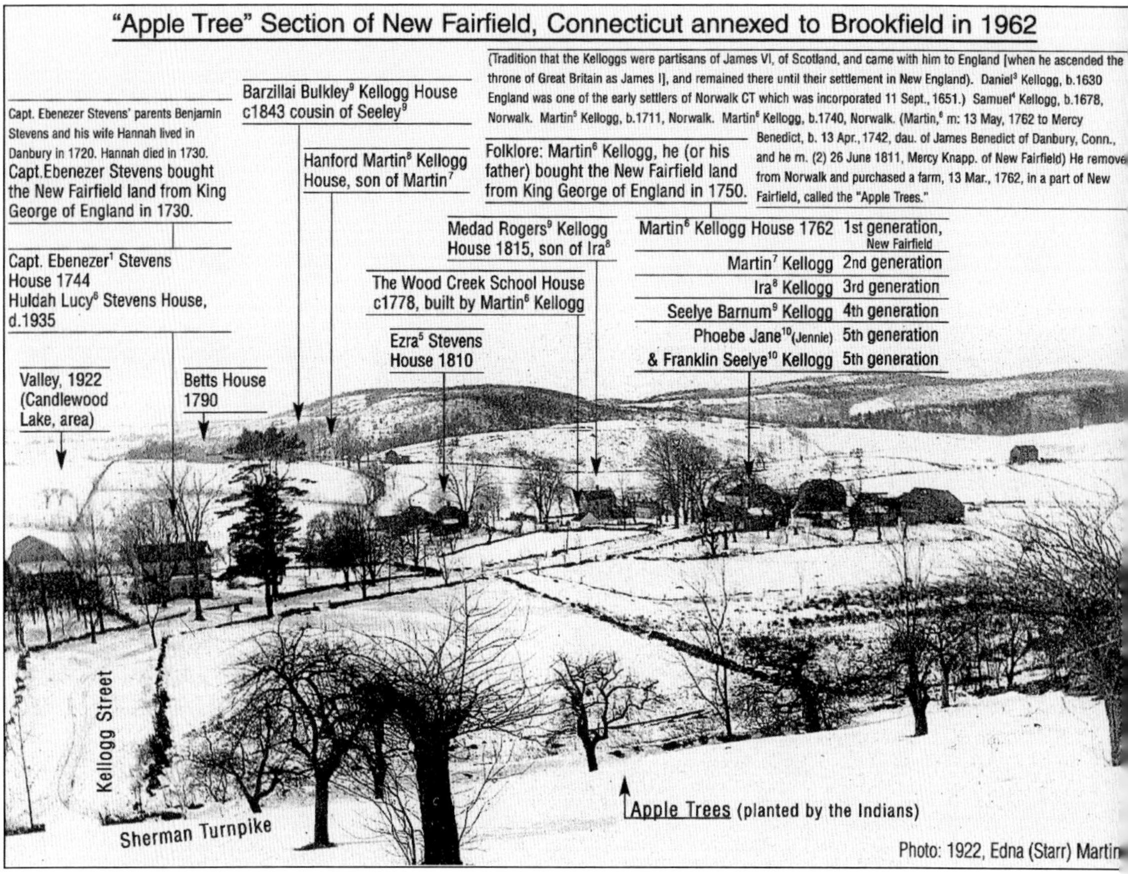

The Martin Kellogg house was the second one constructed in the Apple Trees section of New Fairfield, the first being Capt. Ebenezer Stevens's house, built c. 1744, next door. The Stevens family built up the south side of the road, and the Kelloggs built up the north side. Martin paid for the construction of the schoolhouse and the Wood Creek School, which was built c. 1778 and was located on Stevens family property. Kellogg also took in the schoolmaster and subsequent schoolmasters as boarders in his home. Both family farms held property in Brookfield, Danbury, and New Fairfield.

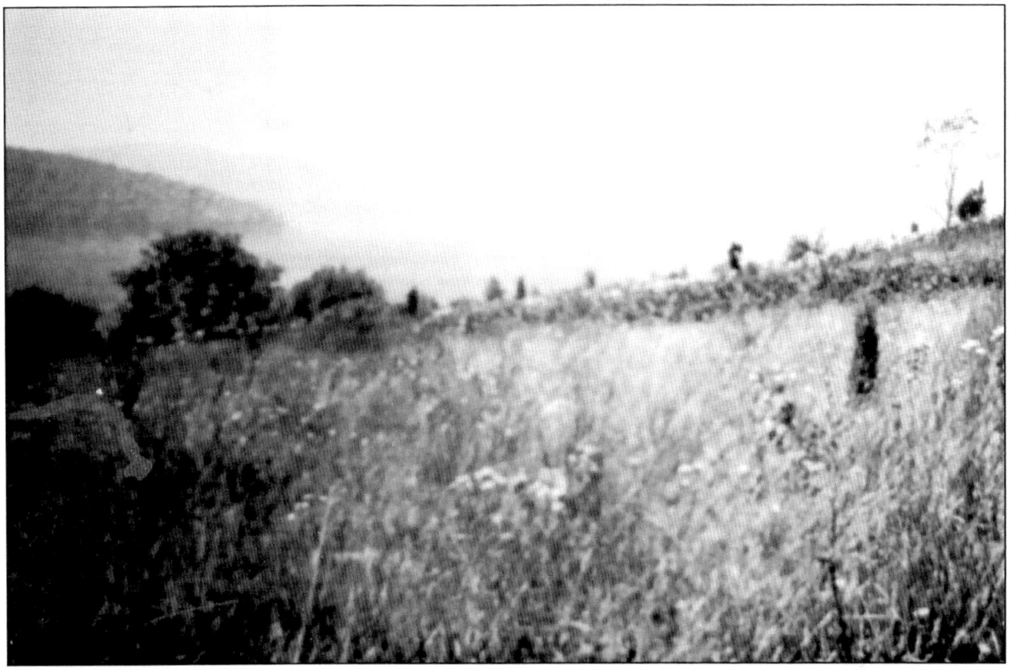

This view looks west from the Kellogg School in Brookfield over the area that was flooded to form the lake. Before the area was under water, there were houses, stone walls, barns, orchards, bridges, a cemetery, and farms on this land. Some vestiges of the old structures, now under water, can be seen when scuba diving in the lake. The majority of the bodies in the cemeteries were removed to graveyards in New Fairfield and Brookfield, but some families chose not to move the remains of their loved ones. Today Arrowhead Point is on the right.

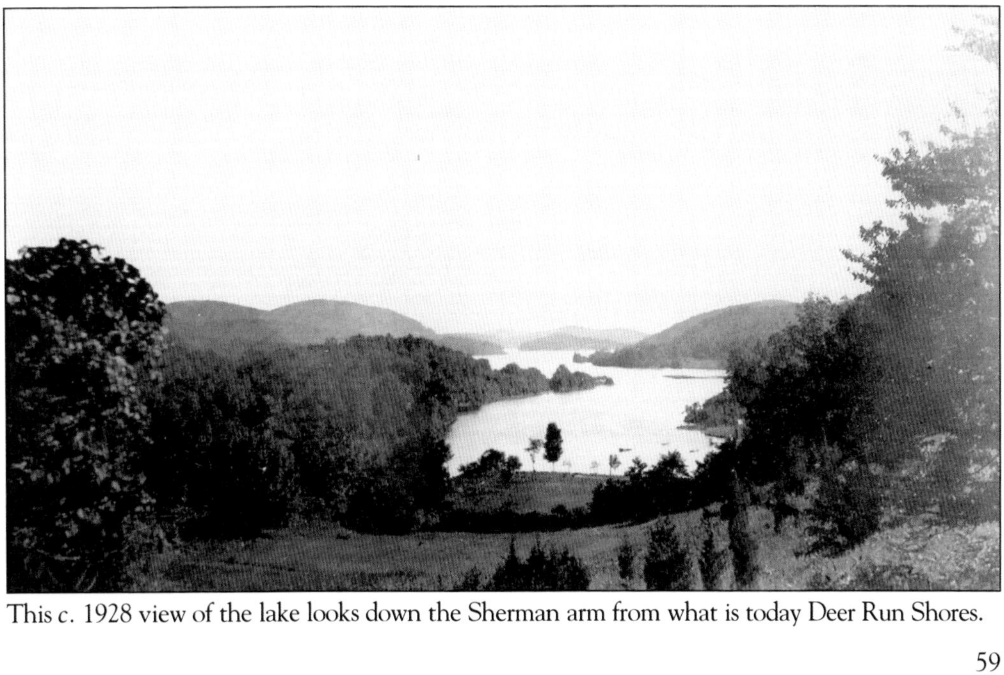

This *c.* 1928 view of the lake looks down the Sherman arm from what is today Deer Run Shores.

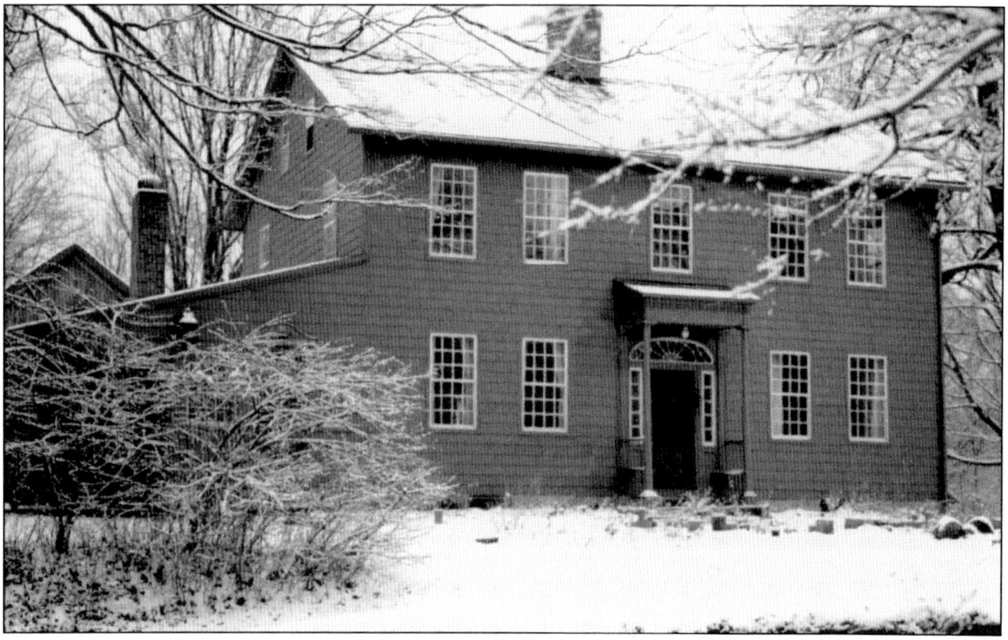

Martin Kellogg bought a 110-acre working farm and built his house c. 1762. That same year he married Mercy (Kemp) Benedict of Danbury. Kellogg had extensive land holdings. Evidence of his wealth is in the house he built at the time. Five generations of Kelloggs lived in the house. They were farmers and prominent New Fairfield residents. All of the Kelloggs on the street descended from Martin. The Kelloggs' summer boarder, Jean Webster, niece of Mark Twain, wrote her first book, *Daddy Long Legs*, at the house.

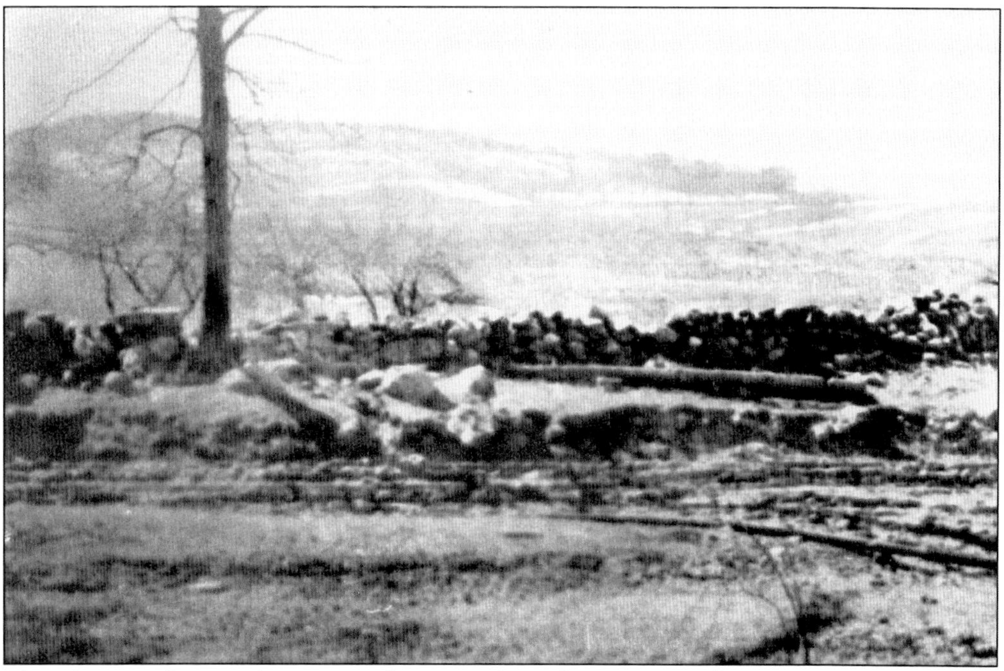

This photograph was taken across the street from the Martin Kellogg House in Brookfield, before the flooding of the lake. Arrowhead Point is seen on the left.

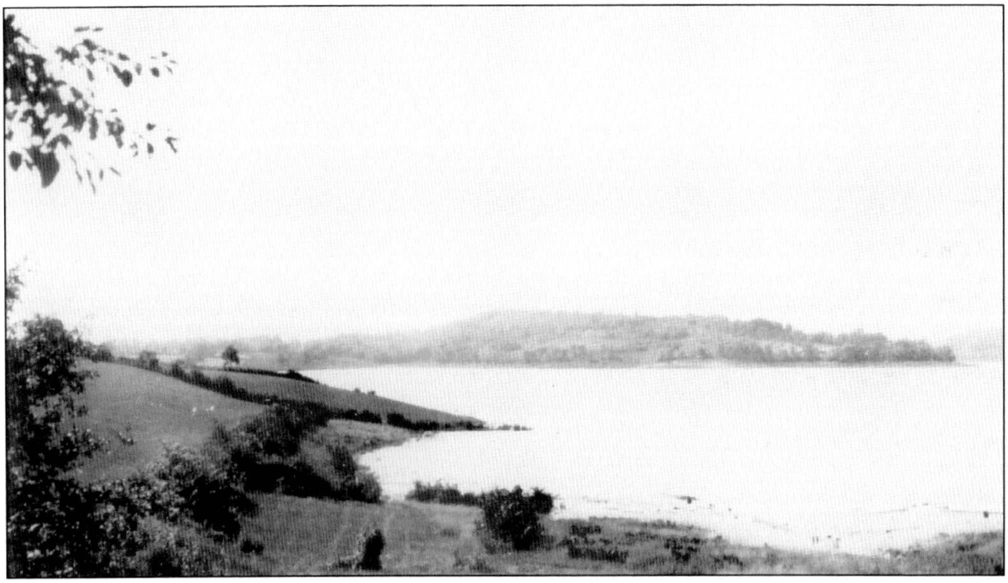

Candlewood Lake has begun to fill with water. Notice the logs and debris along the shoreline. These were trees that were cut down to make way for the lake. The hill on the left later became Candlewood Orchards, and the hill in the distance became Hawthorne Terrace.

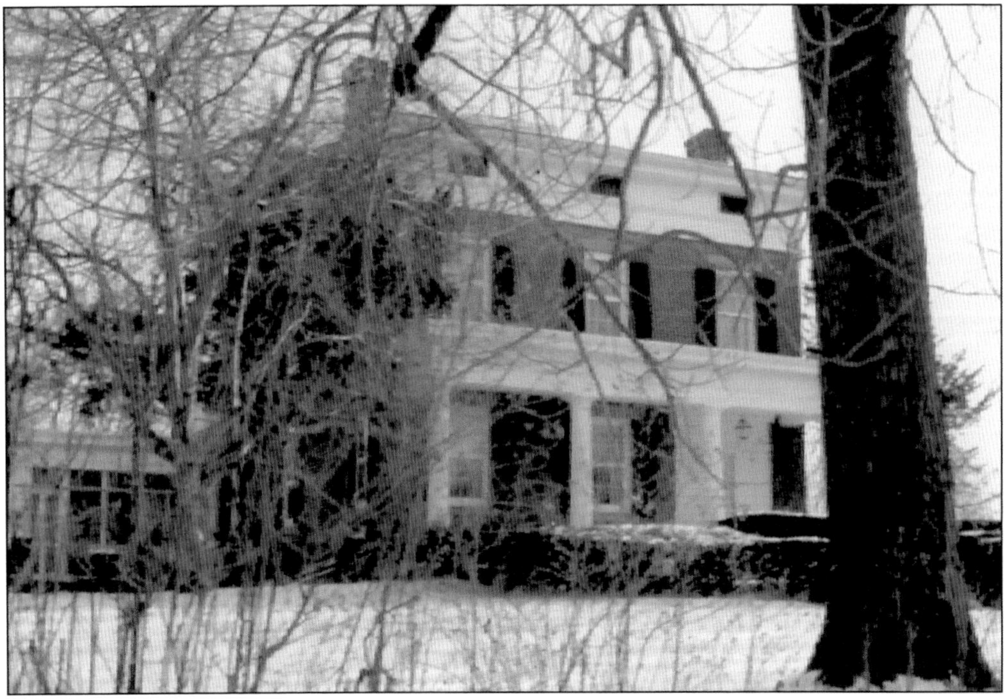

Barzillai Bulkey Kellogg was a successful and prosperous banker. He was elected state senator for the eleventh senatorial district, and from 1869 to 1880 he was elected first selectman of New Fairfield. His house, built *c.* 1845, is in the classical Greek Revival style. Kellogg owned a large farm and made bricks here. His first wife was Emeline Johnson, and his second wife was Florida Merwin. Both were Brookfield residents. The house was called Breezy Top because of its location at the top of Kellogg Street. The area is now called Arrowhead Point.

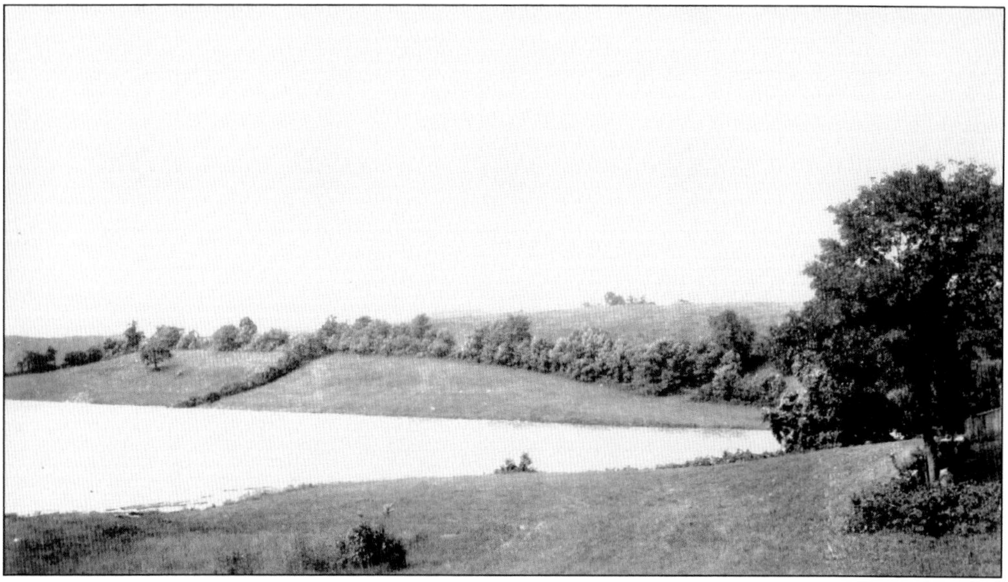

This southwestward view of the valley shows the area before Candlewood Lake was created. Some of the farmers sold their land for prices such as $2,300 for 53 acres and $100 for 3 acres. Other landowners traded land with the power company and ended up with lakefront property.

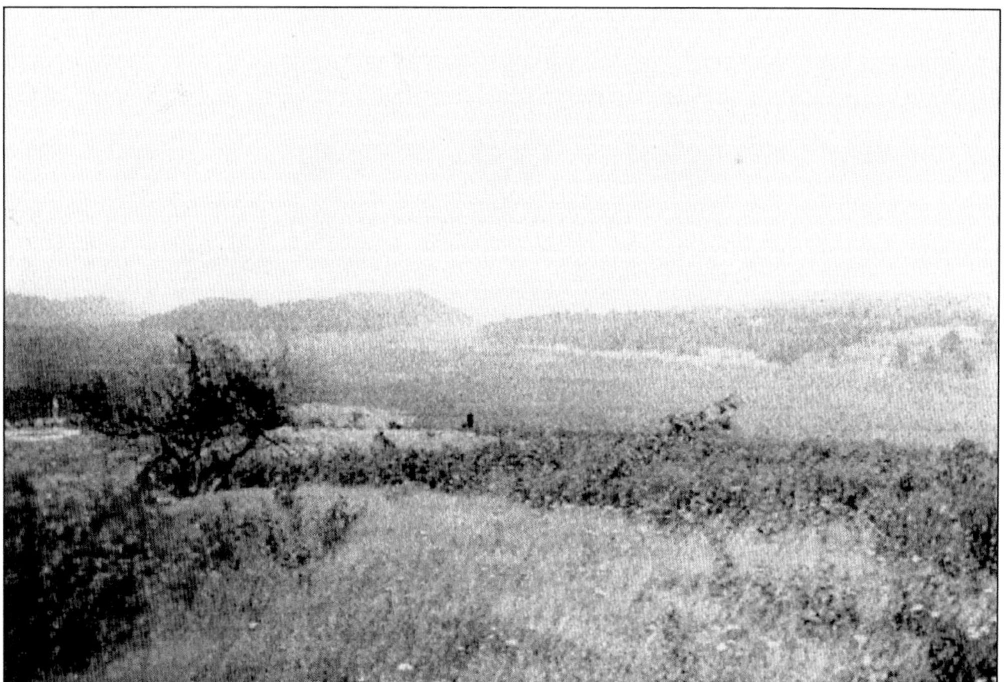

This view of the area before the lake was created looks north from Hatch's Pond, now Candlewood Shores. Vaughn's Neck is in the center, and Candlewood Lake Club is now located on the right.

Four

DEVELOPMENT THROUGH THE YEARS

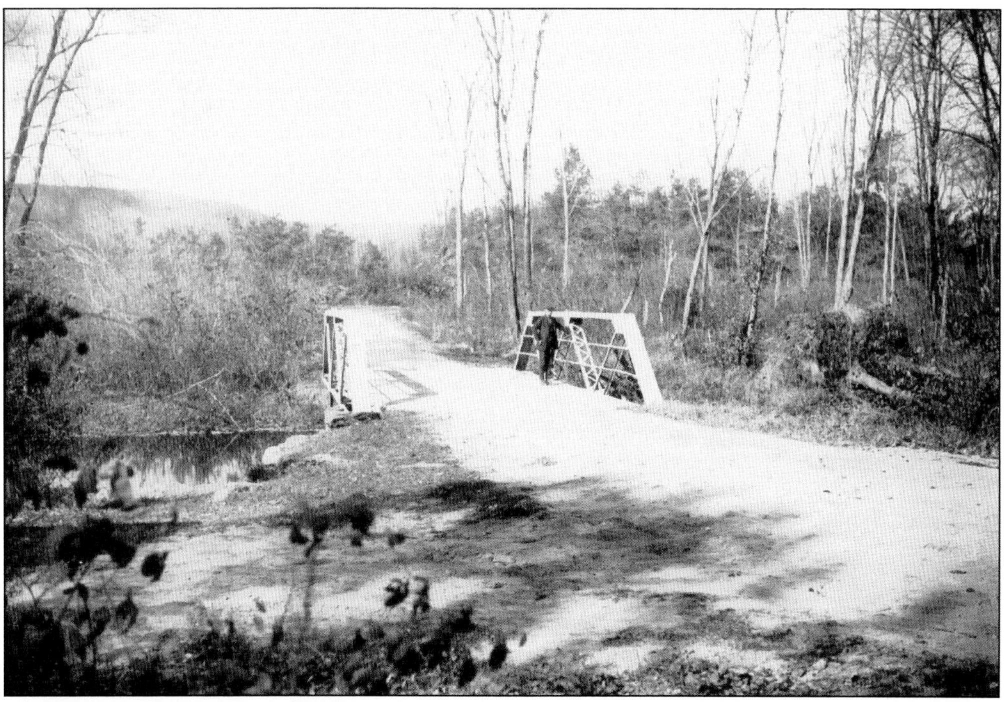

The Neversink Bridge in Danbury is seen here in 1927. The bridge was located south of Candlewood Isle, between Driftwood Point and an island. The bridge is now under the lake, and parts of the rust-covered stanchions on the lake bed can still be seen by divers.

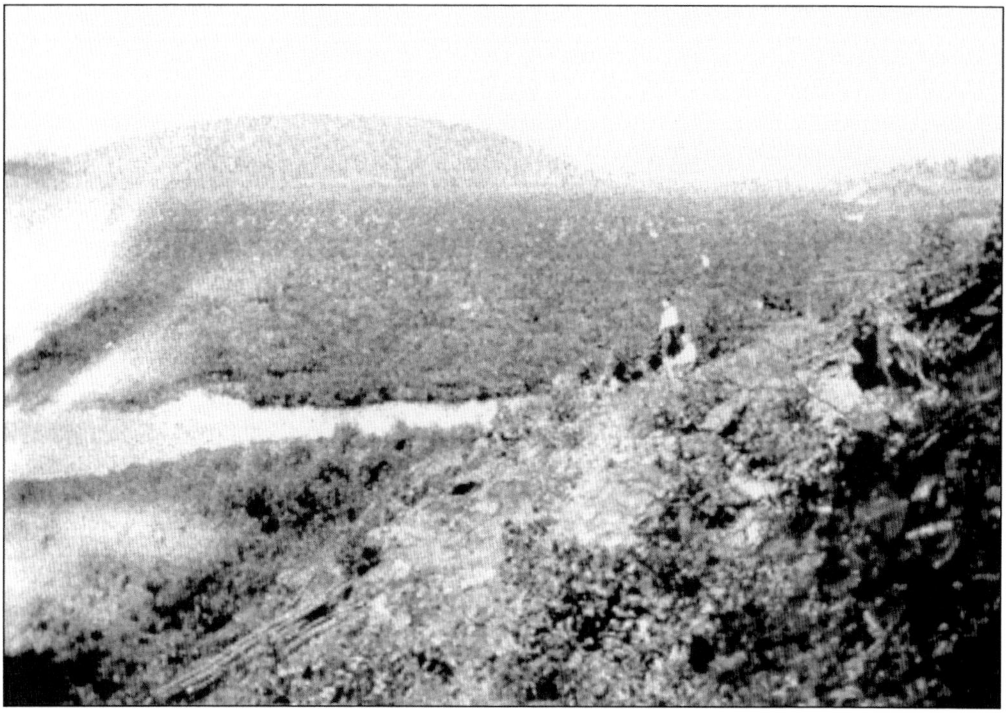

Seen here is the area of Neversink Pond before Candlewood Lake was constructed. This was one of five ponds that were flooded by the lake.

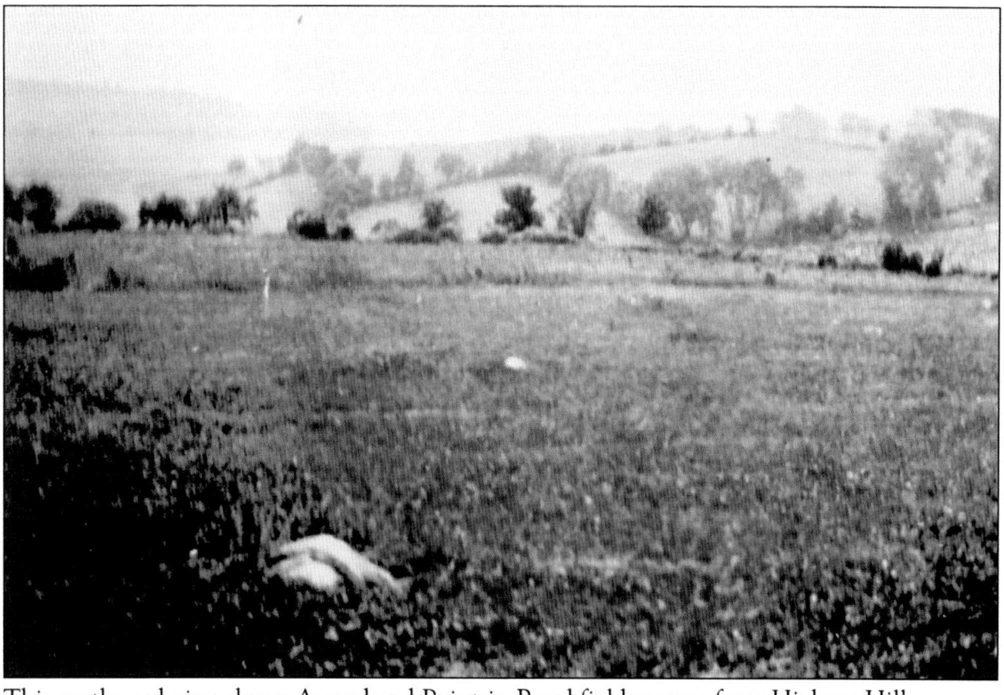

This southward view shows Arrowhead Point in Brookfield as seen from Hickory Hill.

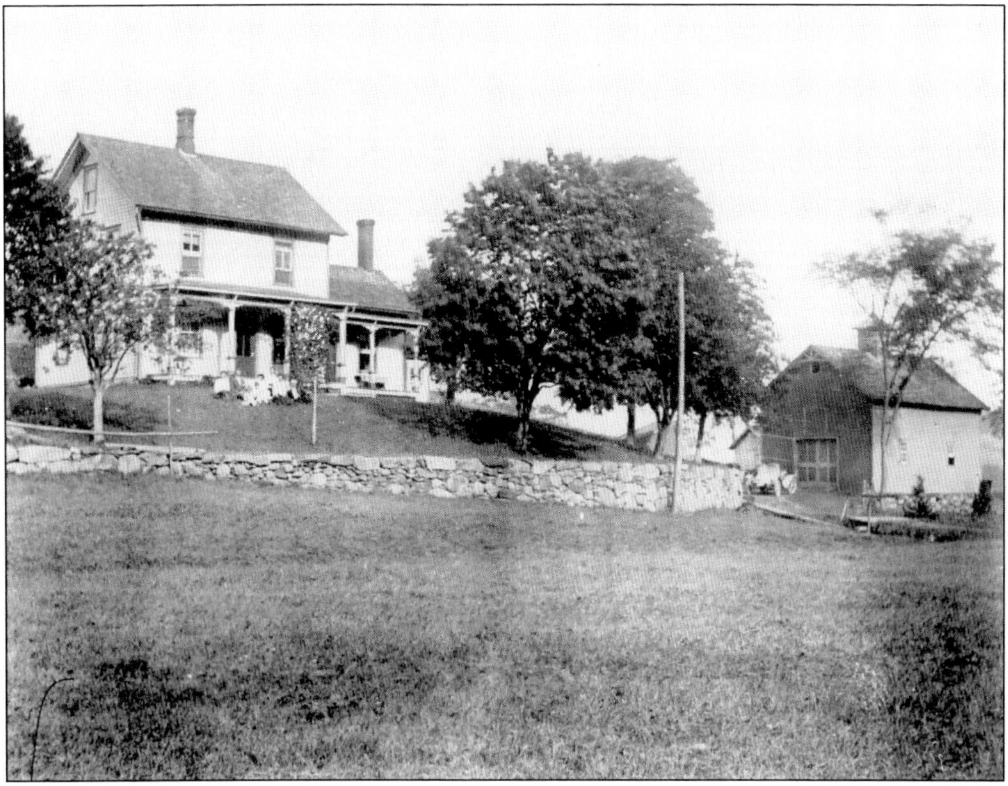

This photograph shows the house and barn of Walter Chatterton, a longtime resident of New Fairfield. These structures were torn down to clear the way for the flooding of the lake. The stone wall most likely remained and is now under water in the vicinity of the present-day New Fairfield Town Beach.

75 years ago (1926)

In clearing land for the great basin north of the city for the lake soon to be created by the United Gas Improvement Co. of Philadelphia for its subsidiary, the Connecticut Light and Power Co., it has been necessary to move four cemeteries in New Fairfield and Sherman to new locations.

The work of removing 412 bodies in these cemeteries commenced a month ago and is now practically completed (Nov. 26, 1926). The cemeteries are Wanzer, Green Pond, Leach Hollow and Turrell.

Most of the bodies have been re-interred in Wood Creek Cemetery, on the New Fairfield-Patterson Road.

The oldest grave disinterred was in the Wanzer Cemetery, that of Ichabod Leach who died 139 years ago (1787).

■

This newspaper clipping dates from 1926.

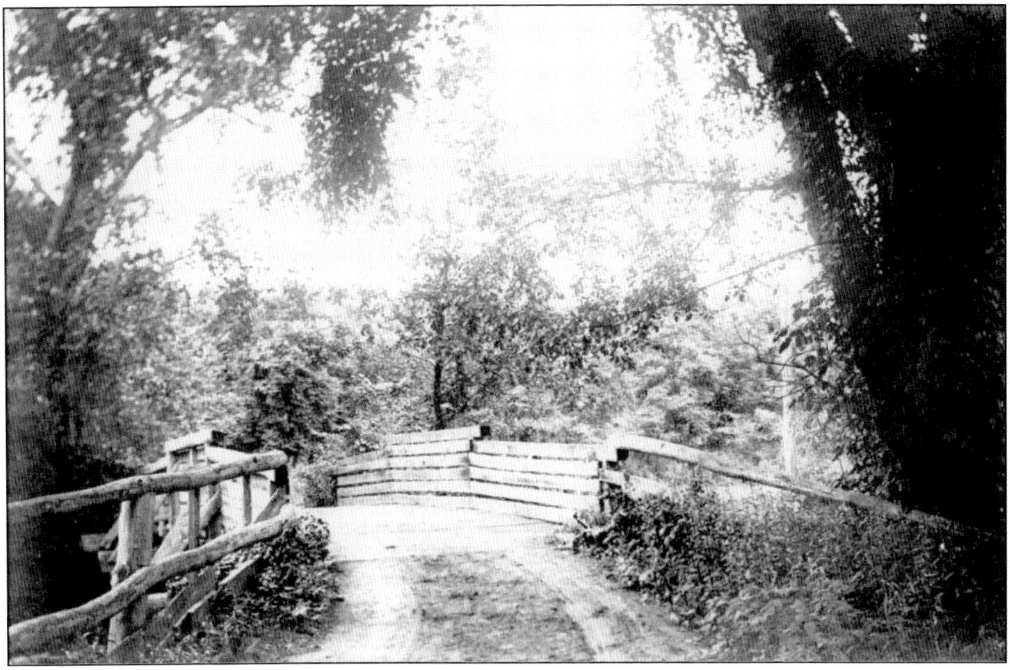

In Allie Giddings book, *A History of Sherman*, this bridge is identified as the "bridge near Creek Pond, flooded by Candlewood Lake, on the old road crossing the valley from Leach Hollow to Mill Pond and Green Pond."

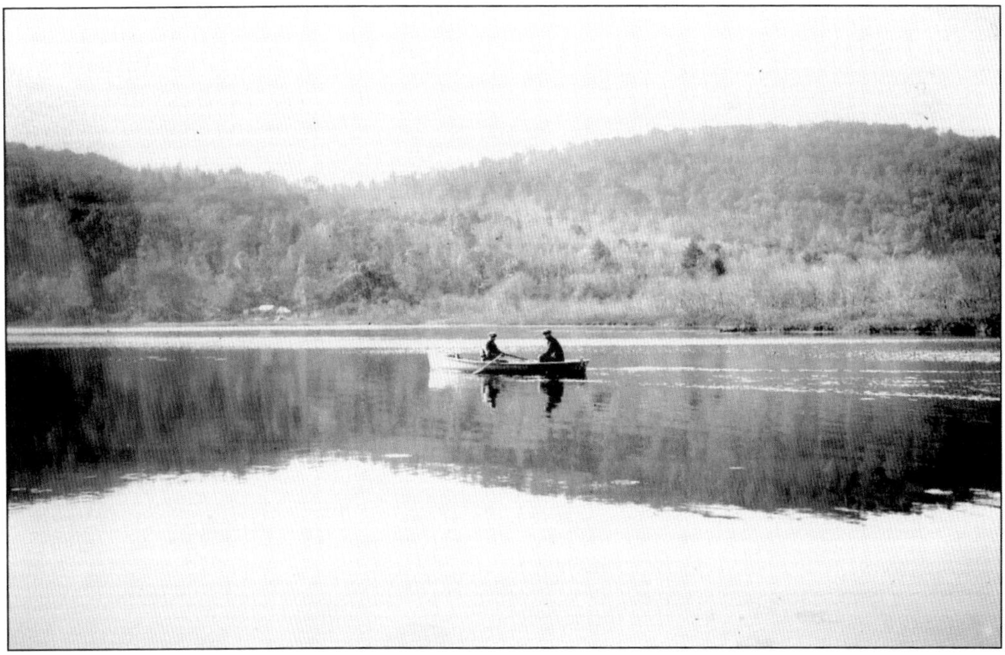

Two rowers are seen on the lake in 1927.

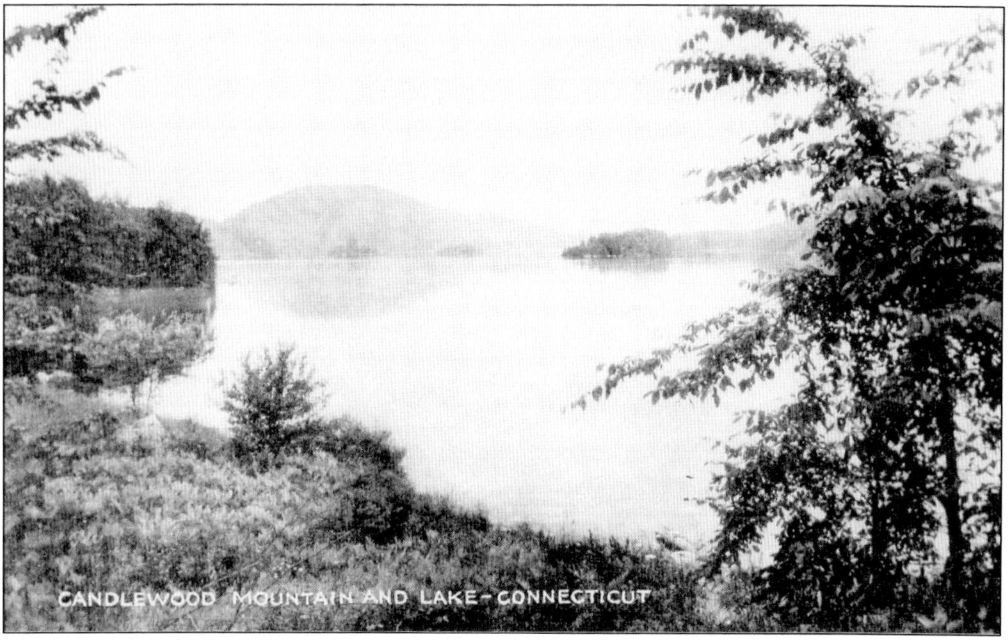

Candlewood Lake was named in honor of the candlewood trees that grew on nearby Candlewood Mountain. The name candlewood derives from early Colonial times, when the settlers cut down the saplings, lit them, and used them as candles.

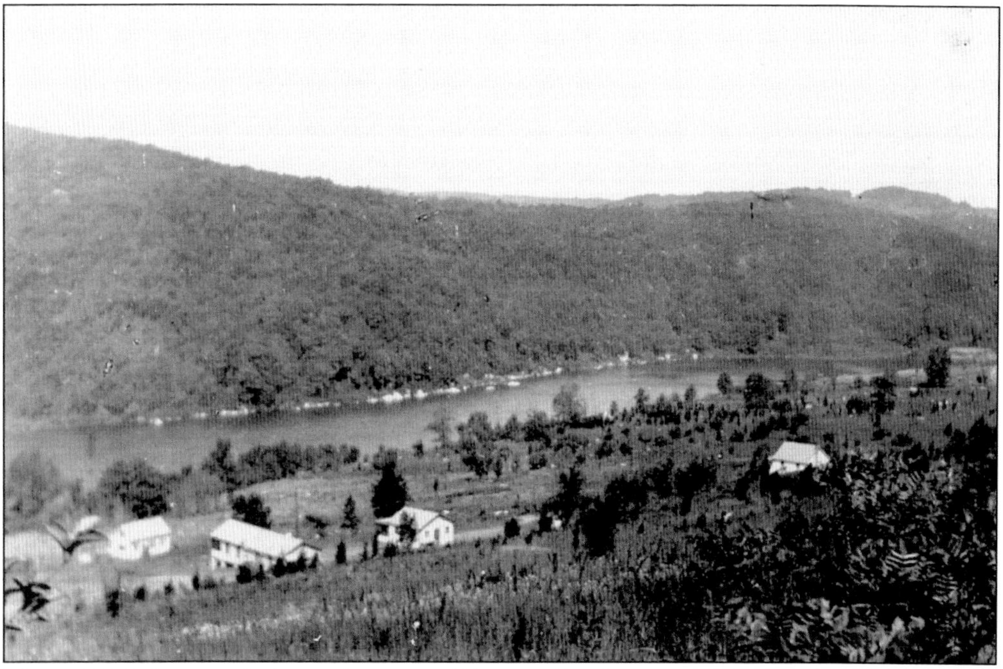

This c. 1926 photograph shows the original Squantz Pond prior to the creation of Candlewood Lake. The land in the foreground is under water today. Squantz is separated from the main body of Candlewood by a causeway that carries Route 39 from New Fairfield to Sherman. However, an aqueduct maintains the same water level on both sides. Most people consider Squantz a part of the "big lake."

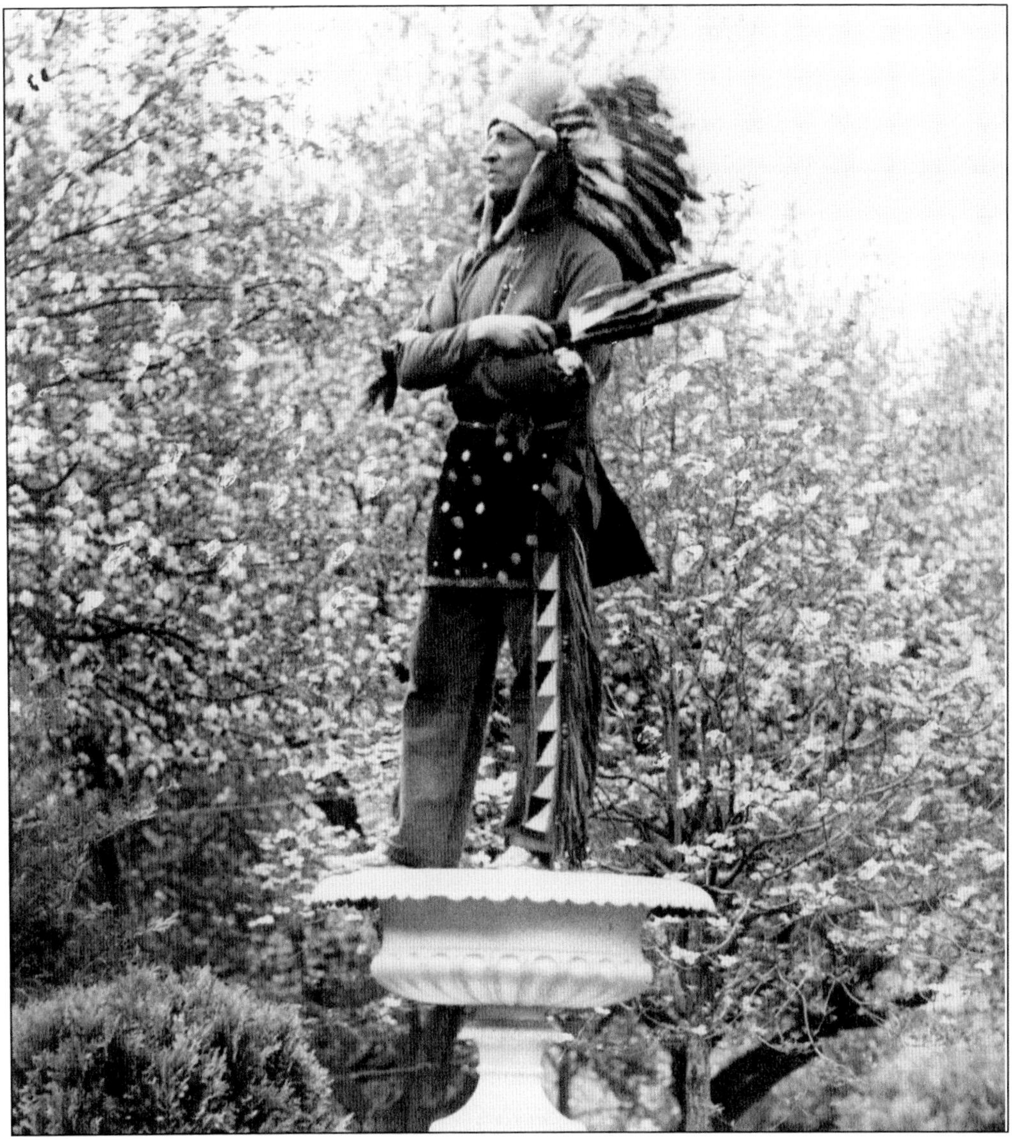

This is a c. 1938 photograph of Chief Come With the Dawn. He is a distant relative of Chief Squantz, for whom Squantz Pond is named. A peaceful man who accepted renegades from the neighboring tribes, Chief Squantz lived in the valley close to the pond in the early 1700s. Many artifacts have been found on the lake's eastern shore, which was the area of the chief's base camp. This territory had been retained by the Native Americans when the original grant of this section of the state was made to settlers. In 1724, 12 men from Fairfield came to purchase this piece of land, which is today known as New Fairfield. They made a verbal contract with Chief Squantz, and then returned to Fairfield to have the deeds drawn up. But when the men returned to meet with the chief in the spring of 1725, they learned that their negotiating efforts had been in vain—Chief Squantz had died during the winter, and his four sons refused to sign the deeds. It was not until 1729 that the Native Americans deeded the property to the white men. Story has it that Chief Squantz was buried where the Keith Joyce Homestead now stands. When the home's foundation site was dug, the body of a Native American, buried in a sitting position, was uncovered. It was reputed to be that of Chief Squantz.

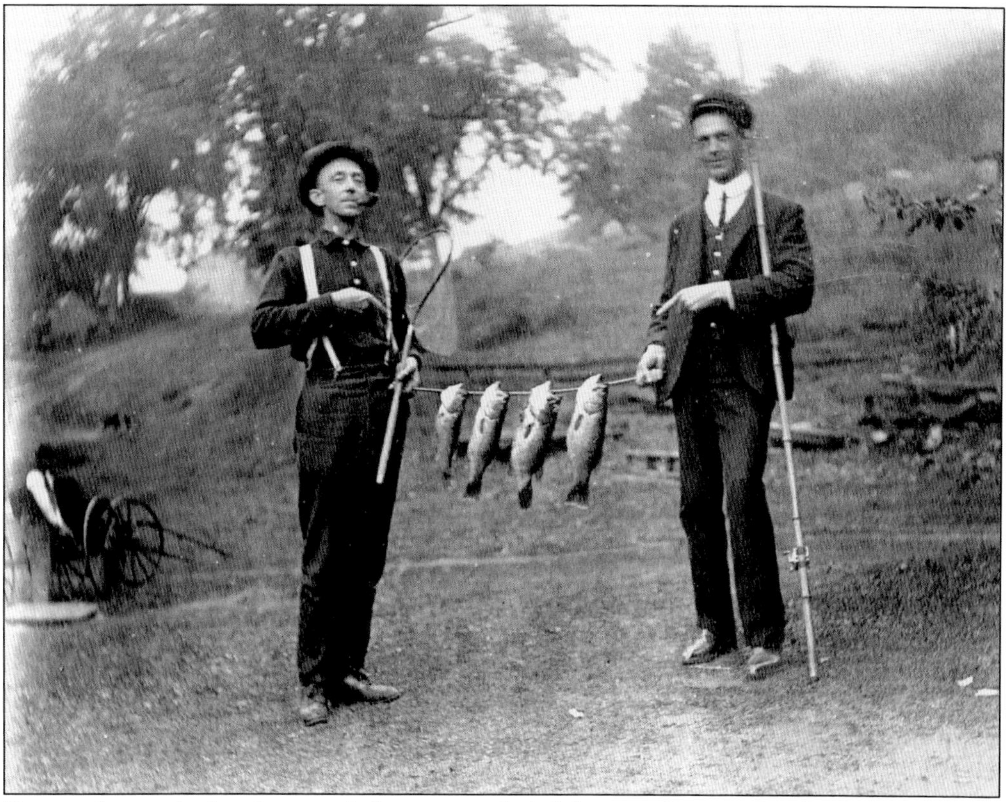

Two gentlemen display their catch from a nice day's fishing on Squantz Pond c. 1928. Note the formal fishing apparel, a far cry from today's garb.

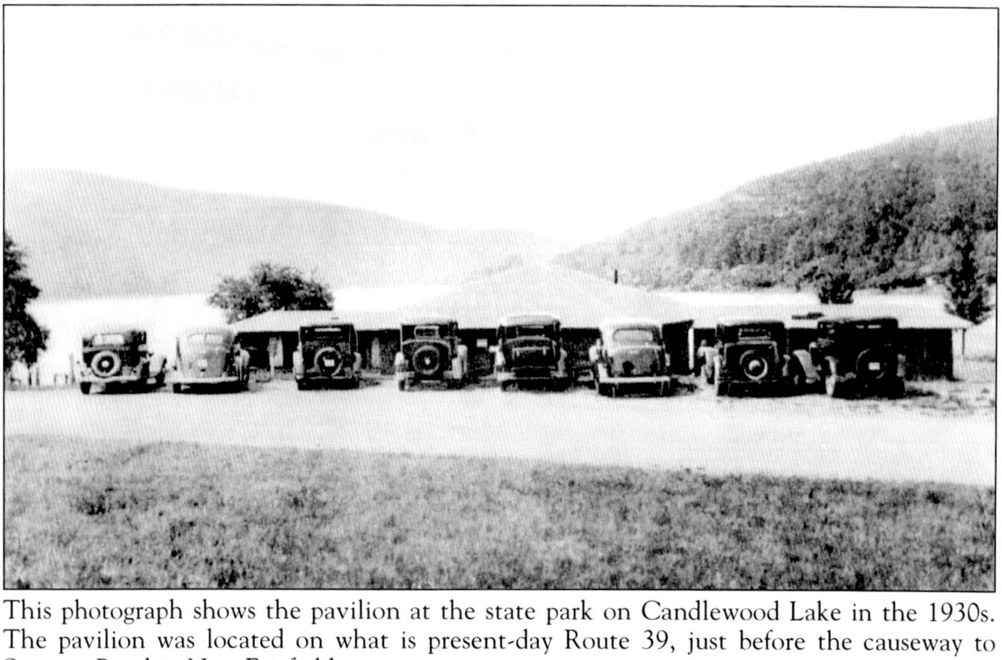

This photograph shows the pavilion at the state park on Candlewood Lake in the 1930s. The pavilion was located on what is present-day Route 39, just before the causeway to Squantz Pond in New Fairfield.

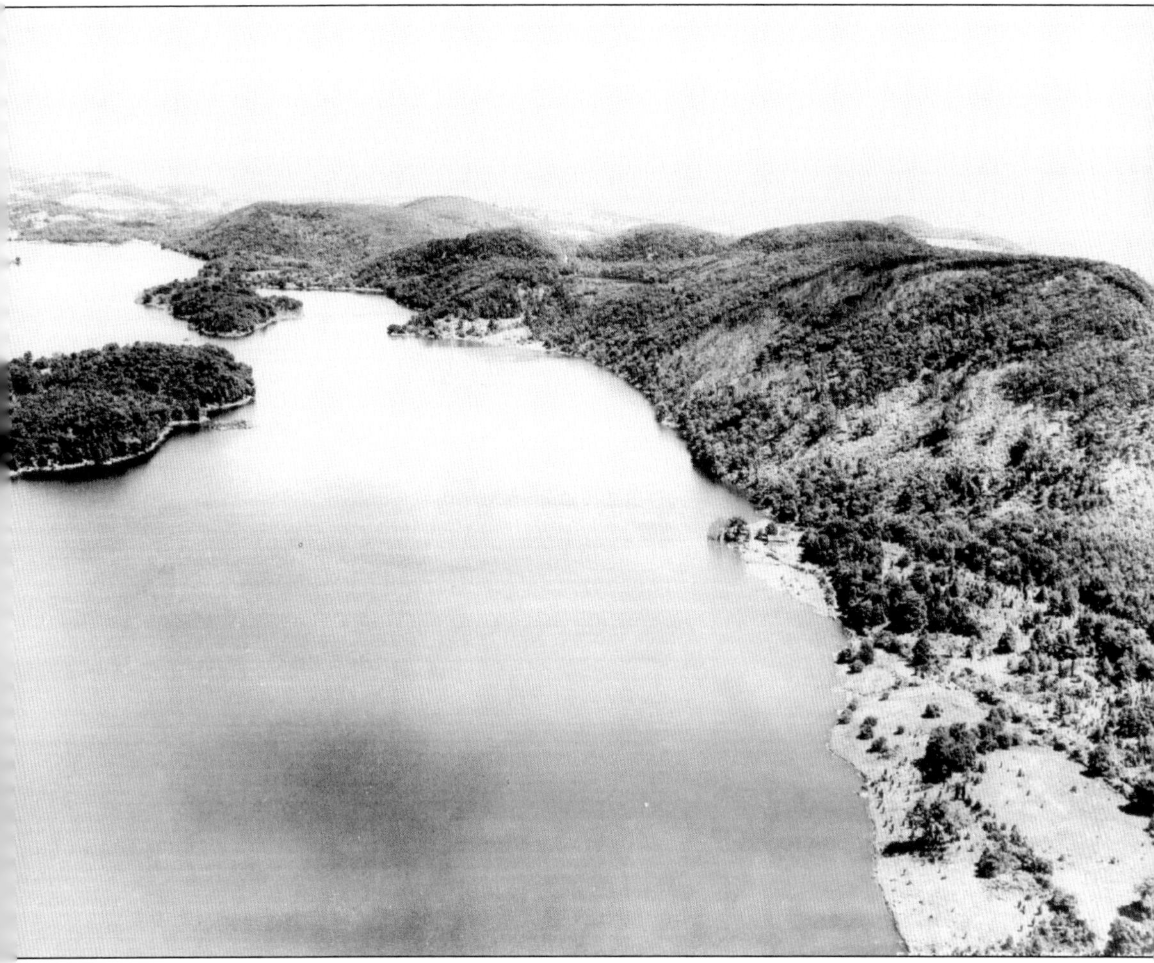

This view of Candlewood Lake in 1929 looks north, toward New Milford. This photograph was likely taken as a part of a survey of the lake after it was formed. The original copy of the photograph is kept in a fireproof cabinet at the New Fairfield Historical Society.

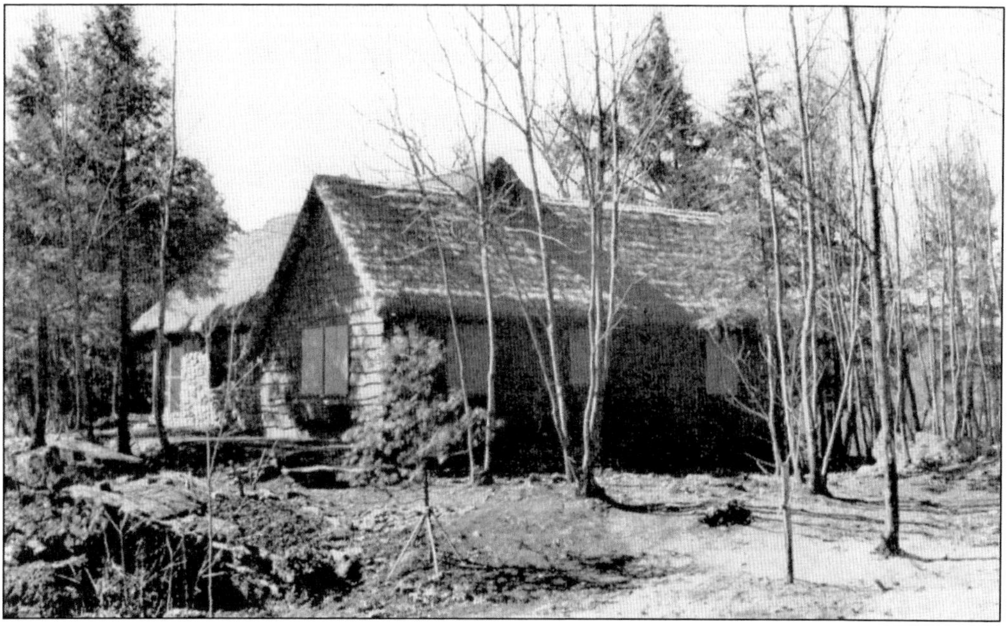

This is one of the many summer homes found around the lake during the 1930s. Most of the summer cottages during the early years of the lake were austere and had large fireplaces for use in the fall and spring months. Most of the communities were closed down during the winter months, and the cottages were deserted.

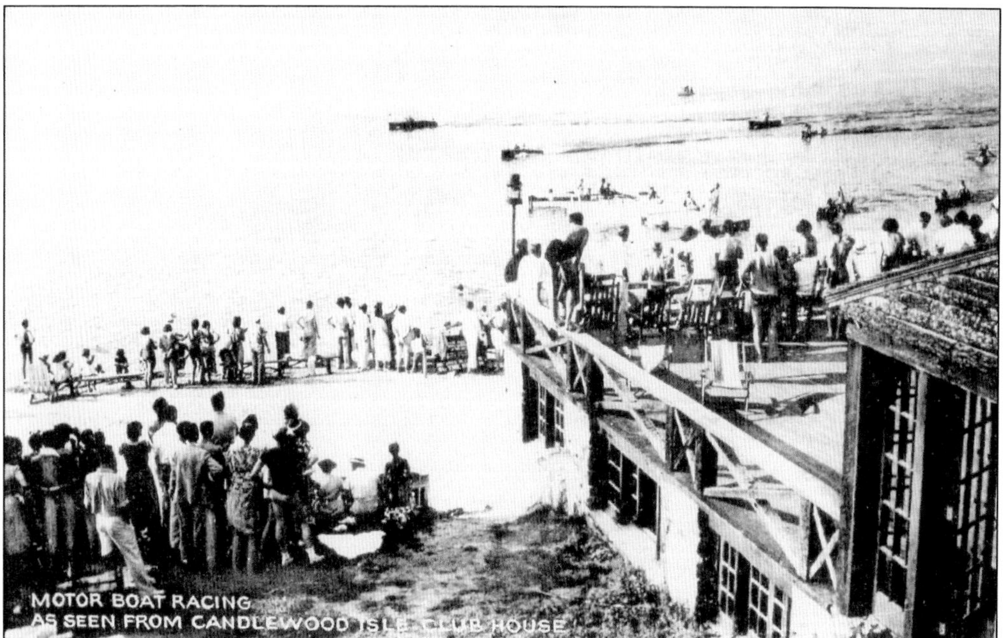

A 1930s motorboat race is seen from Candlewood Isle Clubhouse in New Fairfield. Note the many families who congregated to watch—the ladies are attired in dresses and the men in suits.

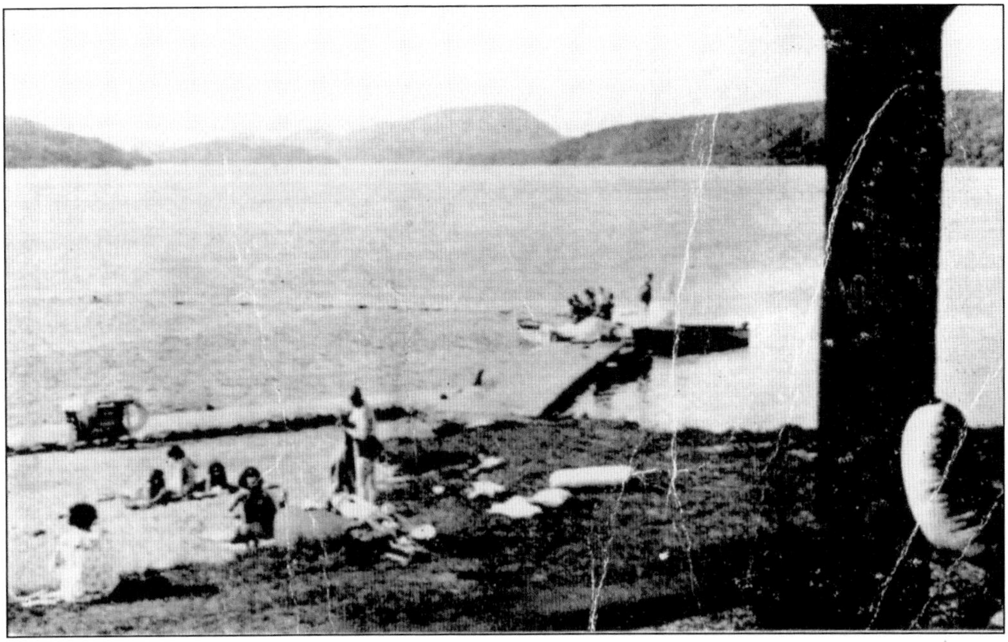

The beach at Candlewood Isle in New Fairfield is seen in this photograph, which is believed to be from the 1930s. Candlewood Isle is one of the original private summer colonies on the lake. Today it is primarily a year-round community, as are most of the private neighborhoods around the lake.

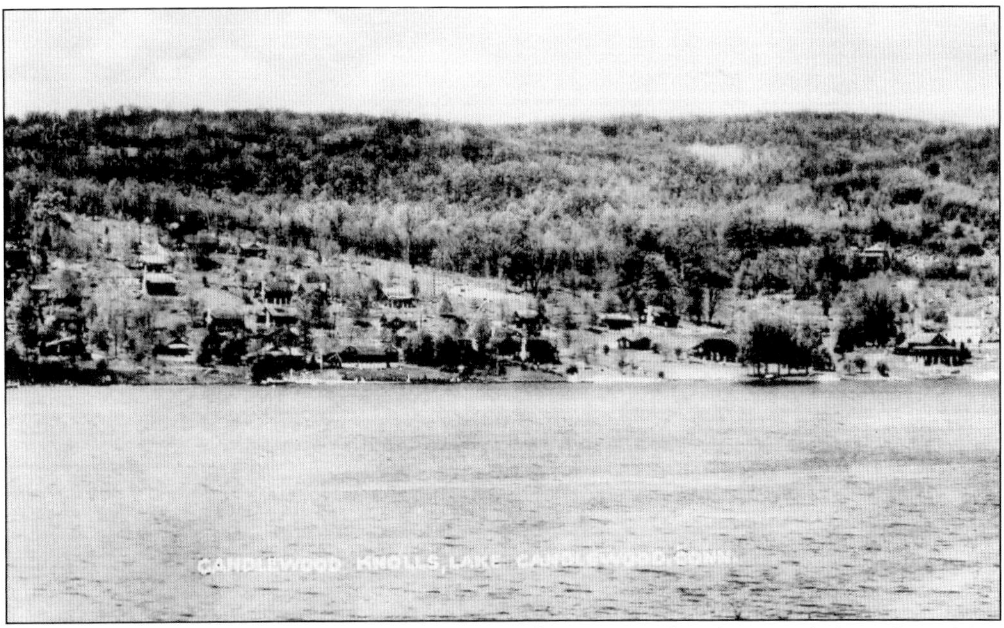

Candlewood Knolls in New Fairfield in seen from the water in this photograph from the 1930s.

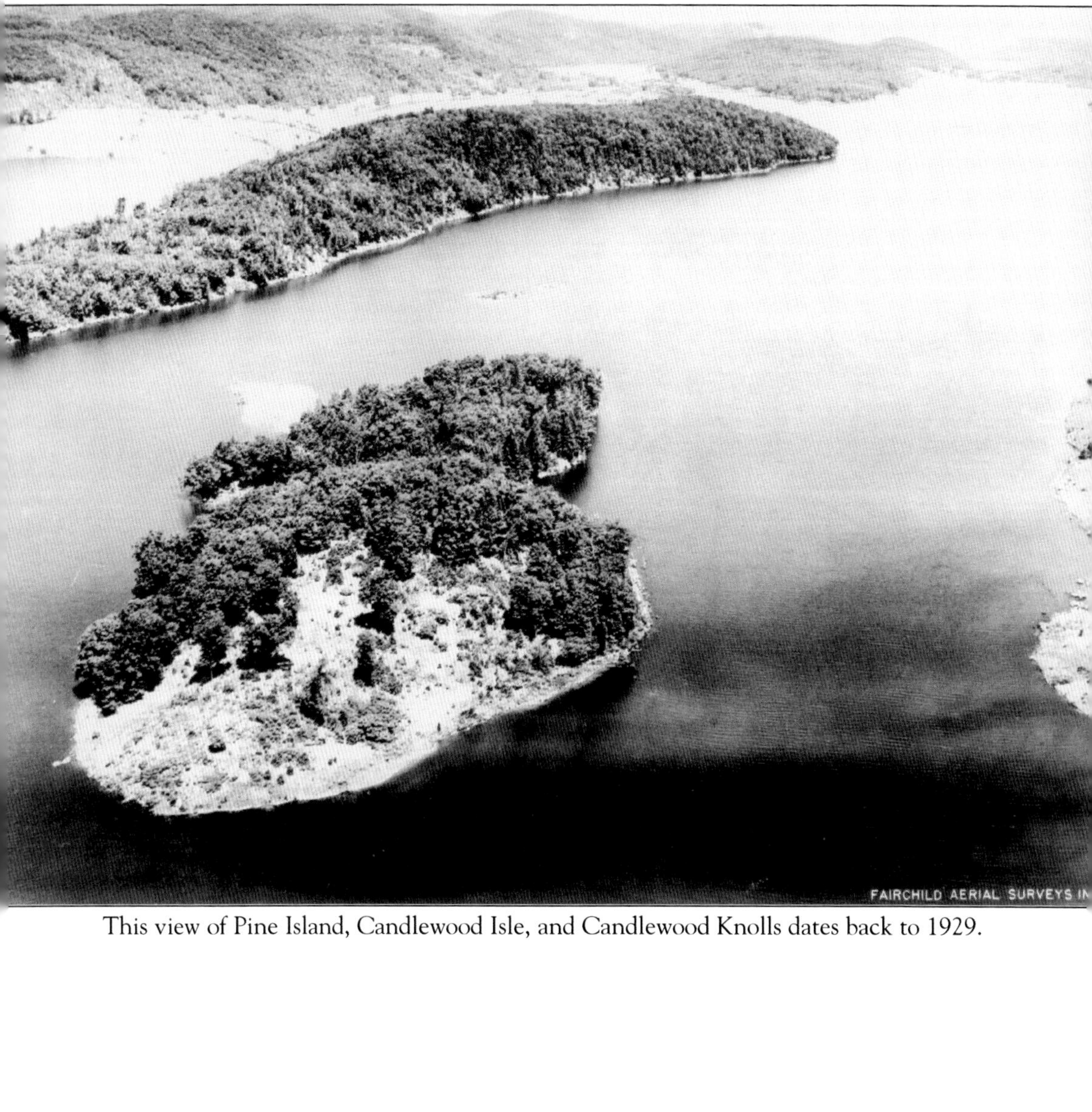

This view of Pine Island, Candlewood Isle, and Candlewood Knolls dates back to 1929.

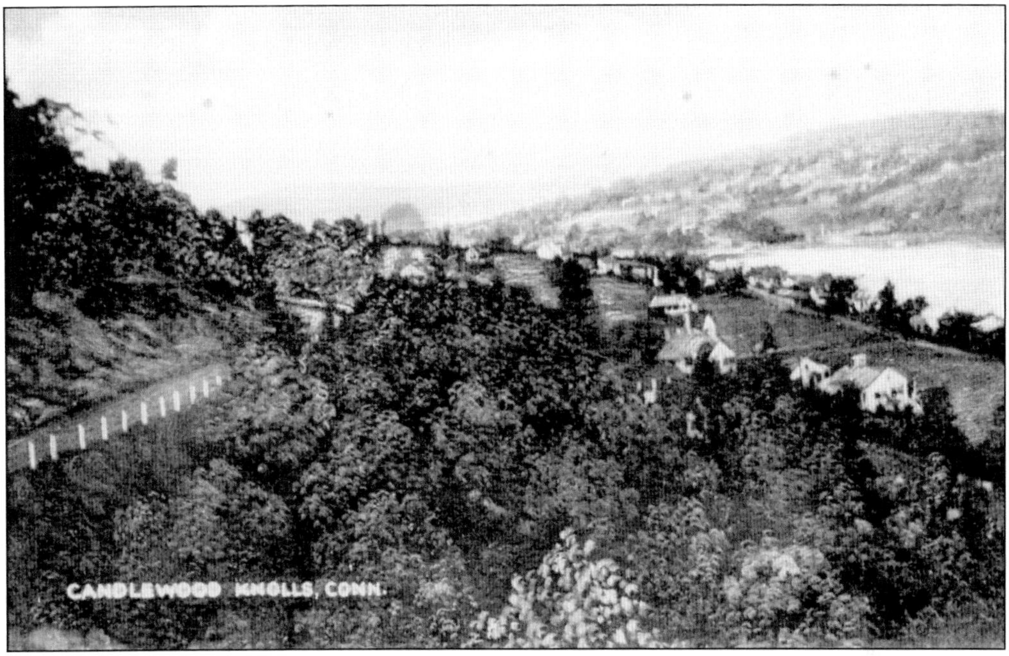

This view of Candlewood Knolls in New Fairfield looks north, toward Sherman. Notice the rather narrow Route 39 on the left side of the photograph.

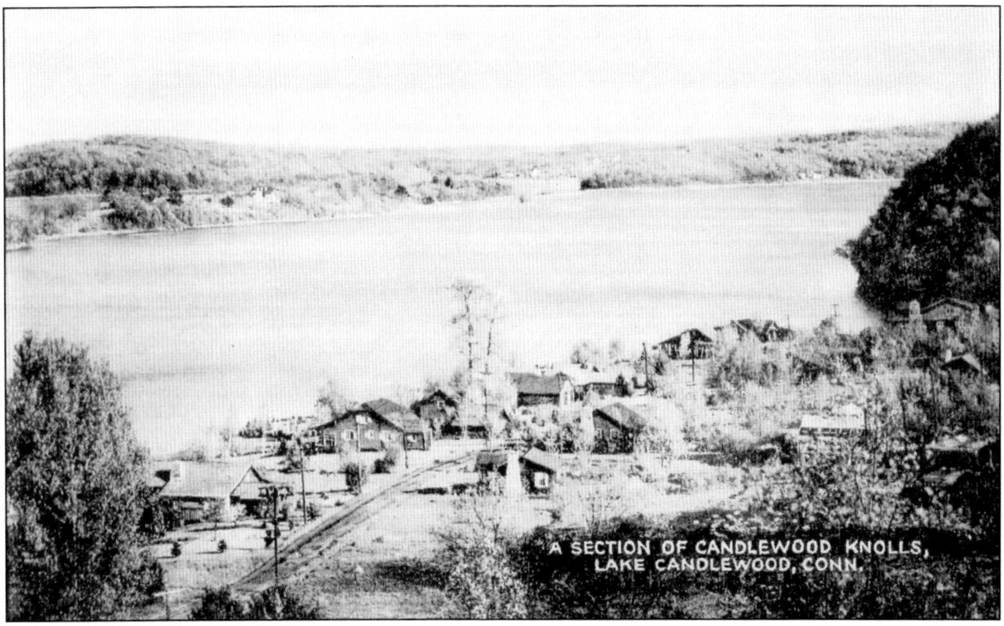

Notice the lack of mature trees around Candlewood Knolls in this view, looking south toward Danbury.

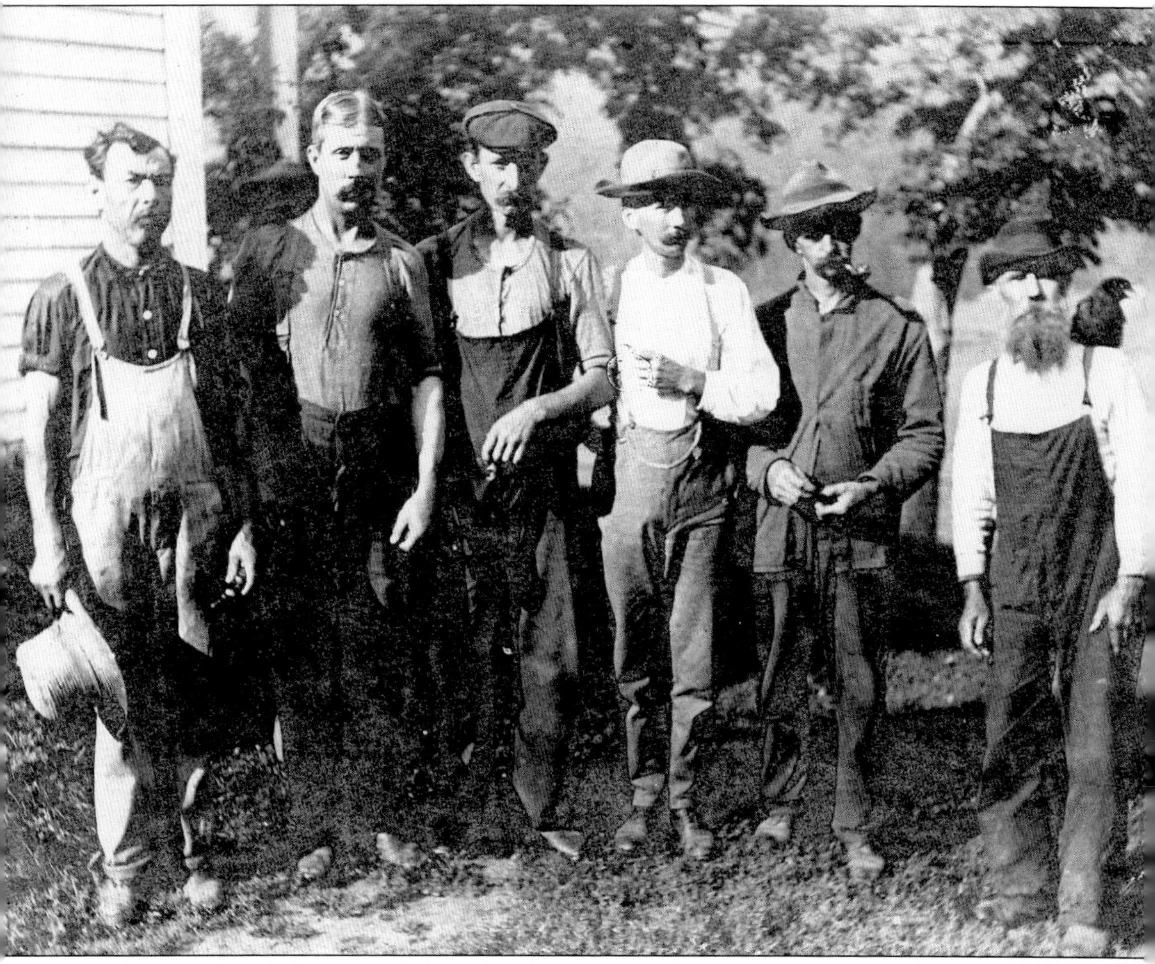

These unidentified men are believed to be workers who were constructing the Joyce House at Squantz Pond in New Fairfield *c.* 1929. The house later became the dance hall/casino known as Joyceland, which burned down in 1955. Joyceland sold ice cream and gas, and held dances every Saturday night during the summer months. There were cabins around Joyceland that visitors could rent for the season. These cabins still exist today. Joyceland itself was built by Keith Joyce and Carrie Chatterton Joyce. Even though the dance hall was called a "casino," it did not have the gambling casinos are known for today. In this photograph, note the friendly crow on the shoulder of the gentleman at the far right.

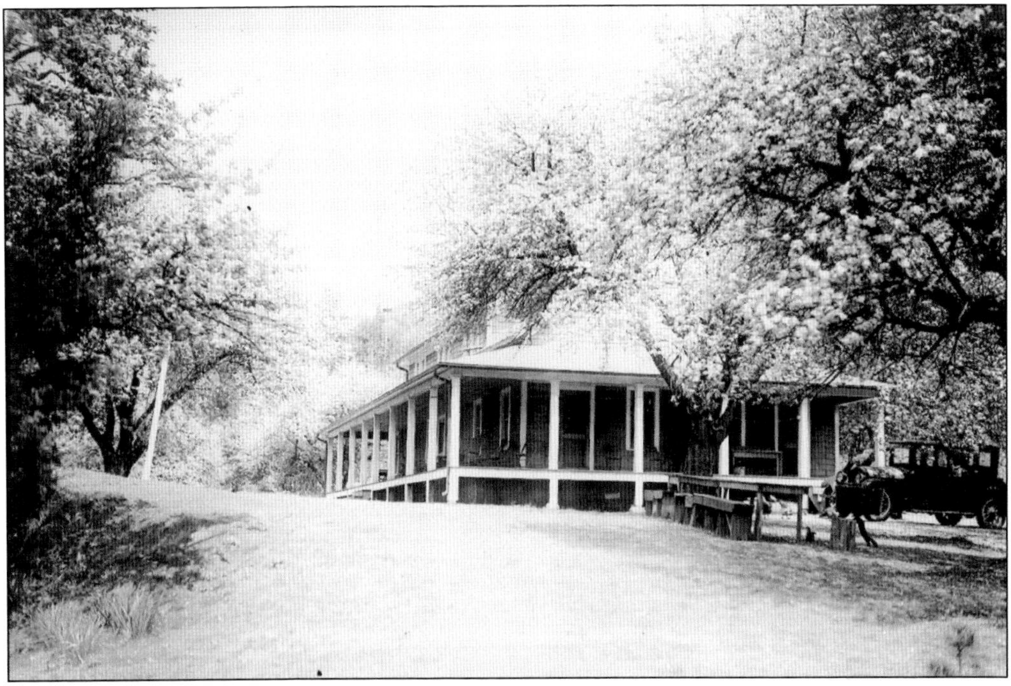
The Joyceland Tourist Home on Squantz Pond was built in 1927.

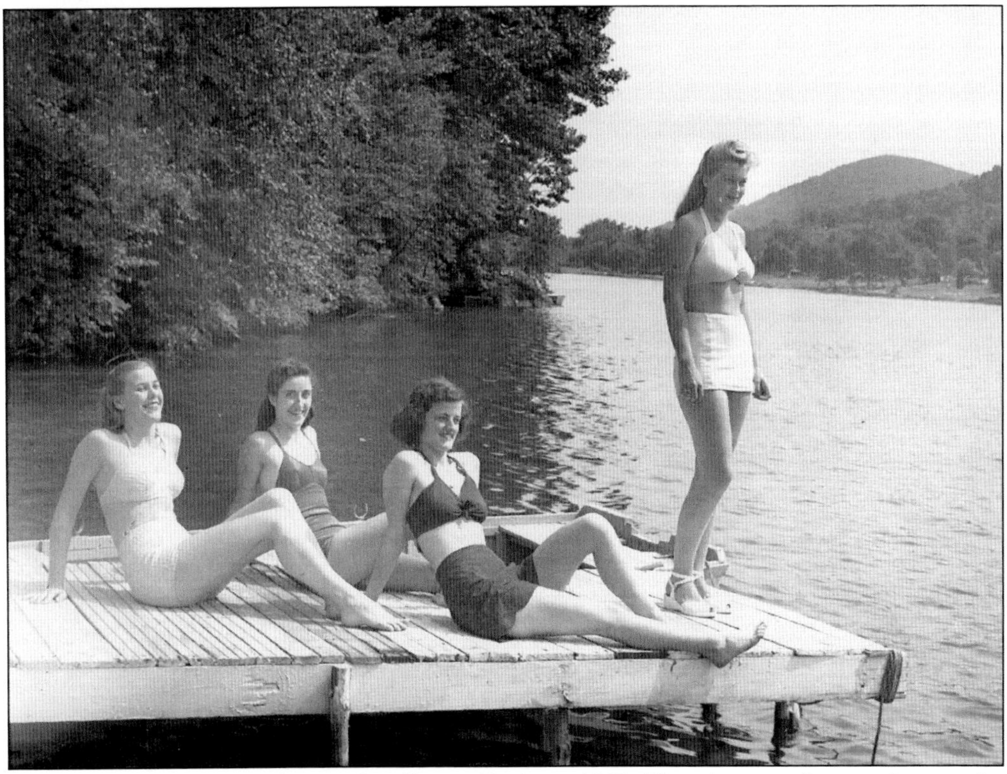
Bathing beauties enjoy a day on Candlewood Lake c. 1948. This photograph was taken on the dock of Joyceland, in New Fairfield.

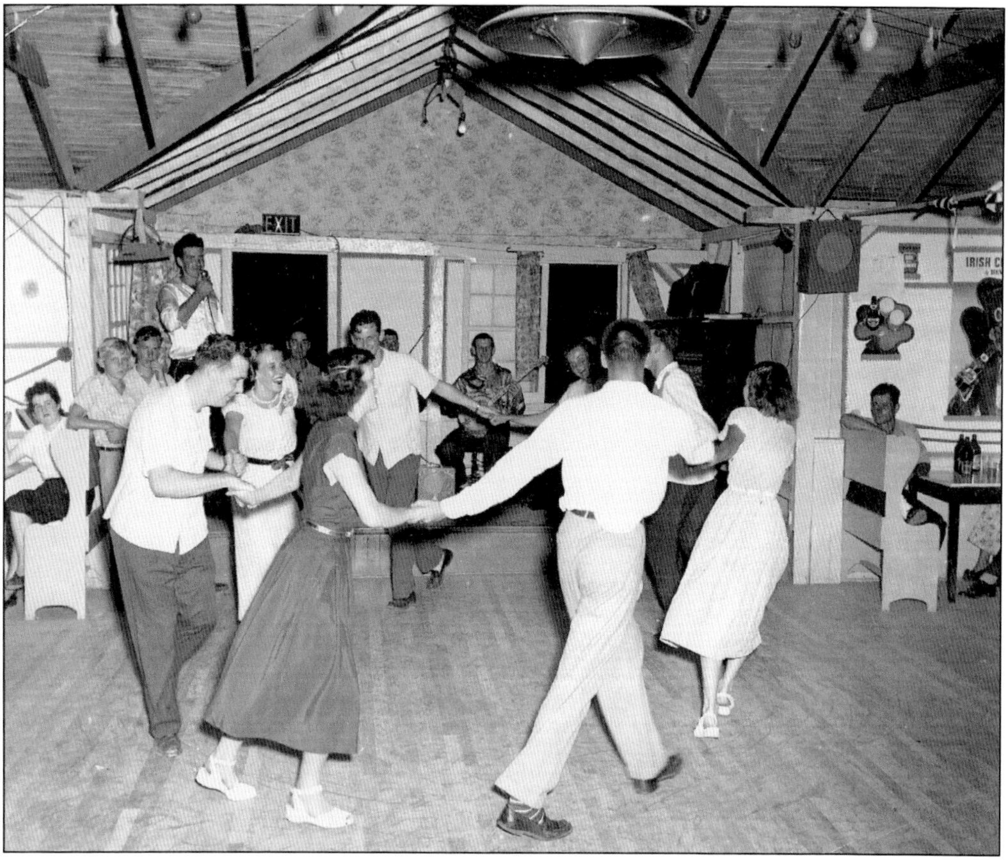

Built in 1927, Joyceland, which is now Shelter Isle, promoted its "dining, dancing, beer, tourists, boating, swimming, gasoline and oils." An advertisement for a picnic at Joyceland read: "Eat, drink, play games, free boating, dance orchestra. Admission $2.00."

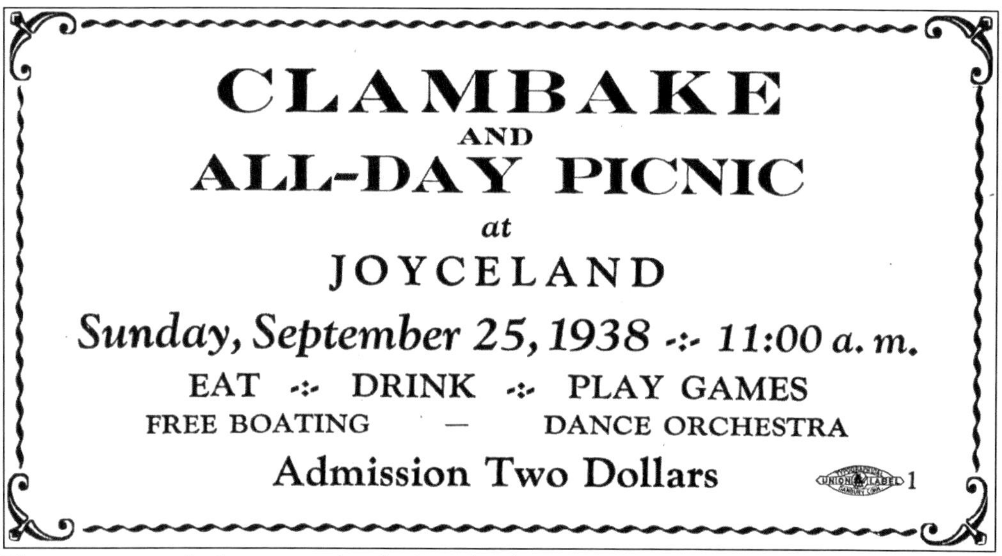

CLAMBAKE
AND
ALL-DAY PICNIC
at
JOYCELAND
Sunday, September 25, 1938 -:- *11:00 a. m.*
EAT -:- DRINK -:- PLAY GAMES
FREE BOATING — DANCE ORCHESTRA
Admission Two Dollars 1

This is an original admission ticket for Joyceland.

Candlewood Lake at Sunset Cove is seen here *c.* 1930.

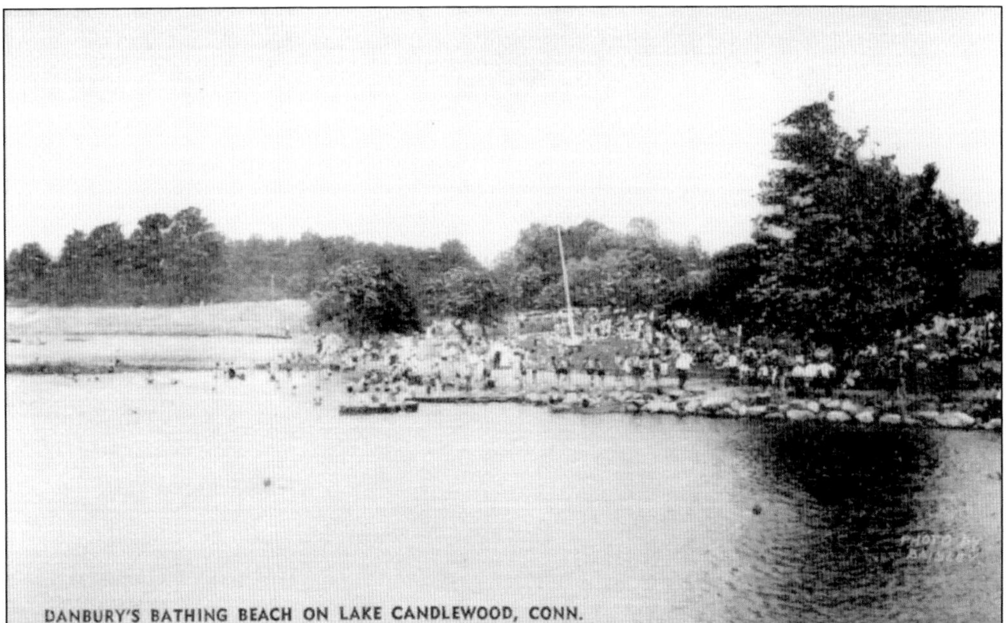

Danbury's bathing beach is shown during the 1930s. Note the limited facilities, as well as the lack of floats and beach. Additional land and facilities were later added to create today's Danbury Town Park.

Candlewood's
Ideal Vacation Resort

WILDMAN'S LANDING

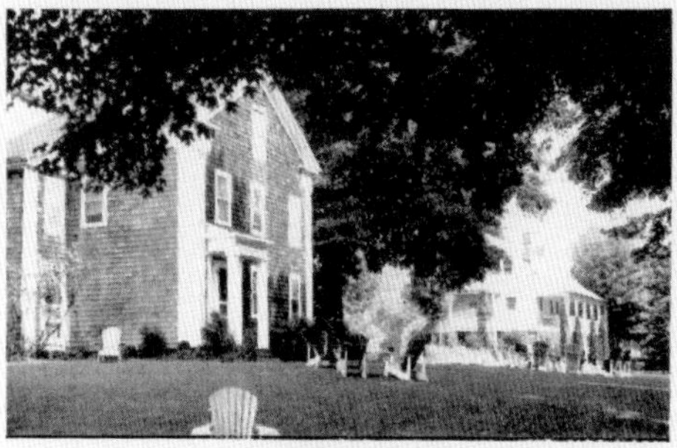

- RESTAURANT — *at the Lodge*
- COCKTAIL LOUNGE
- BATHING BEACH — *Large Parking Area*
- SNACK BAR — *On the Waters Edge*
- ROW BOATS, CANOES, OUTBOARDS — *for Hire*
- SPEEDBOAT RIDES
- SIGHTSEEING TRIPS — *Around Lake*

Wildman's Landing Lodge is a spacious Homestead with cozy and quaint bedrooms. On the main floor you will find three attractive dining rooms where you will enjoy a superb French cuisine. The finest food obtainable is expertly prepared by our internationally known Chef Del. You will enjoy a new thrill in fine dining served in delightful surroundings.

DOCKING FACILITIES AVAILABLE
FOR DINNER GUESTS ARRIVING BY BOAT

OPEN ALL YEAR

SEND FOR ILLUSTRATED COLOR FOLDER TO

WILDMAN'S LANDING LODGE

DANBURY, CONN. TEL. 8-2621

IDEALLY LOCATED NEAR CHURCHES
SHOPPING AND THEATRES.
FREQUENT BUS SERVICE AVAILABLE

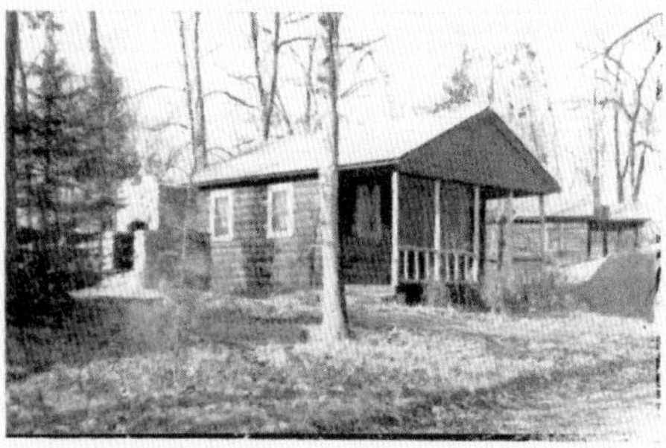

Twenty deluxe rustic cabins situated in a wooded section commanding a beautiful panoramic view of the lake area. All cabins are completely and tastefully furnished for housekeeping. Delightful for honeymoons or carefree vacationing.

Wildman's Landing also offers you a Club Building with lounging room, guest rooms with twin or double beds, private tile bathrooms with showers, steam heat.

Several inns were located around Candlewood Lake's 60 miles of shoreline during the 1940s and 1950s. This is a c. 1948 advertisement for Wildman's Landing Lodge, which was on the Danbury side of the lake.

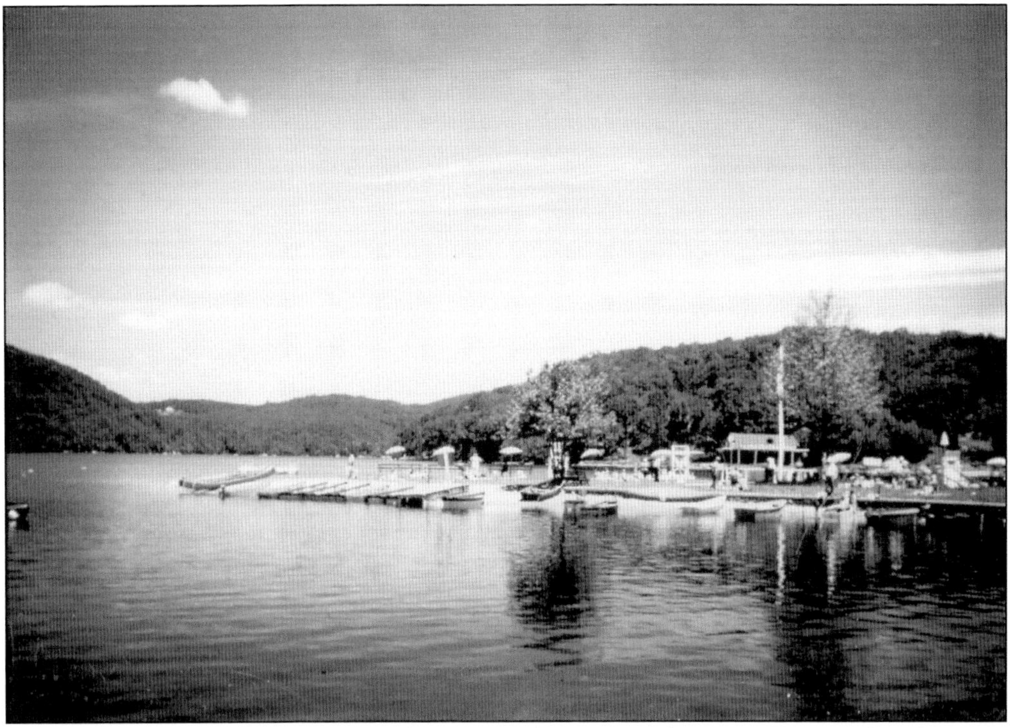

This photograph was taken at Wildman's Landing in Danbury in 1949. Today this area is occupied by the Crystal Bay development—the only condominiums on Candlewood Lake—located at the southern tip of the lake in Danbury.

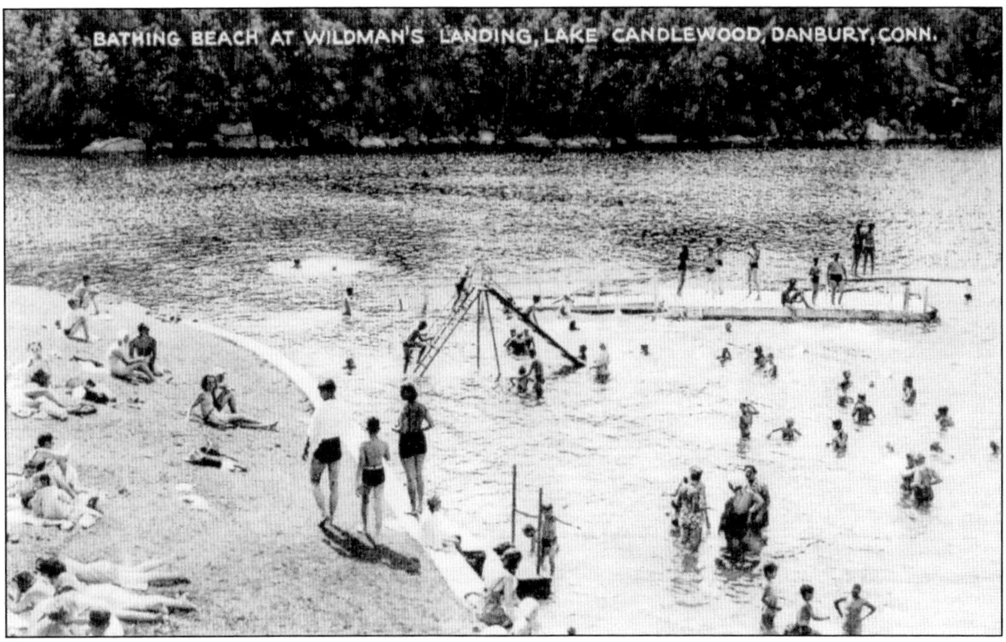

The bathing beach at Wildman's Landing in Danbury is shown c. 1940.

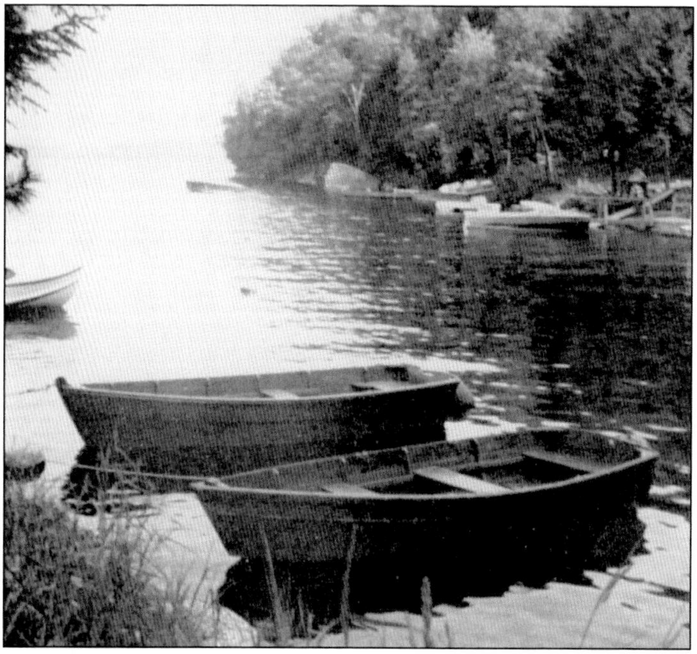

Two lone rowboats are pictured *c.* 1946.

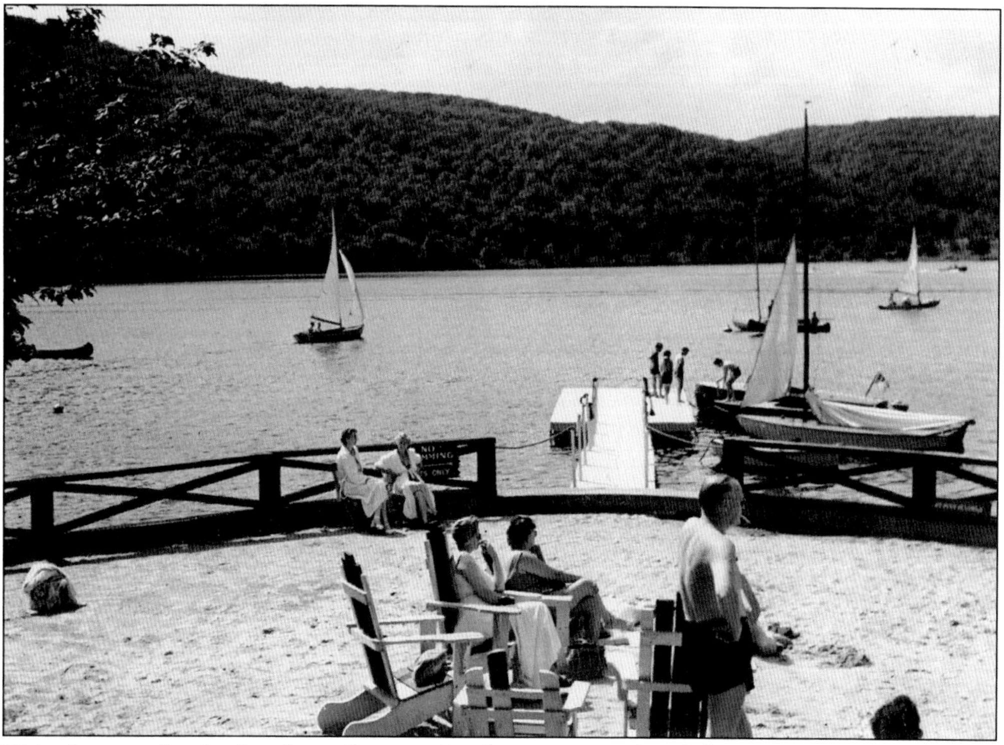

This photograph of a beach on Squantz Pond was captured in July 1944. Squantz Pond and Candlewood Lake are physically separated by the Route 39 causeway. However, water can pass between the two through large pipes under the roadway. Before there was a Candlewood Lake, Squantz Pond did exist; however, the pond was greatly enlarged when the lake was created. Today Squantz Pond is six miles around, and the entire west end of the pond is a state park.

Five

RECREATIONAL USES

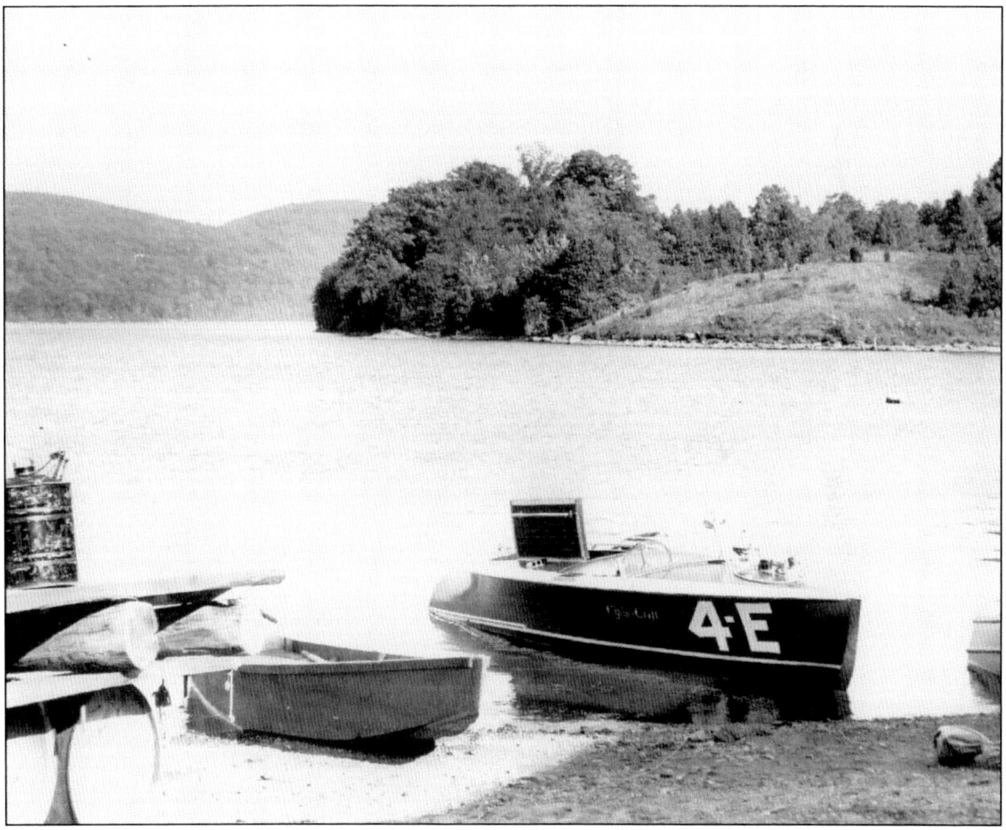

This *c.* 1940 photograph shows Candlewood Lake as seen from the vicinity of Green Pond in Sherman. This boat, a Chris-Craft, was one of the many recreational vehicles found around the lake during the 1940s. It is hard to believe that only 20 years or so earlier there were farmhouses, schools, and churches in this valley now covered by Candlewood Lake. Only the occasional sight of stone walls or house chimneys on the lake bed, glimpsed through the clear lake water, offer proof that boats now travel over an area once occupied by fertile farmlands and comfortable homesteads.

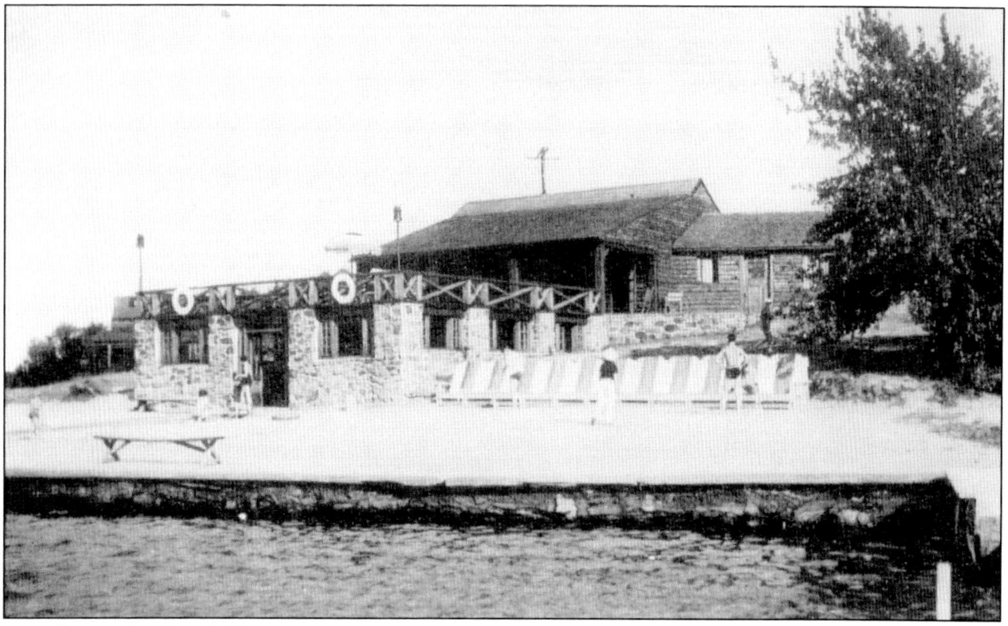

Candlewood Isle Clubhouse and Beach in New Fairfield has been the scene of many social events throughout its history. This 1940s photograph shows the original clubhouse structure; it has since been extensively expanded and renovated.

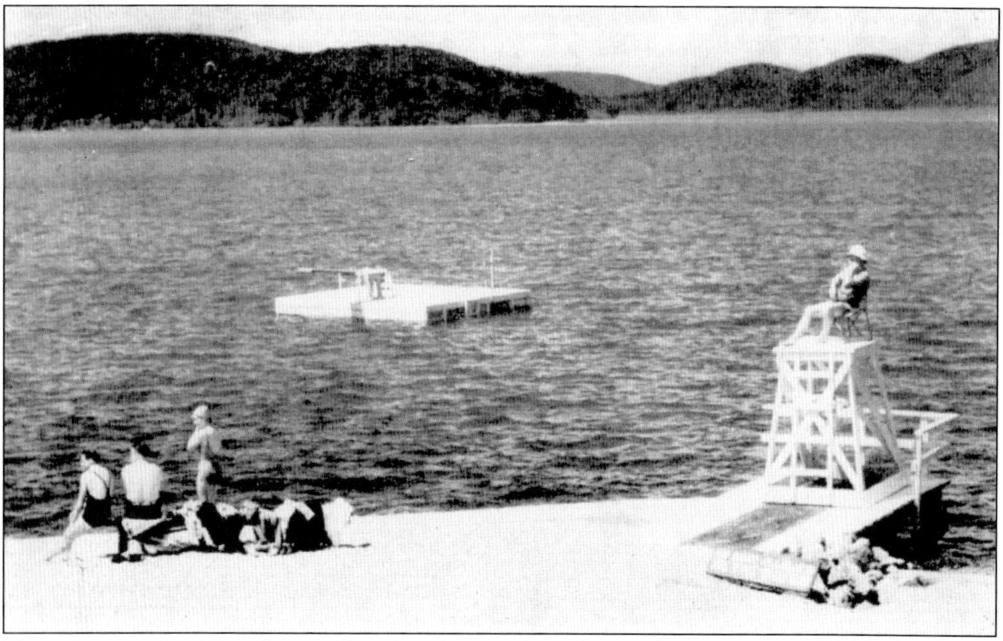

This photograph of Candlewood Isle Beach was taken during the 1940s. Note the lack of boats in the area.

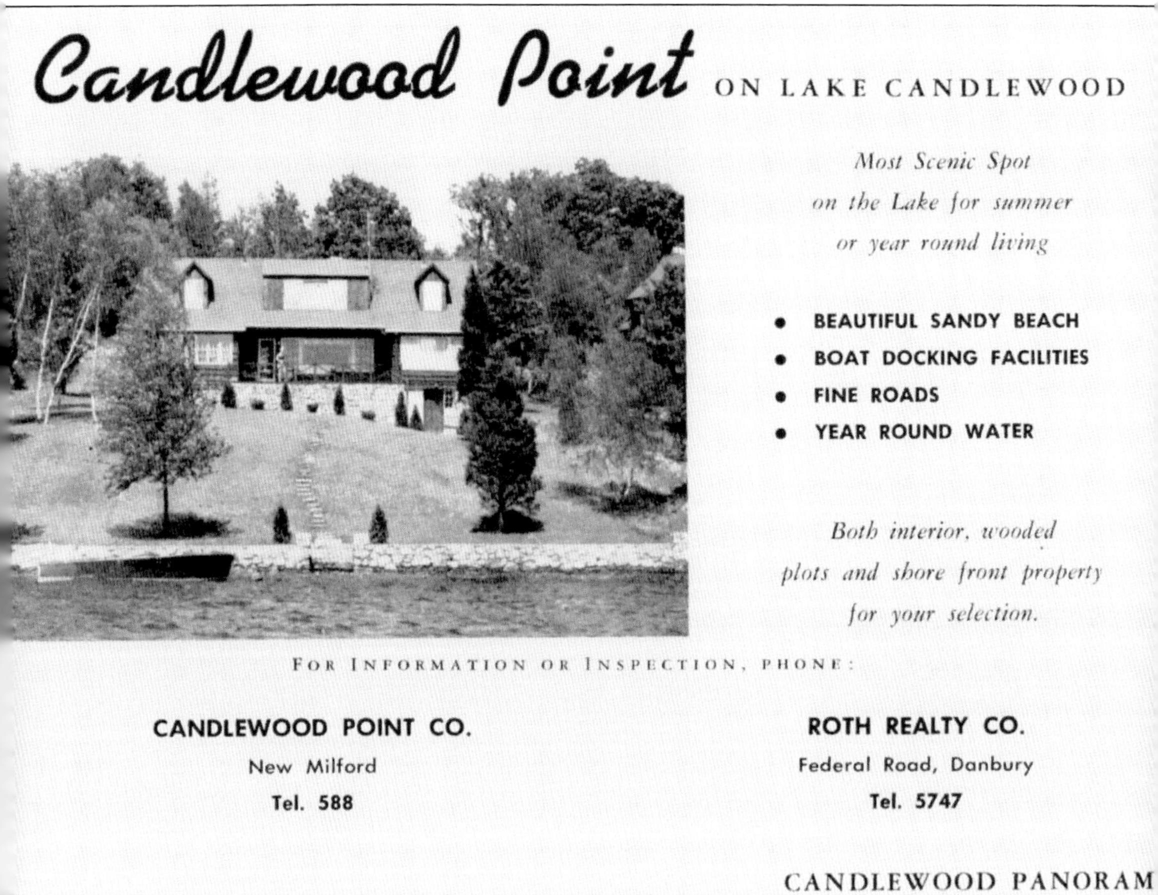

This is a Candlewood Point advertisement from *Candlewood Panorama* magazine in the summer of 1949. Note the telephone numbers.

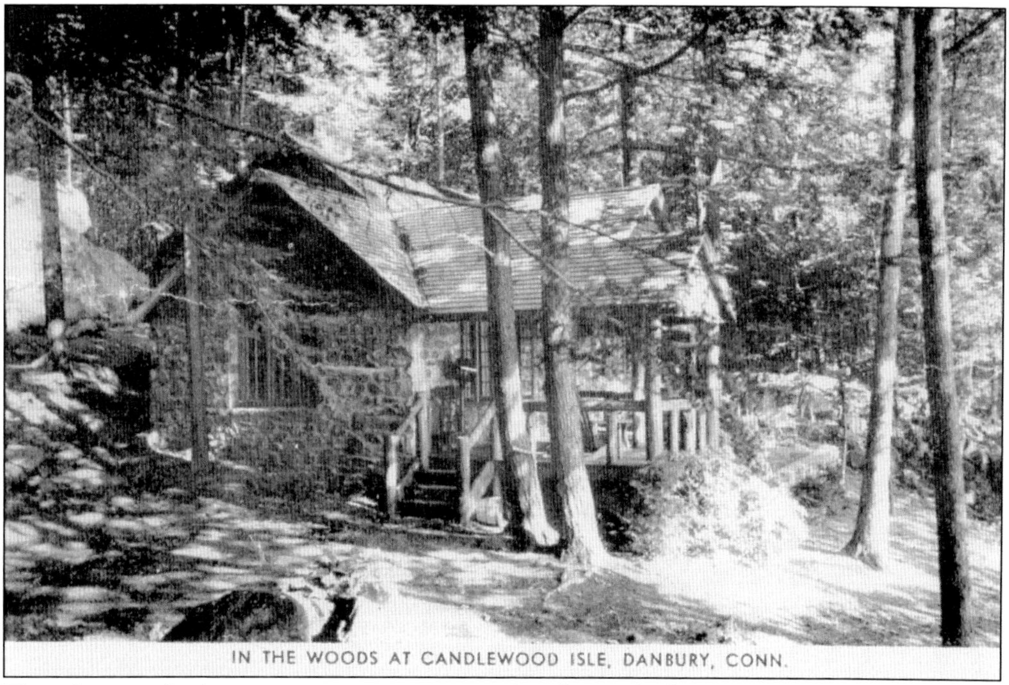

This photograph shows a summer cottage on Candlewood Isle in New Fairfield during the 1940s. Most of the cottages were quite simple in design, but the communities had activities for the entire family to enjoy. The teenagers participated in swim meets, softball games, and dances amongst the communities of Candlewood Knolls, Candlewood Isle, Candlewood Shores, and Candlewood Lake Club during the 1950s and 1960s.

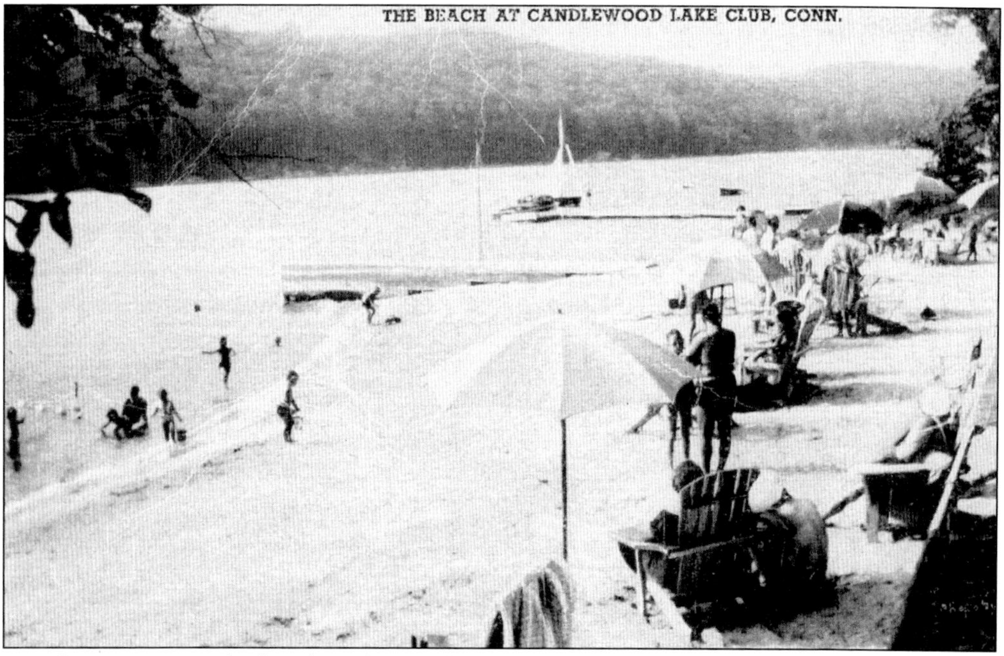

Seen here in 1940 is the beach at the Candlewood Lake Club in New Milford, one of the many private communities around the lake.

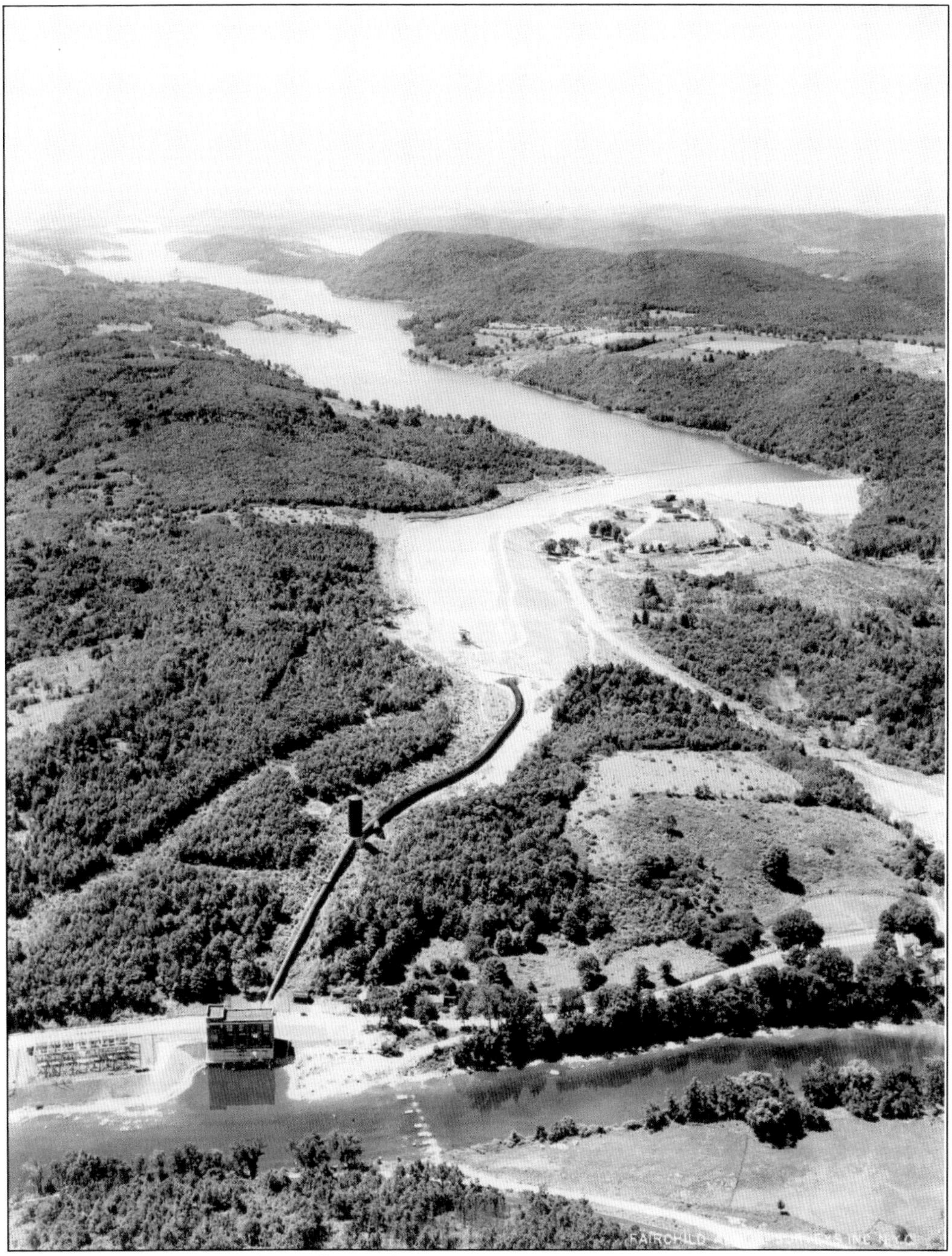

This *c.* 1940 aerial view shows the Rocky River powerplant and penstock, and the New Milford arm of Candlewood Lake. The Housatonic River, in the foreground, is some 230 feet lower than the level of Candlewood Lake.

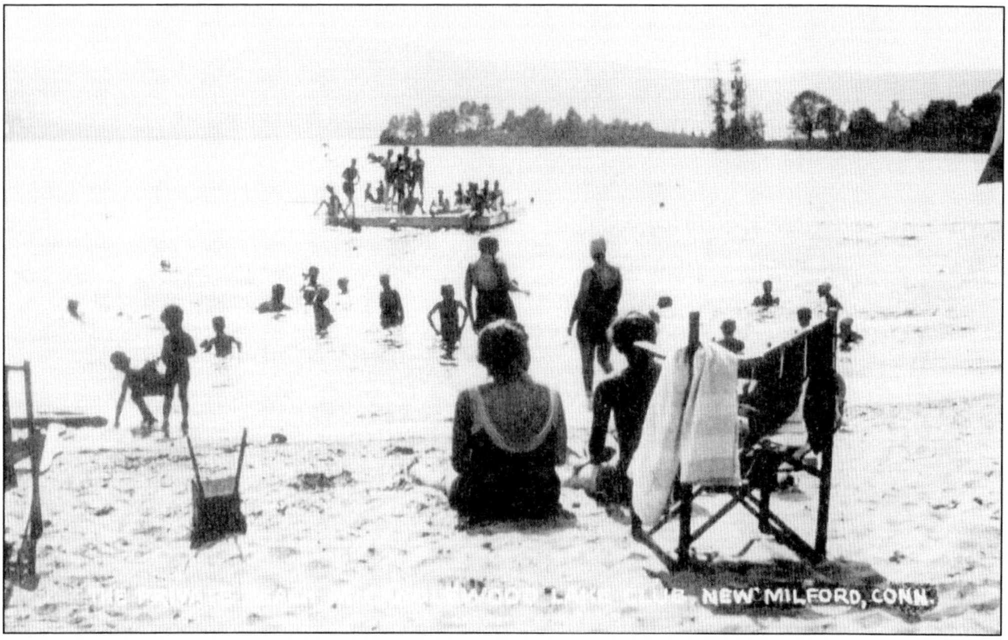

The Candlewood Lake Club Beach, shown here in the 1940s, was a popular spot on a hot summer day.

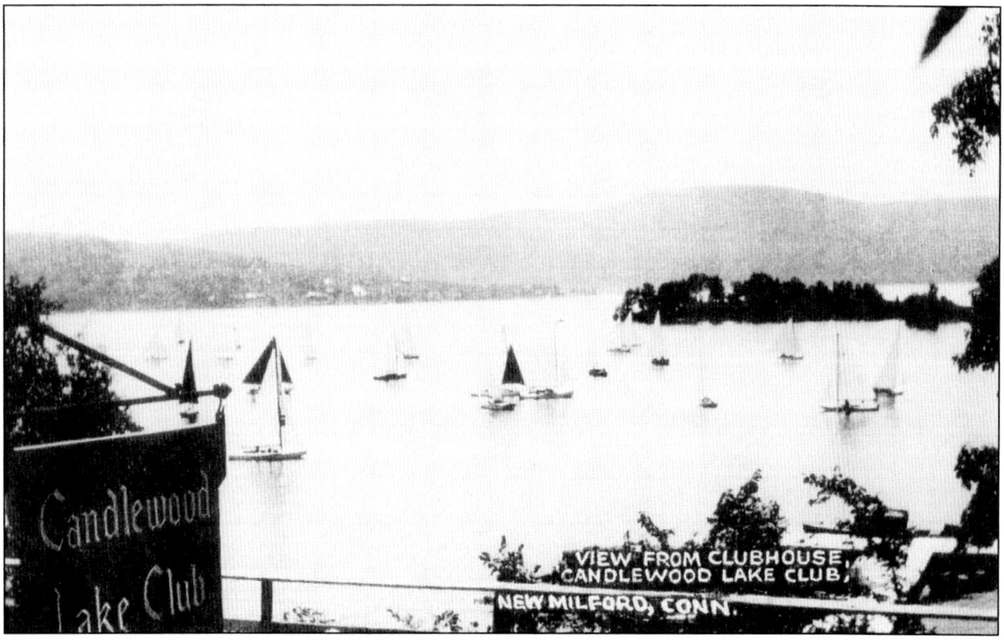

This c. 1940 view looks west from Candlewood Lake to the tip of Vaughn's Neck.

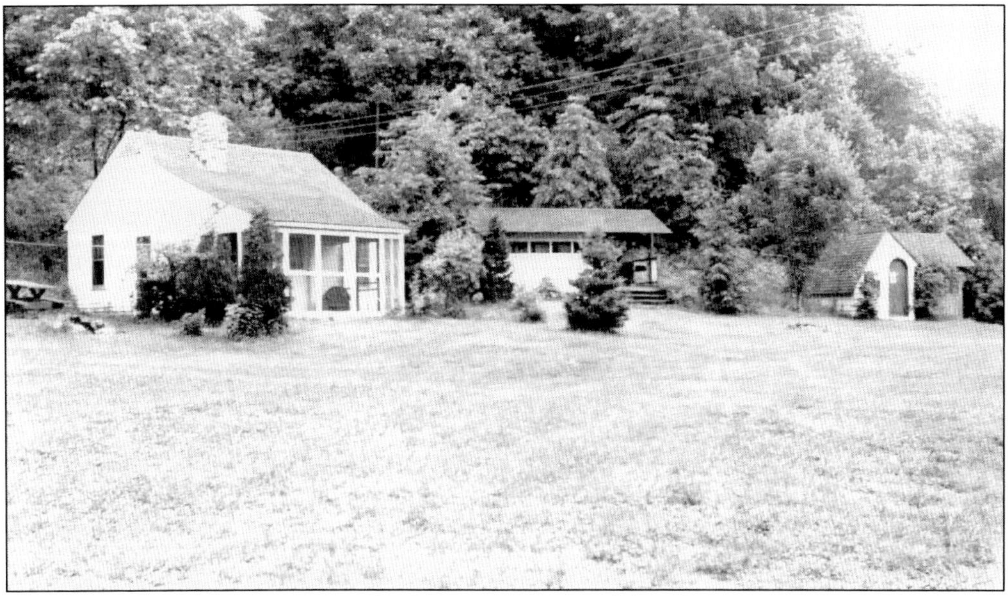

This is the old Allen's Camp, which is now occupied by Sherman Park and Recreation buildings. Today, the business office of the Candlewood Lake Authority is located in this area, which is also the site of the Sherman Town Beach. The office itself is a converted cabin that was formerly part of Allen's Camp. The Candlewood Lake Authority assists Northeast Utilities, the state of Connecticut, the city of Danbury, and the towns of Brookfield, New Fairfield, New Milford, and Sherman in the provision of lake, shoreline, and watershed management to foster the preservation and enhancement of recreational, public safety, and environmental values.

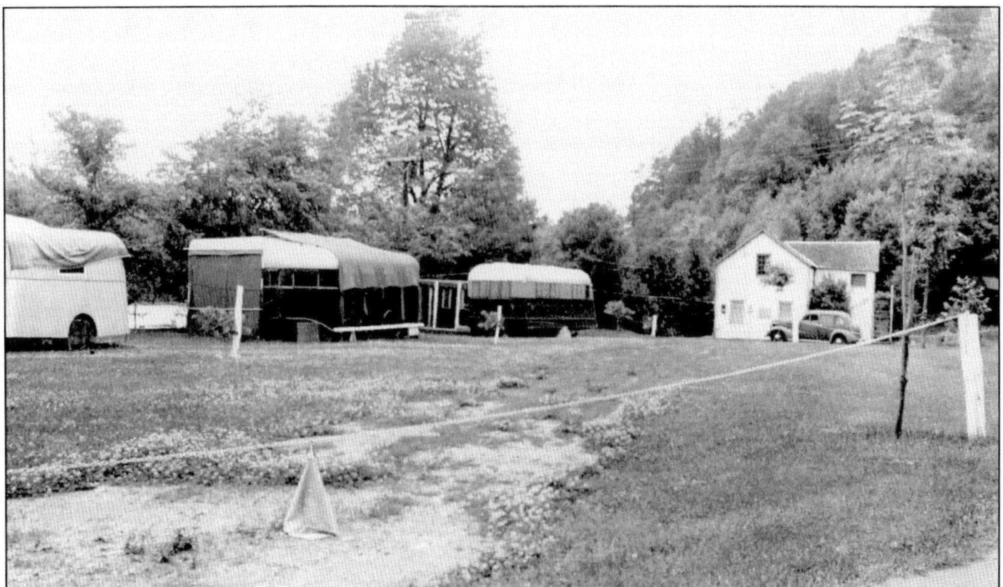

Allen's Camp, today the site of Sherman Beach and headquarters of the Candlewood Lake Authority, is pictured c. 1950, when summer campers could "winter" their trailers here.

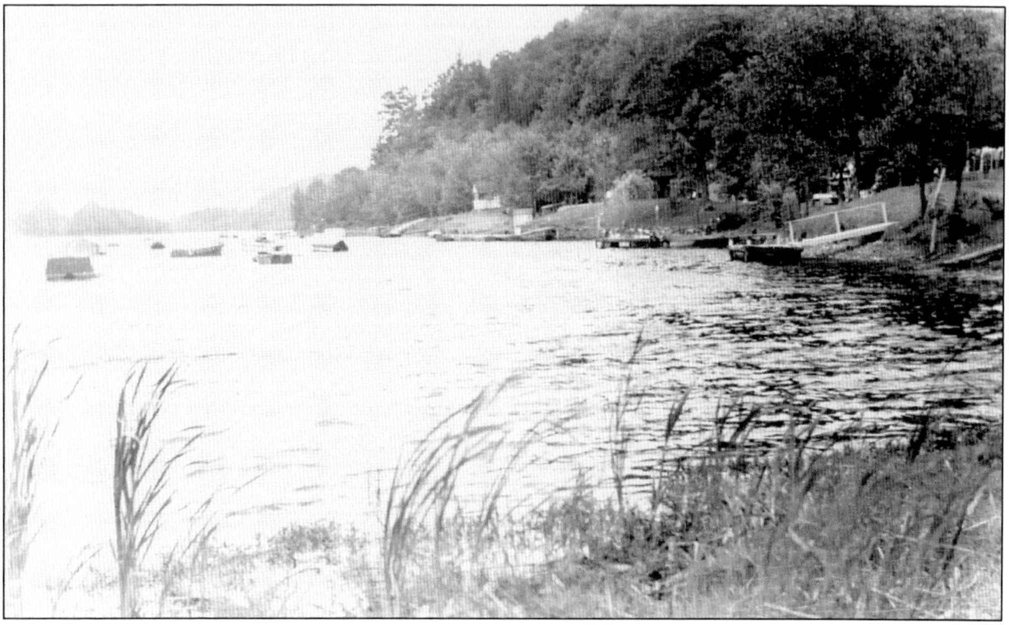

Seen here is the original Allen's Camp Marina, which is the present-day docking site of the Candlewood Lake Authority in Sherman.

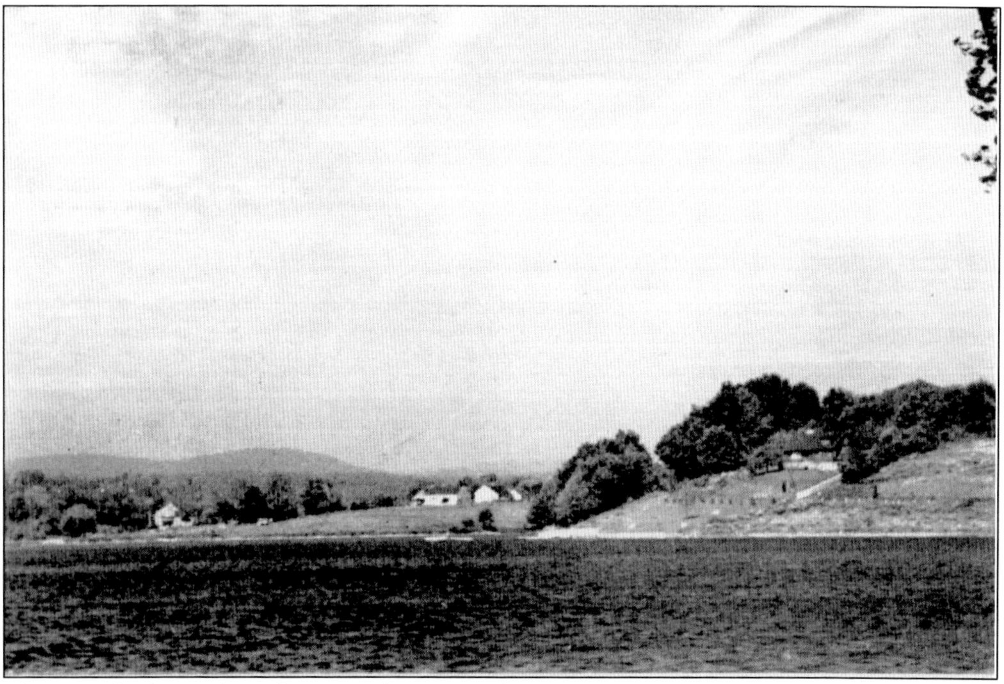

This view looks north in the general vicinity of Down the Hatch Restaurant, a popular eatery on the lake. This photograph shows Candlewood Orchards from Conrad's Landing *c.* 1950.

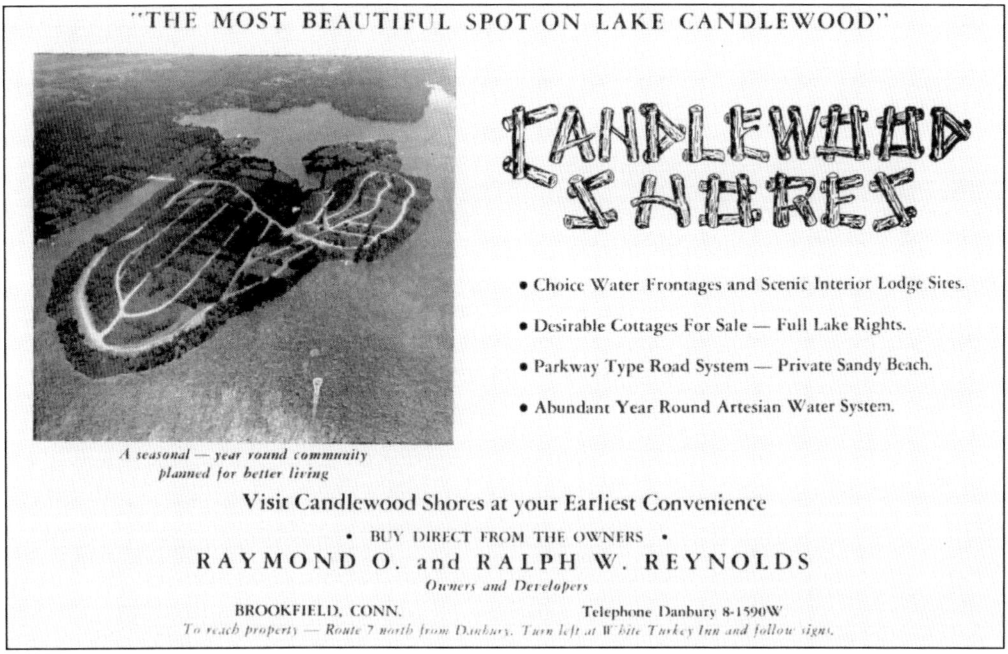

This Candlewood Shores advertisement was featured in *Candlewood Panorama* magazine during the summer of 1949.

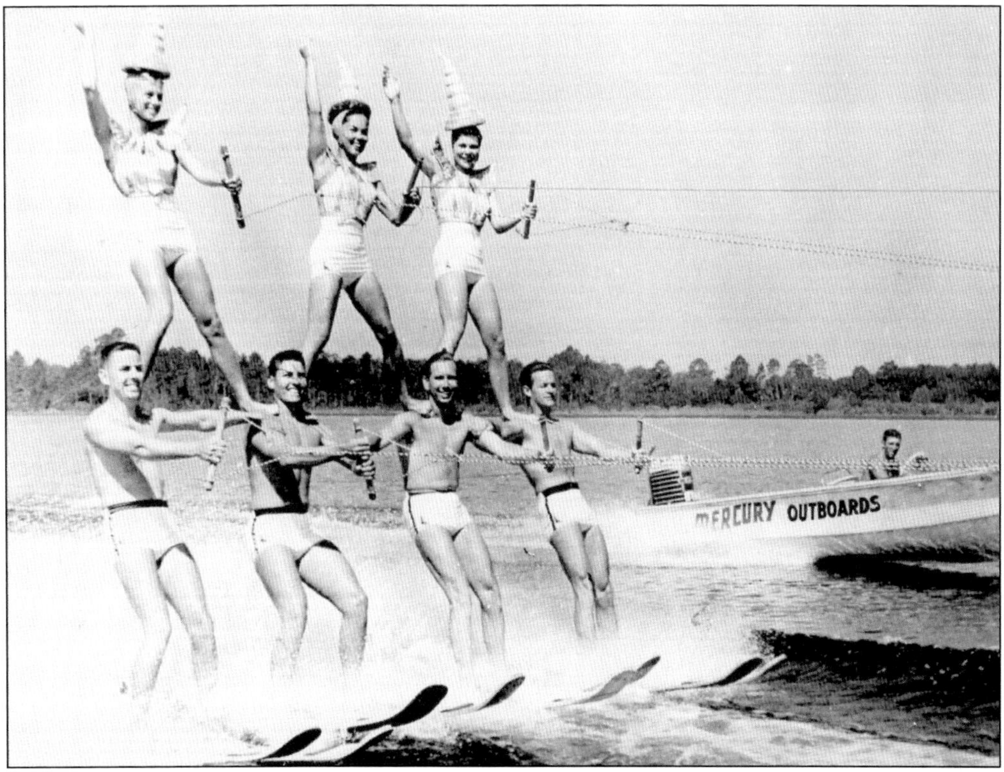

Believe it or not, these water-skiers are performing on Candlewood Lake—not Cypress Gardens. The outboard motor and the bathing suits date this photograph.

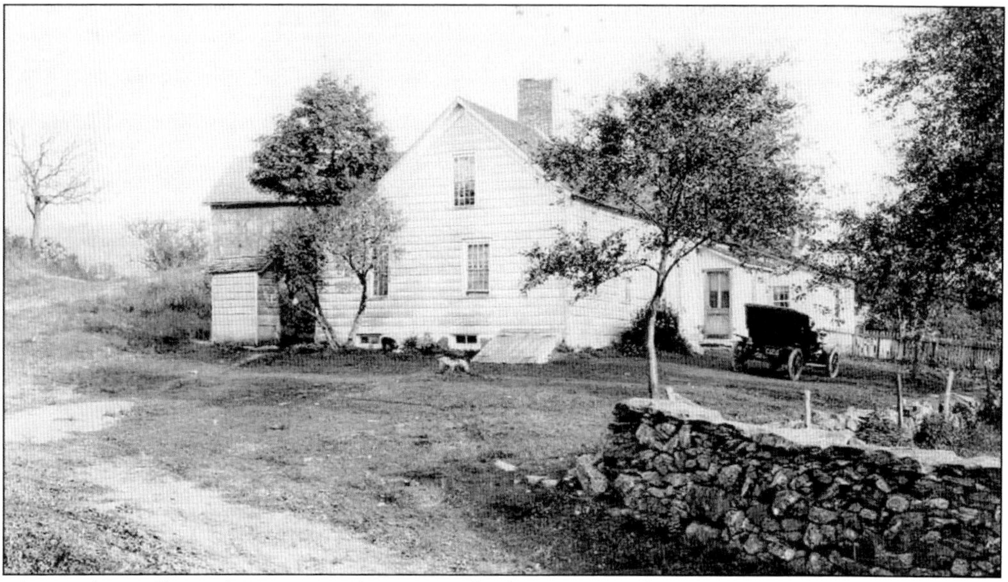

This is the Mill Pond House in Sherman, which was once the headquarters of Camp Aquila, a Boy Scout camp.

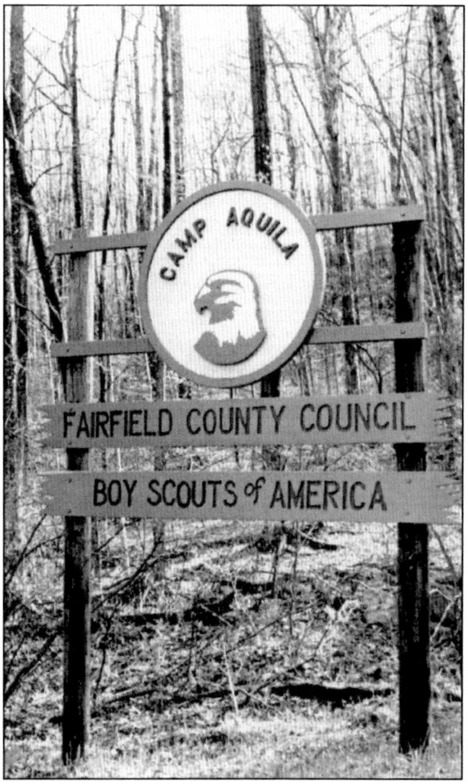

Here is the old Boy Scout camp entrance to Camp Aquila, which is now Mill Pond residential community. The Boy Scout camp was sold to a private developer several years ago.

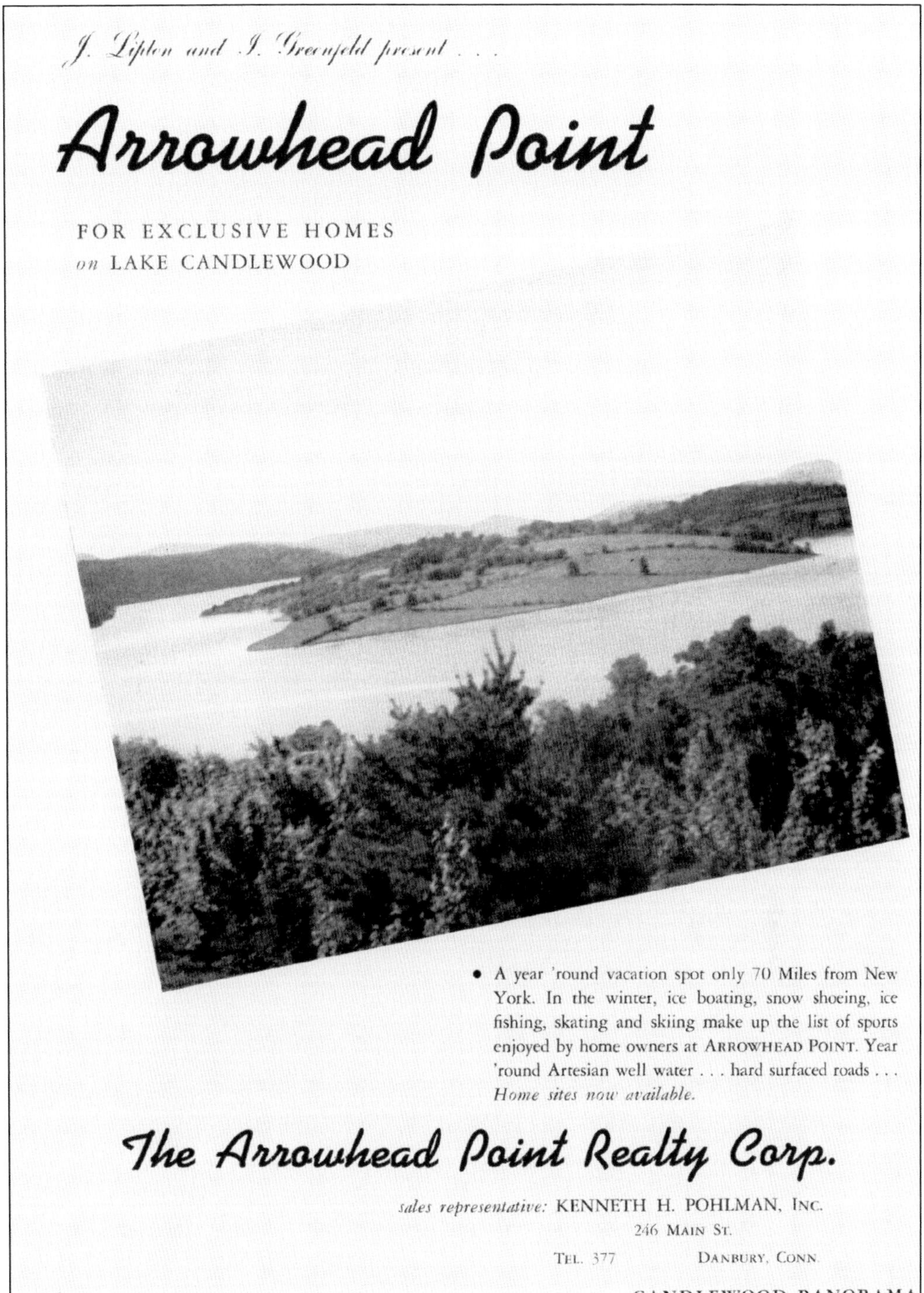

This advertisement for Arrowhead Point in Brookfield ran during the summer of 1949. The ad announces "home sites now available."

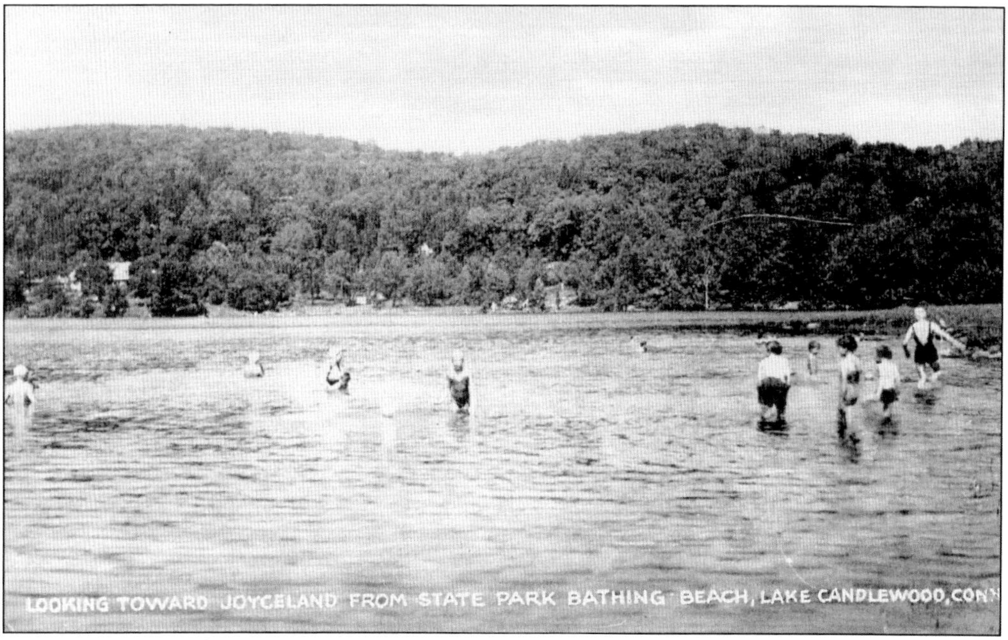

This *c*. 1940 view from Squantz Pond State Park looks toward Joyceland casino.

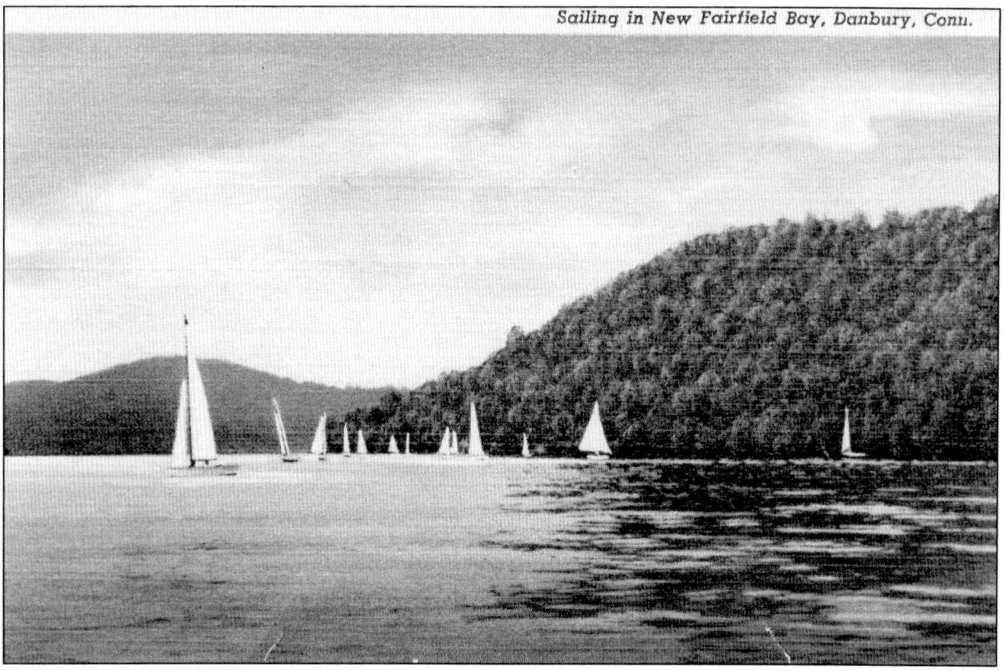

Visitors are pictured sailing on Candlewood Lake during a peaceful summer's day in the 1950s.

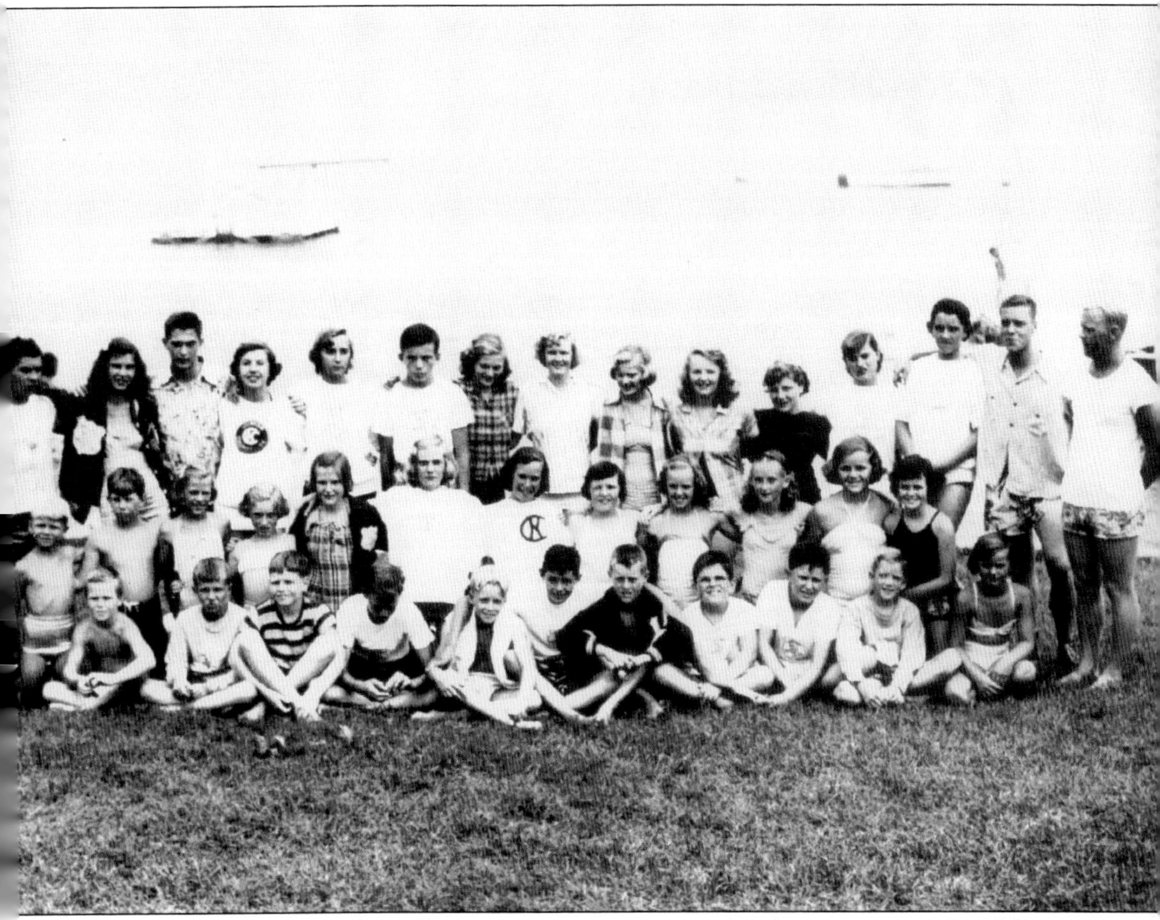

Members of the Candlewood Knolls community swim team gather for a portrait in the 1950s.

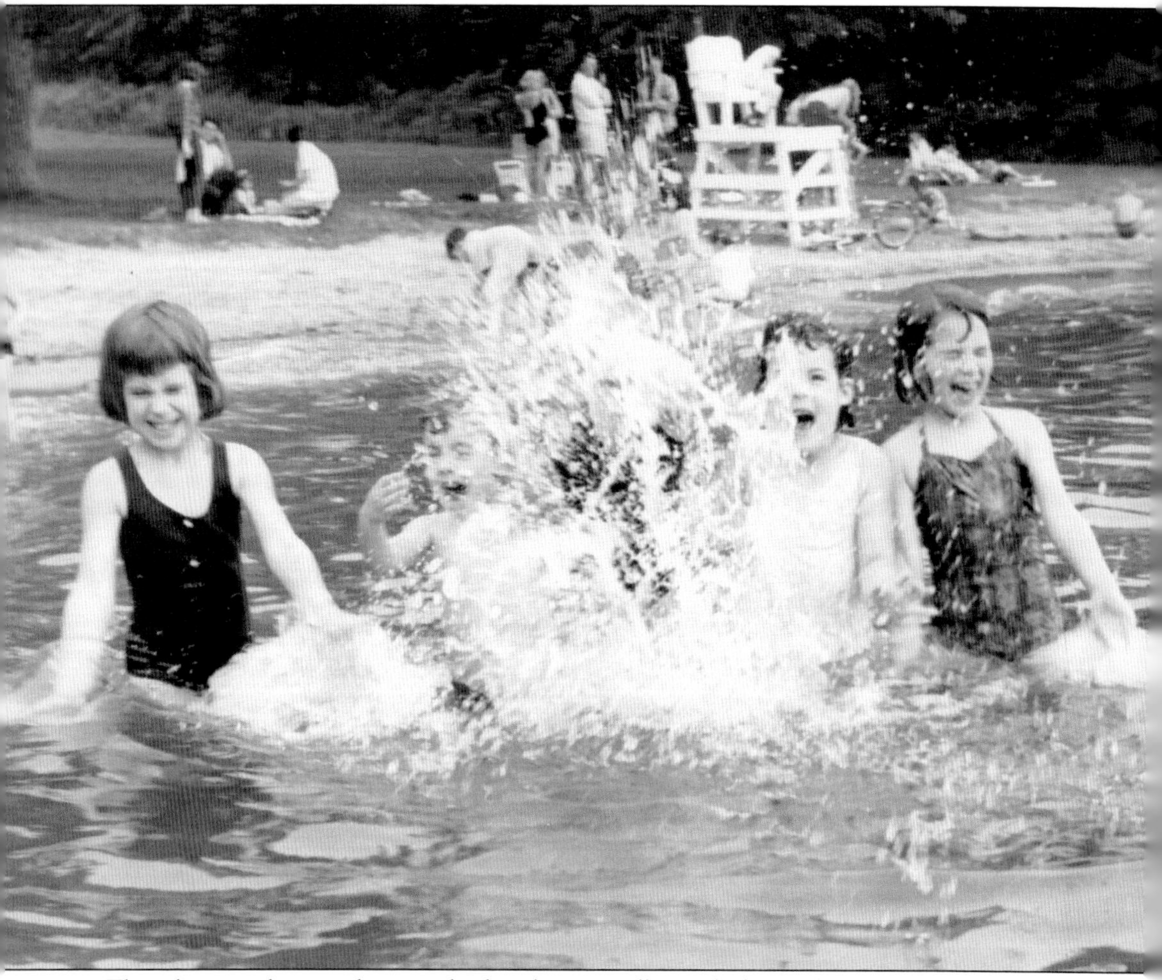

This photograph was taken on the beach at Candlewood Shores during the 1960s. The area that became Candlewood Shores was originally part of New Fairfield, but when the lake was flooded, the land became isolated. During the 1950s Candlewood Shores became part of the town of Brookfield by mutual agreement of the two towns.

Six

The Lake through the Decades

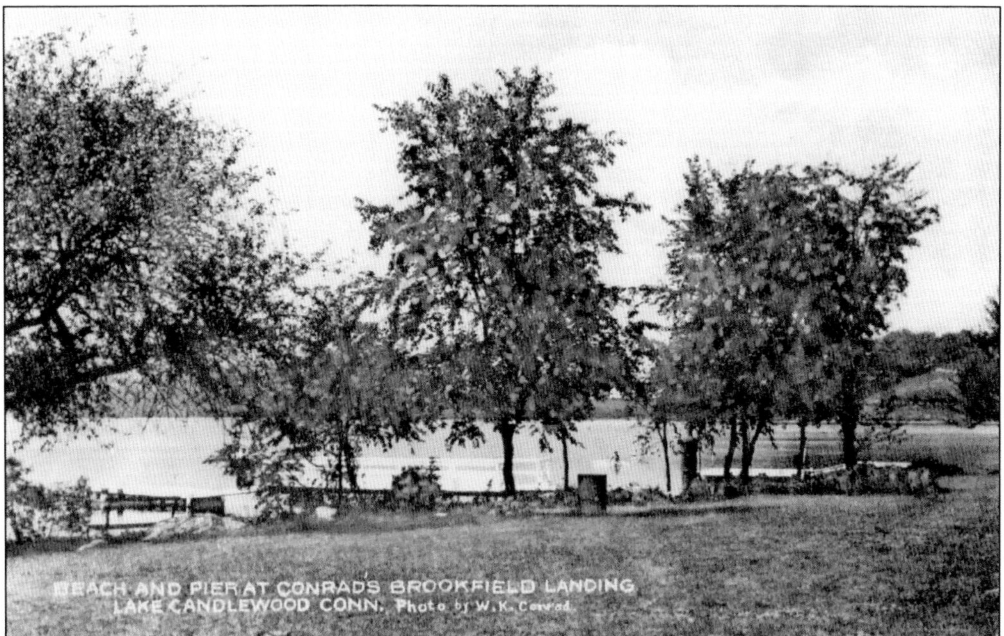

Conrad's Landing beach and piers in Brookfield, which are still in existence today, are shown here in the 1940s. This is now the site of the Candlewood East Marina. There are approximately 250 boats moored there today.

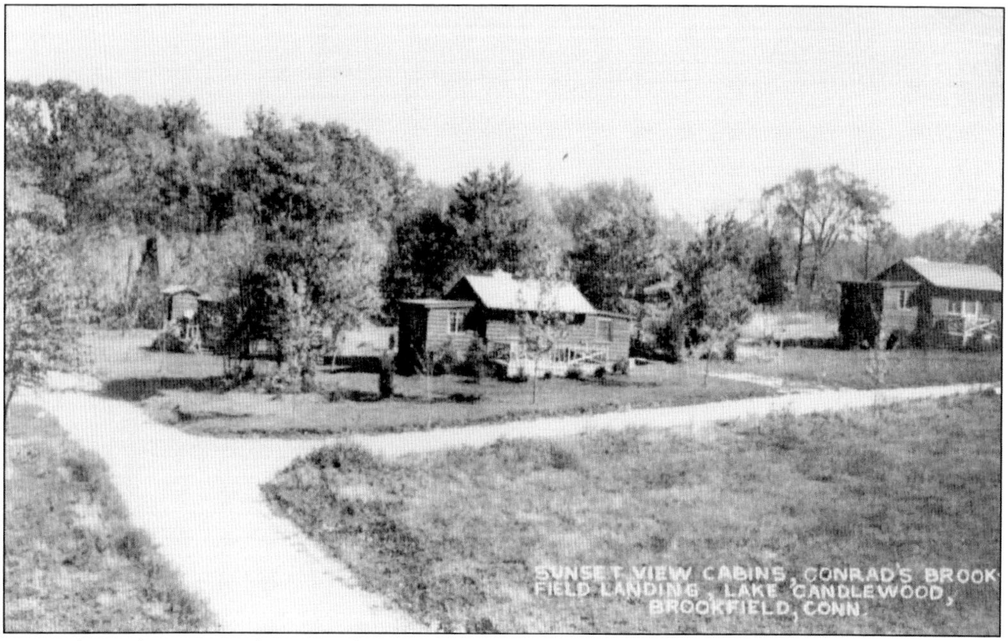

Conrad's Cabins, seen here in the 1930s, remain almost in the same condition today. As one travels north on Candlewood Lake Road, the cabins can be seen directly across from Candlewood East Marina.

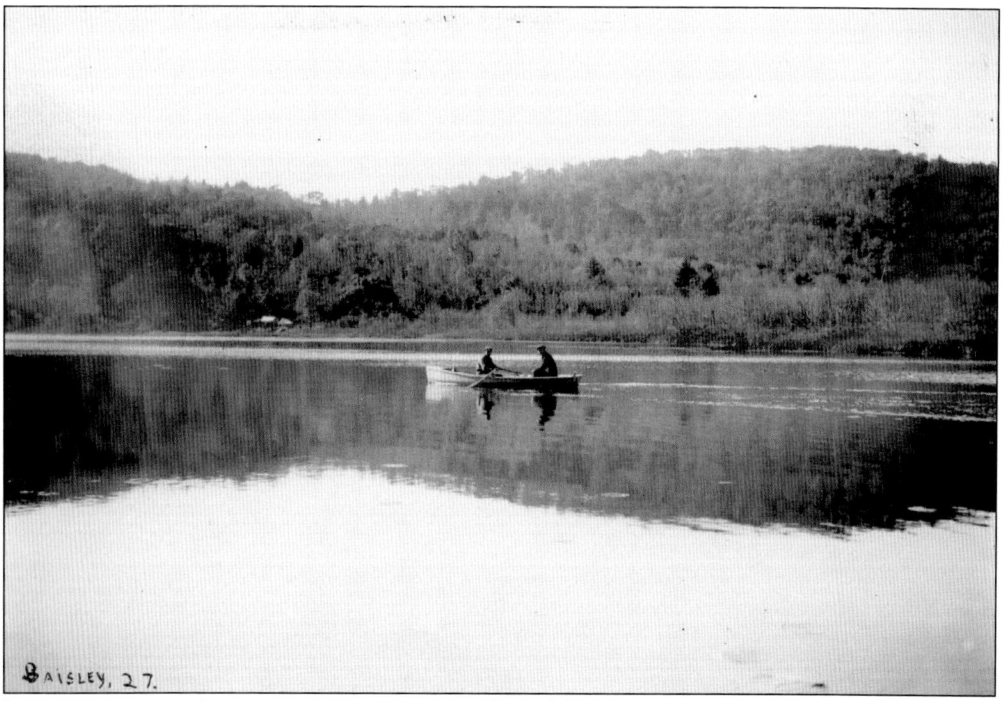

Fishing has always been a popular activity, as these folks demonstrate. They are setting out for a night of fishing as the sun goes down over the lake during the summer of 1950.

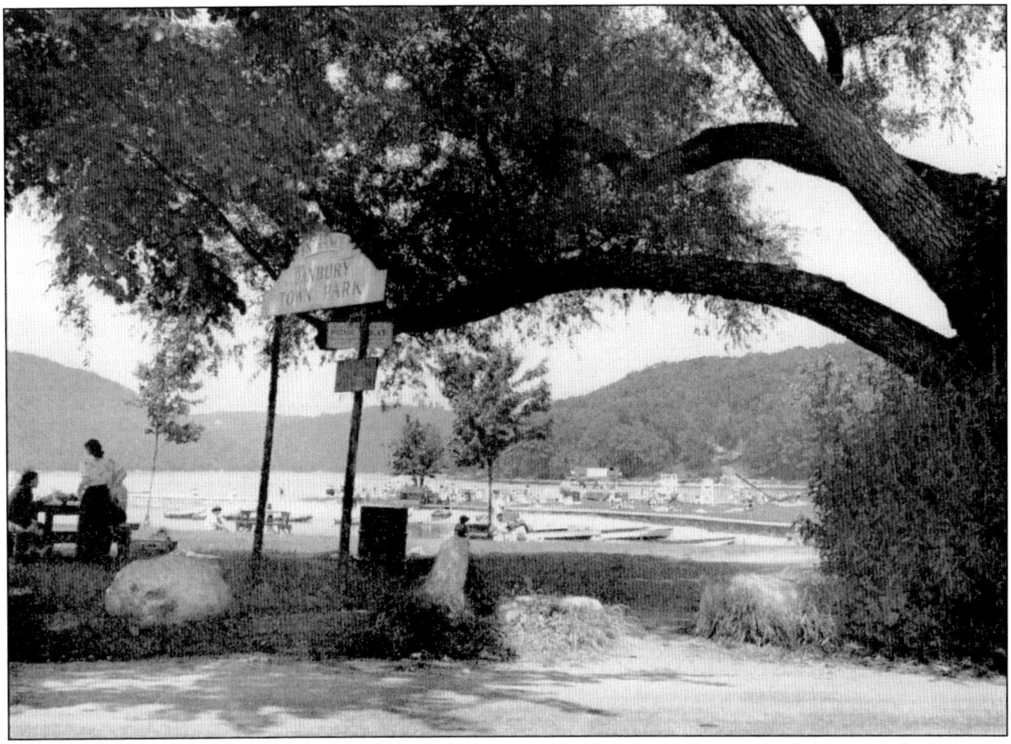

This is a photograph of Danbury Town Park in 1952. All five towns on Candlewood Lake have their own town parks, which are for the use of each community's respective residents. Each of the parks is maintained by the town in which it is located.

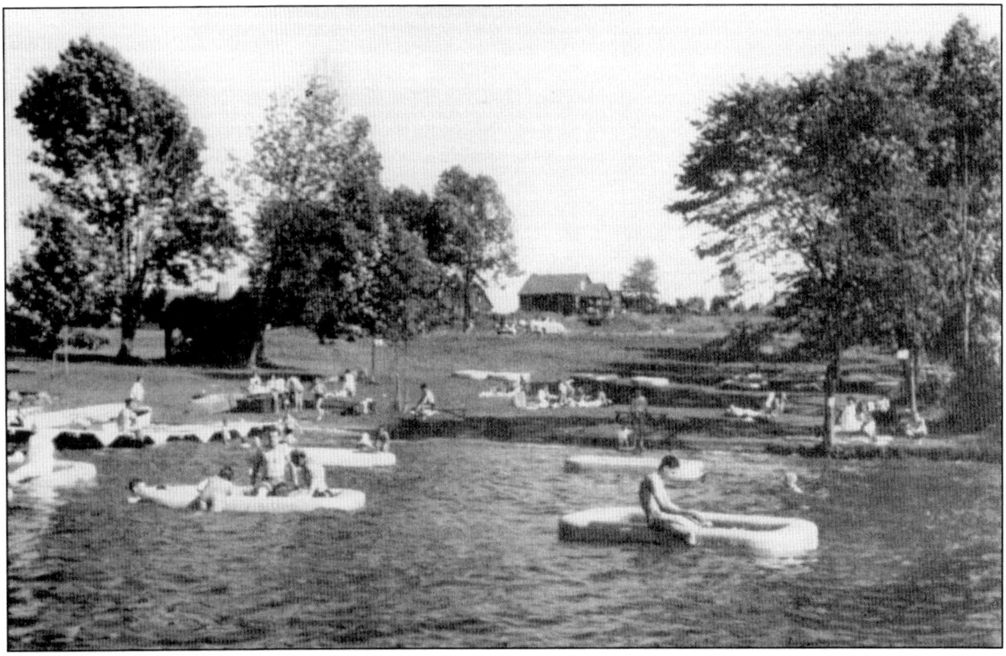

Candlewood Shores on the Brookfield side of the lake is shown during the 1950s. The floats being used by the swimmers appear to be navy life rafts.

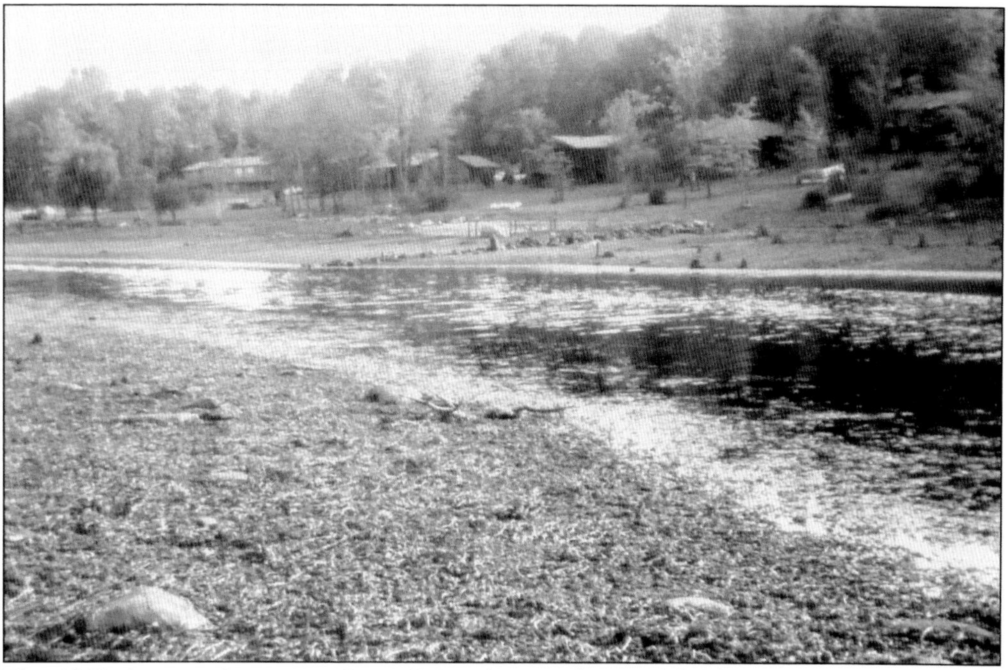

This 1965 photograph captures Conrad's Landing on the Brookfield side of the lake.

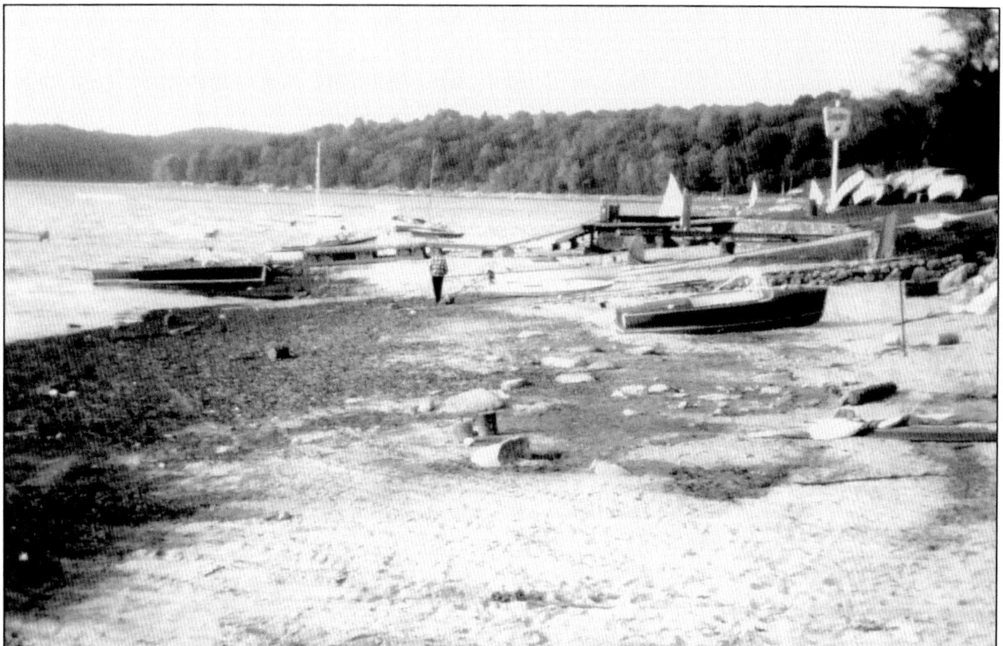

This 1965 photograph was taken in front of what was then Bullock's Marina, now Brookfield Bay Marina. The long boat on the left (middle of view) was a Bullock's Marina work boat for many years. The boat was originally purchased by Ted Farley, the developer of Candlewood Lake Club, as a way to show the lake to potential customers. But he sold the boat when he realized these "customers" were actually folks looking for a free boat ride on the lake.

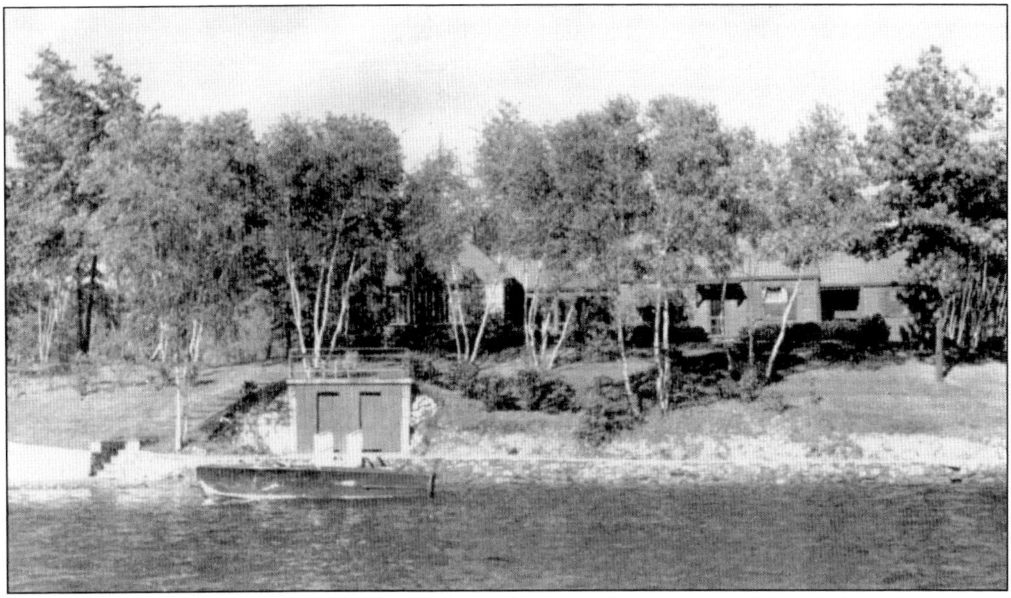

This is one of the many houses located on the lake during the 1950s. Before the days of trailers and winter storage for boats, the vessels were stored in lakeside boathouses. Many of these boathouses are still in existence today, although few, if any, are used for winter storage. Permission for construction of new boathouses is no longer granted by the utility.

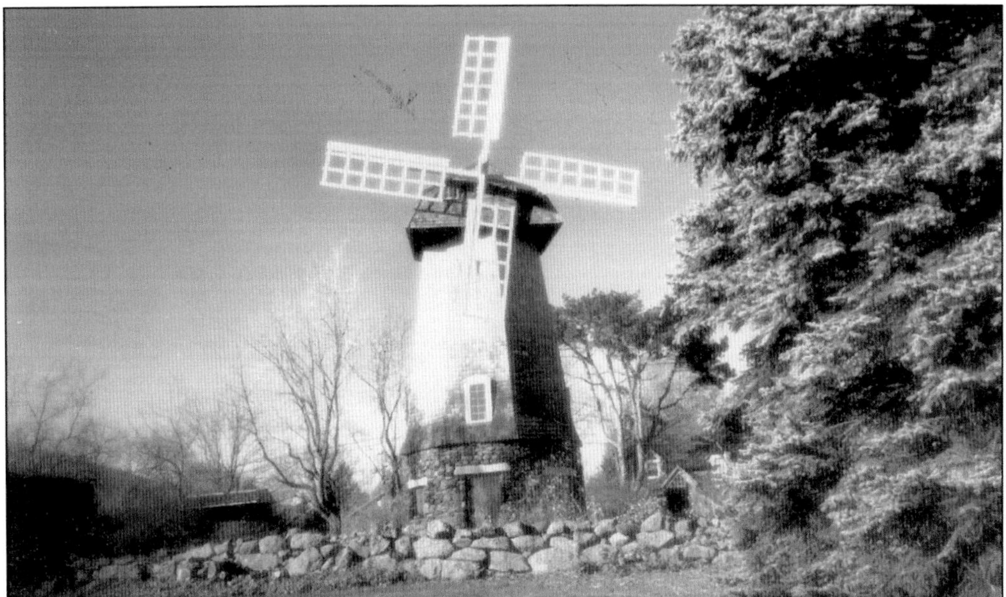

The Windmill at Knollcrest overlooks the New Fairfield side of Candlewood Lake and is situated at the top of a summer community. Built in 1936, the windmill is 80 feet high and features a water-pumping mechanism. (Today, water pumps are powered by electricity.) The top section of the windmill revolves so the sails might be trimmed to the prevailing winds. The walnut shaft for the sails weighs nearly 300 pounds. Although the windmill site was not the best of locations, this landmark stands out as an observation point from which to see a broad panorama of the lake and other major points surrounding the beautiful communities.

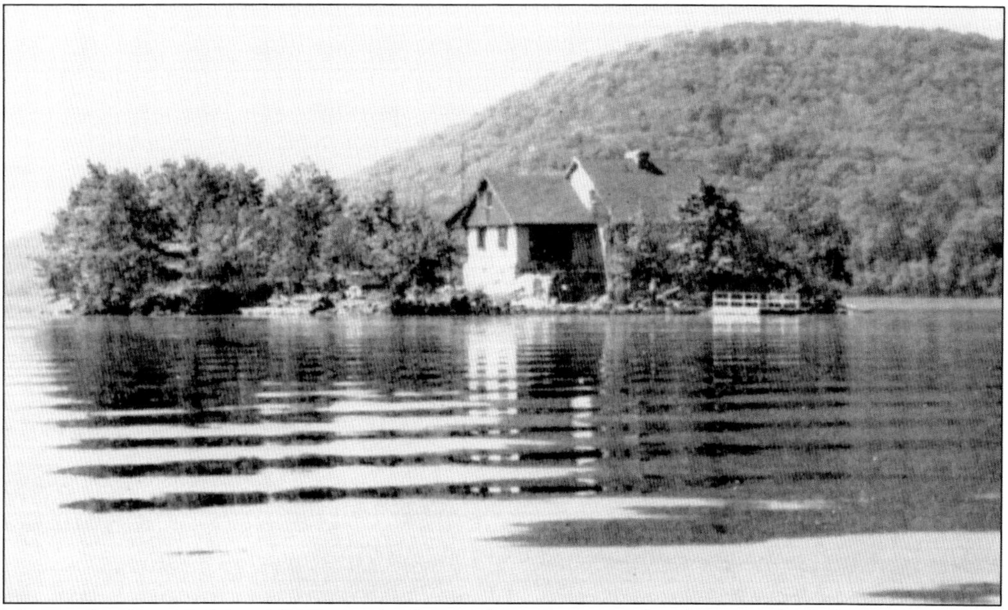

This is the famous Island House, which stands on Sunset Island, located off the southern tip of Candlewood Isle in New Fairfield. This is a private residence that has had many owners over the years, one of whom had access to the mainland via an amphibious car/boat vehicle. This house remains a popular spot today, as boaters can go all the way around the island to quench their curiosity.

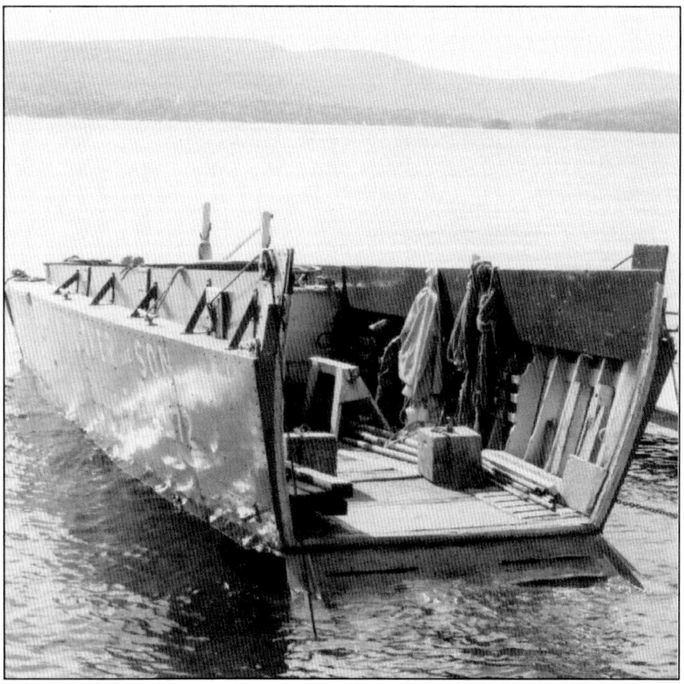

H. T. Tucker and Sons is in the business of building, maintaining, and storing docks and floats on the lake. The third-generation company has been in business since the 1950s. Pictured here is Tucker's landing craft, which is a navy LCVP (landing craft, vehicle, personnel). This is the famous Higgin's boat that was used for many amphibious invasions in the Atlantic and Pacific during World War II. The boat is still used on Candlewood Lake for transporting heavy cargo and material to isolated spots.

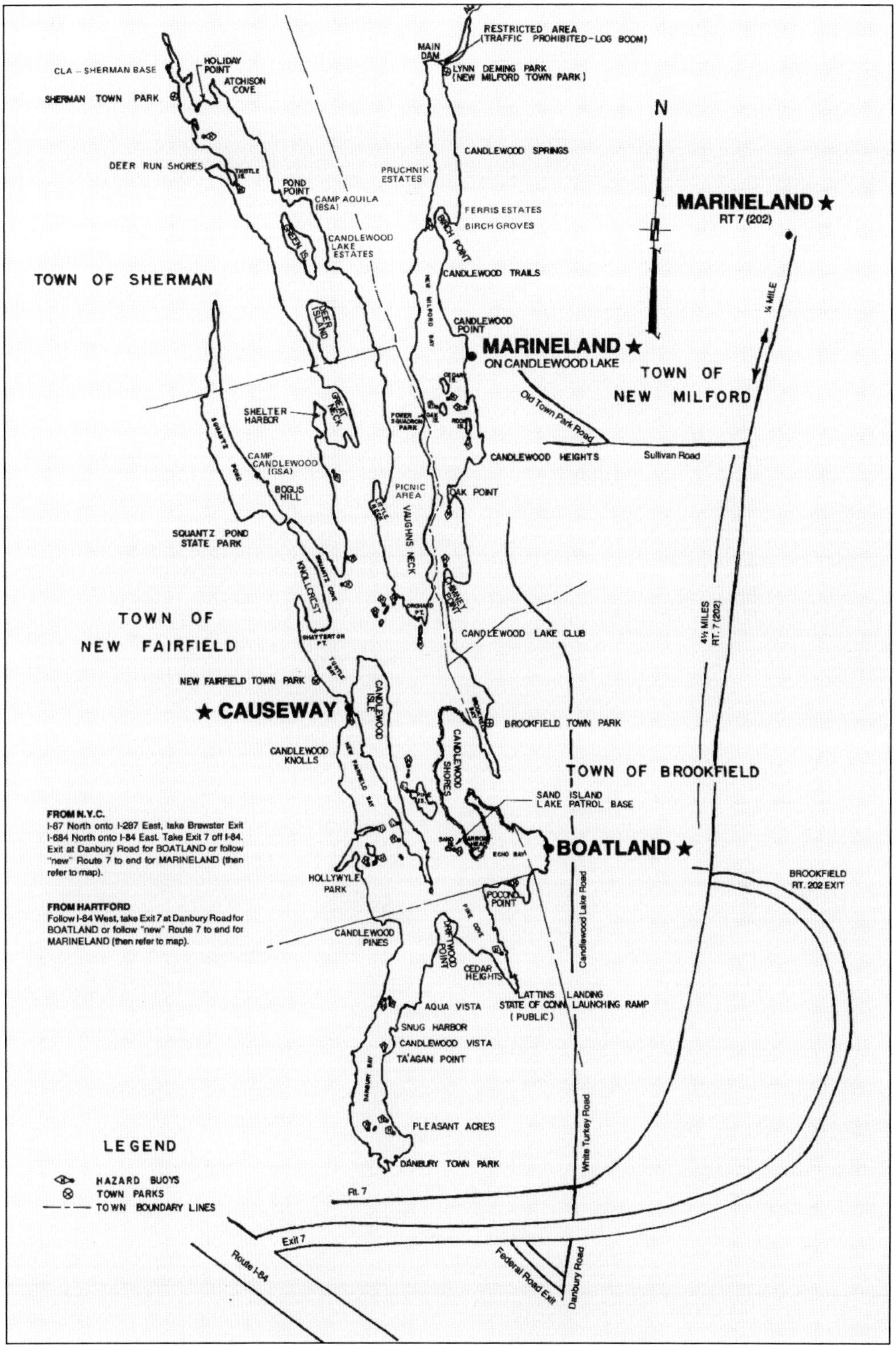

This map of the lake shows the locations of marinas during the 1980s.

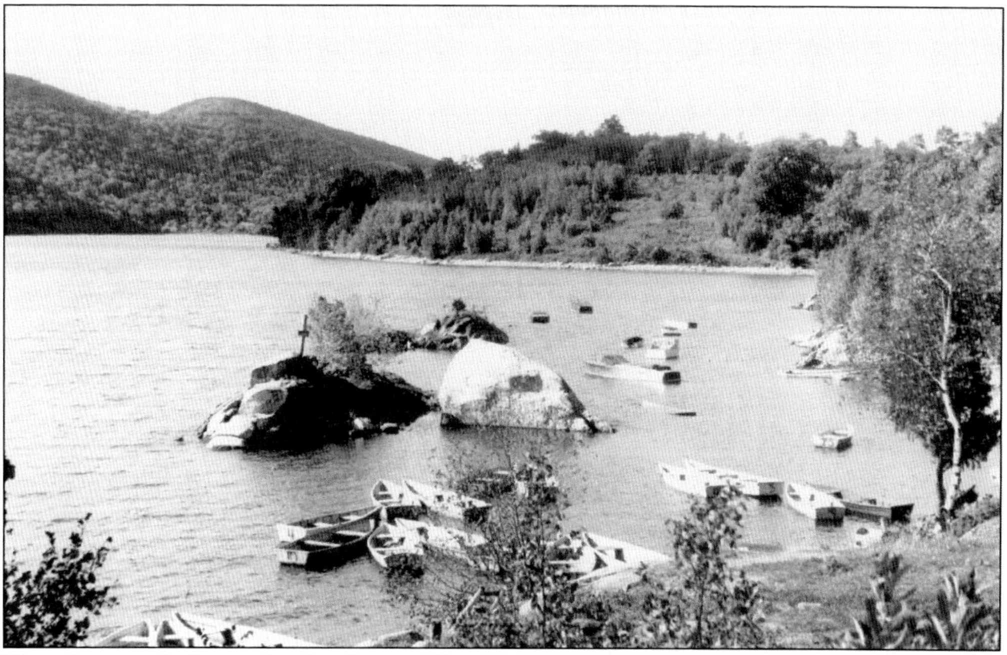

This photograph shows the Candlewood Point section of New Milford in 1952, when the area was void of houses. Today it is a lively year-round community with many homes and docks. At the top left of this view is Candlewood Mountain, and at the bottom right is the area that became the site of Bogie's Marina and is today the home of Gerard's Marina. Note the cross on one of the rocks.

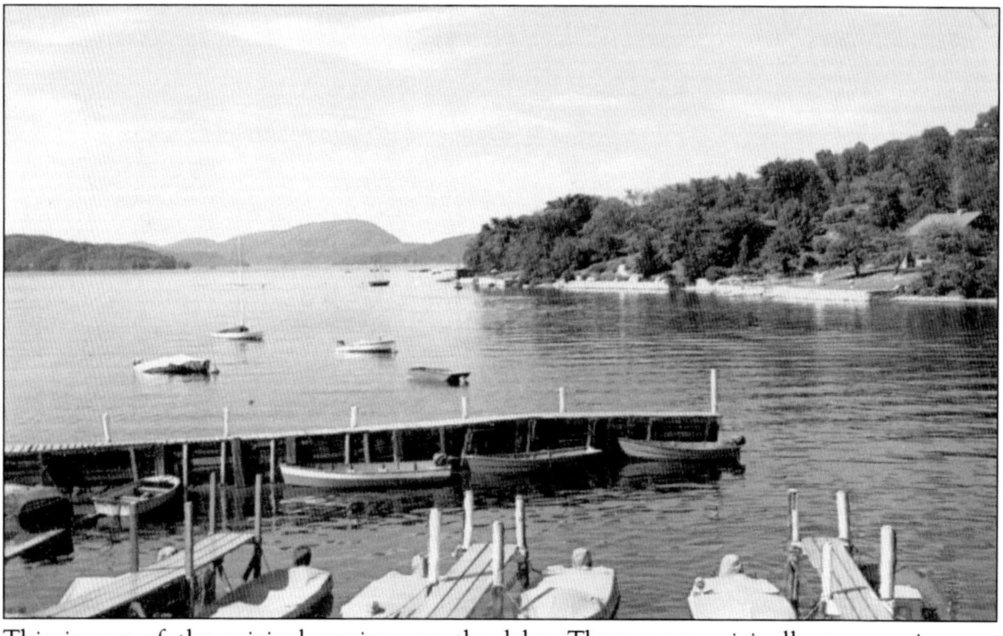

This is one of the original marinas on the lake. There were originally two marinas on Candlewood Lake: Bullock's, located on the Brookfield side of the lake; and Lake Marine, located at the Candlewood Isle Causeway. Today there are several marinas around the lake, all of which are full service and provide dockage.

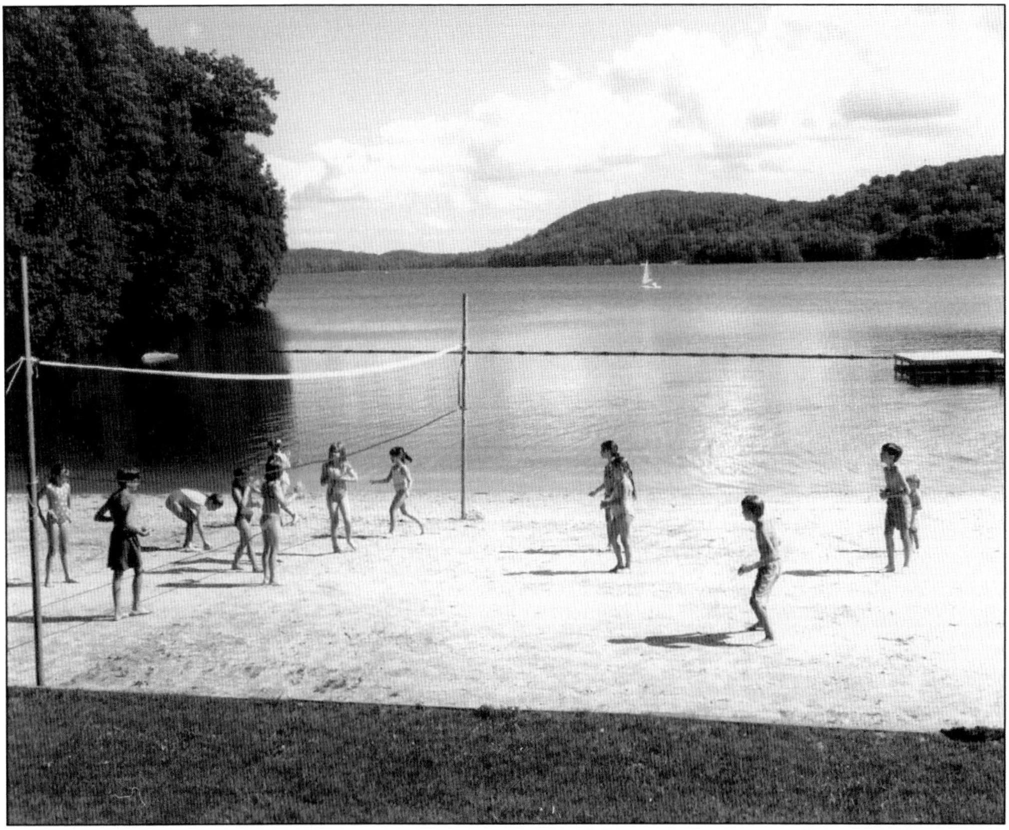

Pictured c. 1986 is the waterfront at Atchison Cove, a lake community in Sherman that enjoys the beauty of Candlewood Lake.

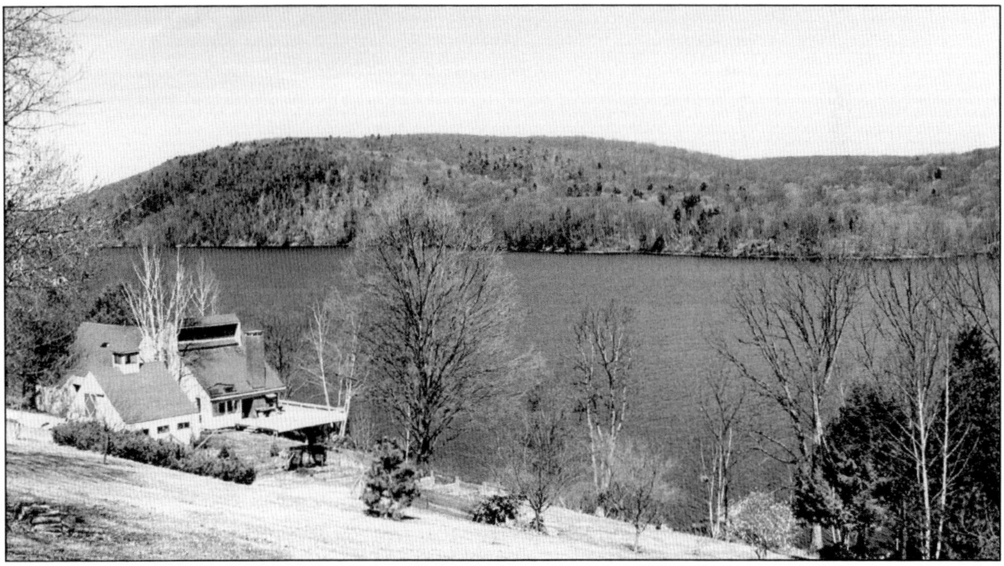

The Kelley family of Sherman purchased this parcel of land from Maltby Leach. The photograph shows Leach Hollow today, in a view across to Mill Pond, an old grain mill and wood mill site.

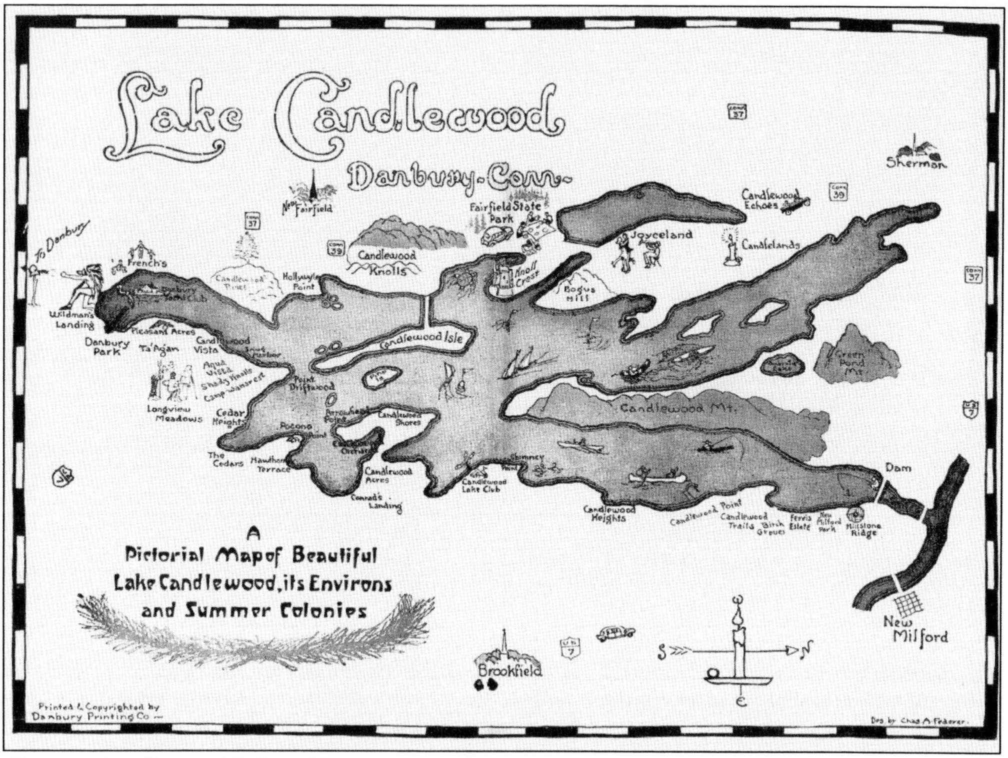

This is a Candlewood Lake advertising map from 1987. It is a reproduction of an old blueprint.

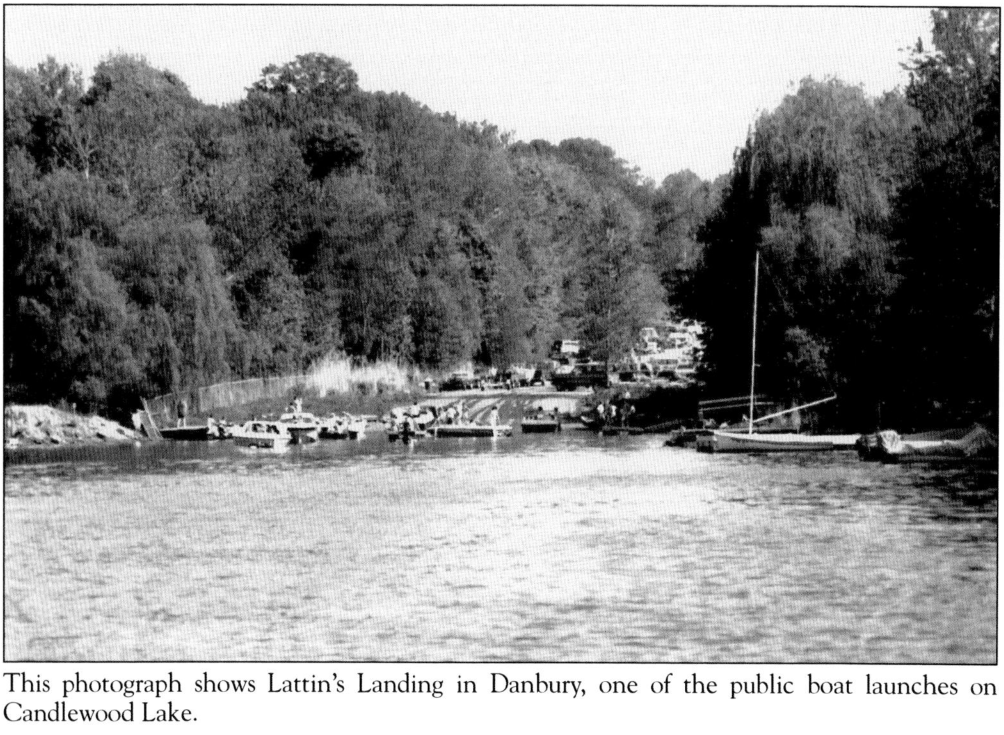
This photograph shows Lattin's Landing in Danbury, one of the public boat launches on Candlewood Lake.

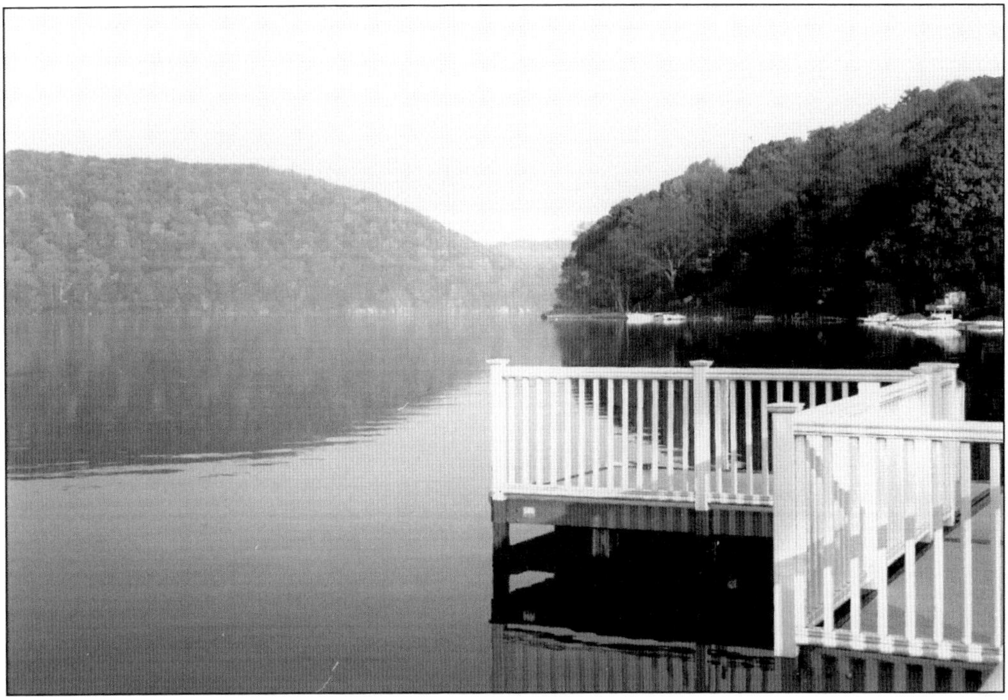
This view looks north from the boat launch ramp at Danbury Town Park.

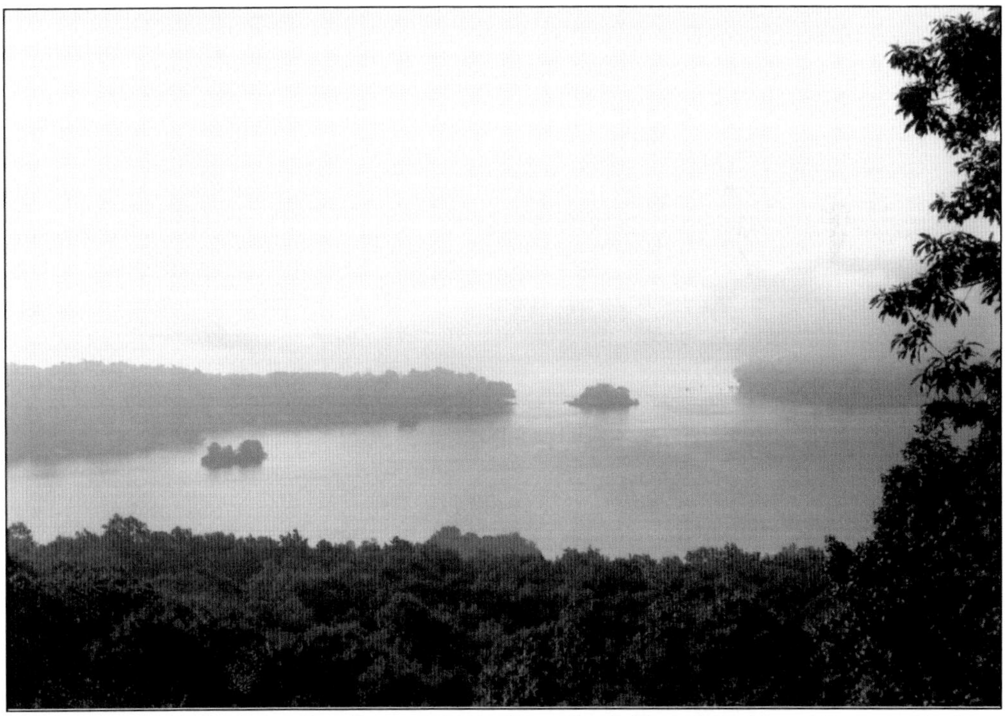
The peninsula on the left is Candlewood Isle in New Fairfield, and Driftwood Point in Danbury is to the right.

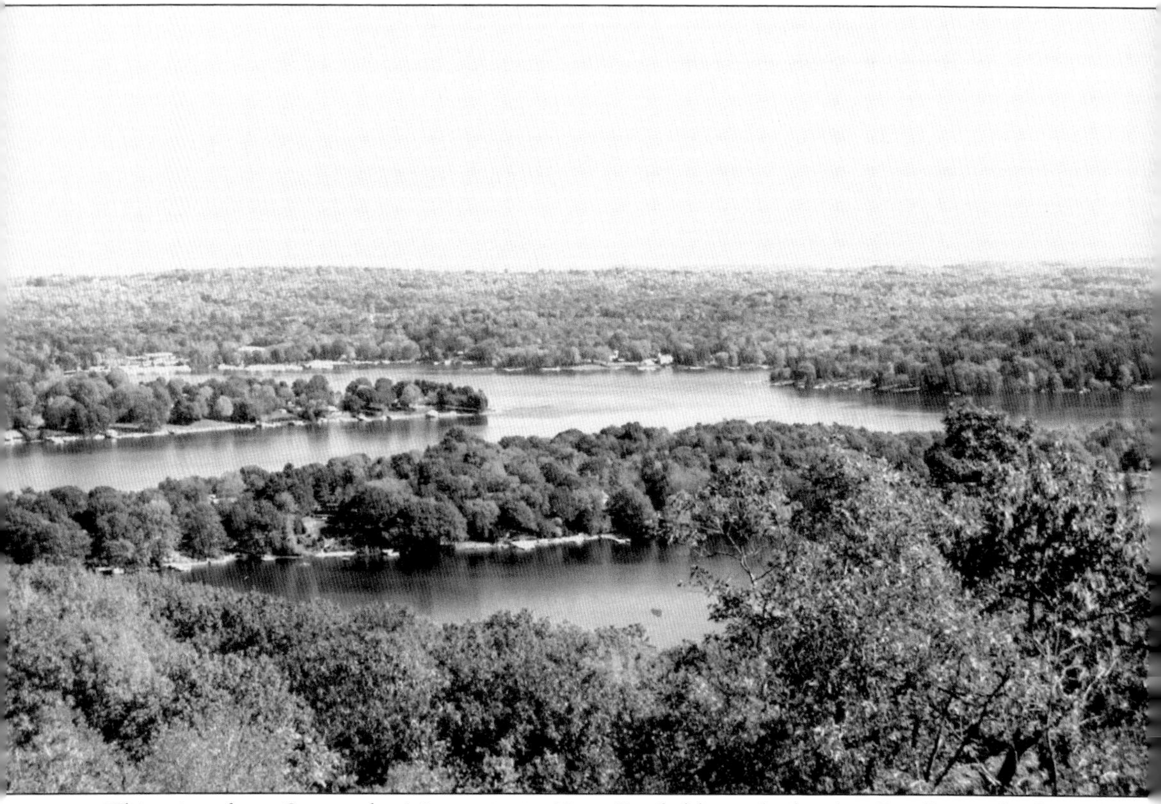

This view from Sweetcake Mountain in New Fairfield overlooks the Candlewood Isle and Candlewood Shores sections of the lake.

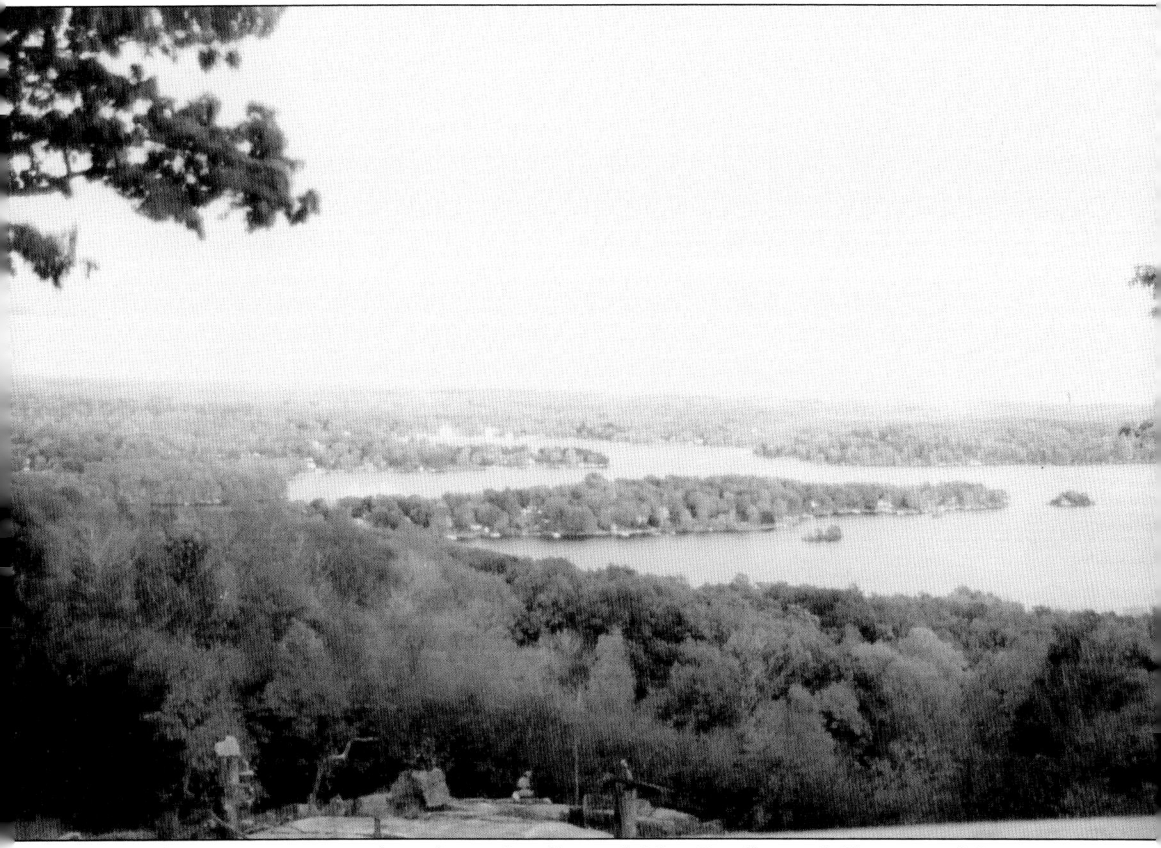

This is a late autumn view of southern Candlewood Isle, Candlewood Shores, and Pocono Point sections of the lake.

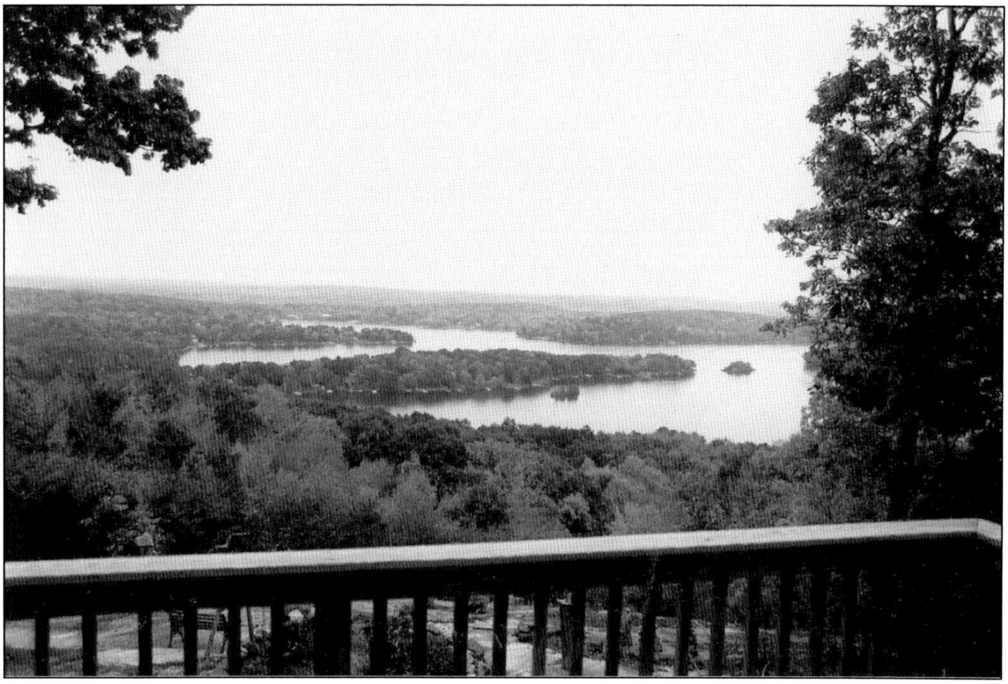

This is a another view from the Sweetcake Mountain section of the lake. This elevation is at 850 feet.

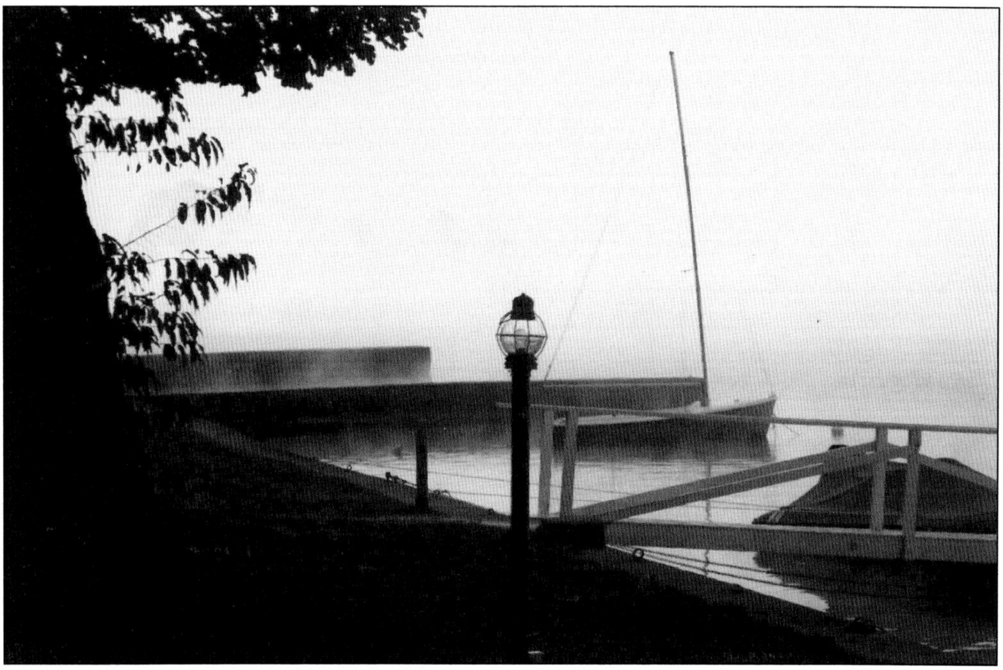

Vaughn's Neck is barely visible in the background of this photograph, taken on a foggy day on the docks of Candlewood Lake Club.

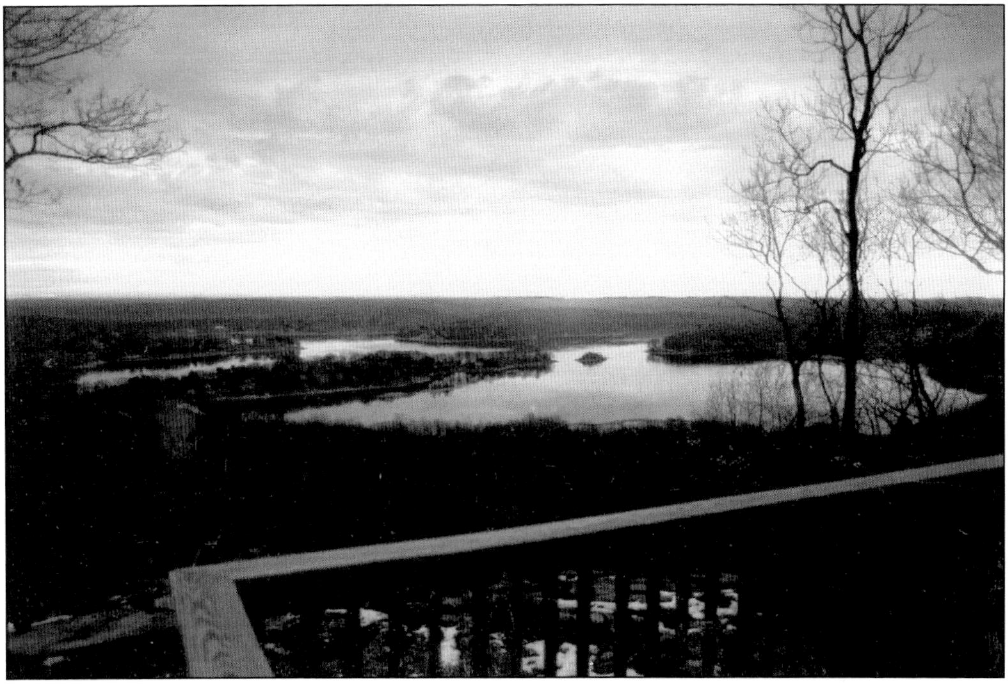

Candlewood Isle in New Fairfield is the scene of this winter view.

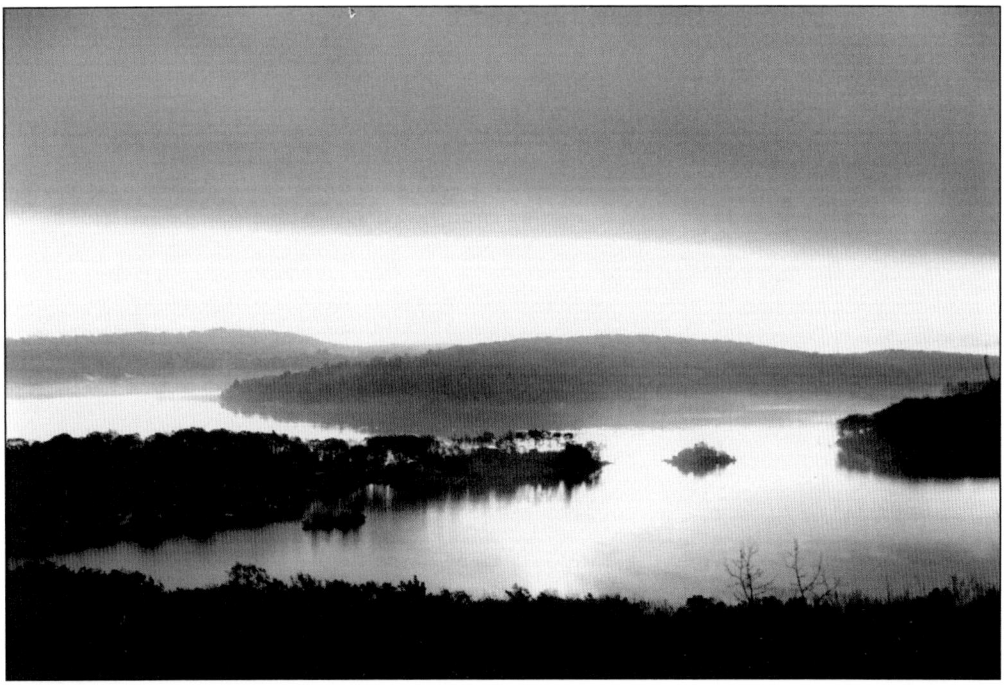

This photograph captures the view overlooking Candlewood Isle in New Fairfield, Driftwood Point, and Pocono Point in Danbury.

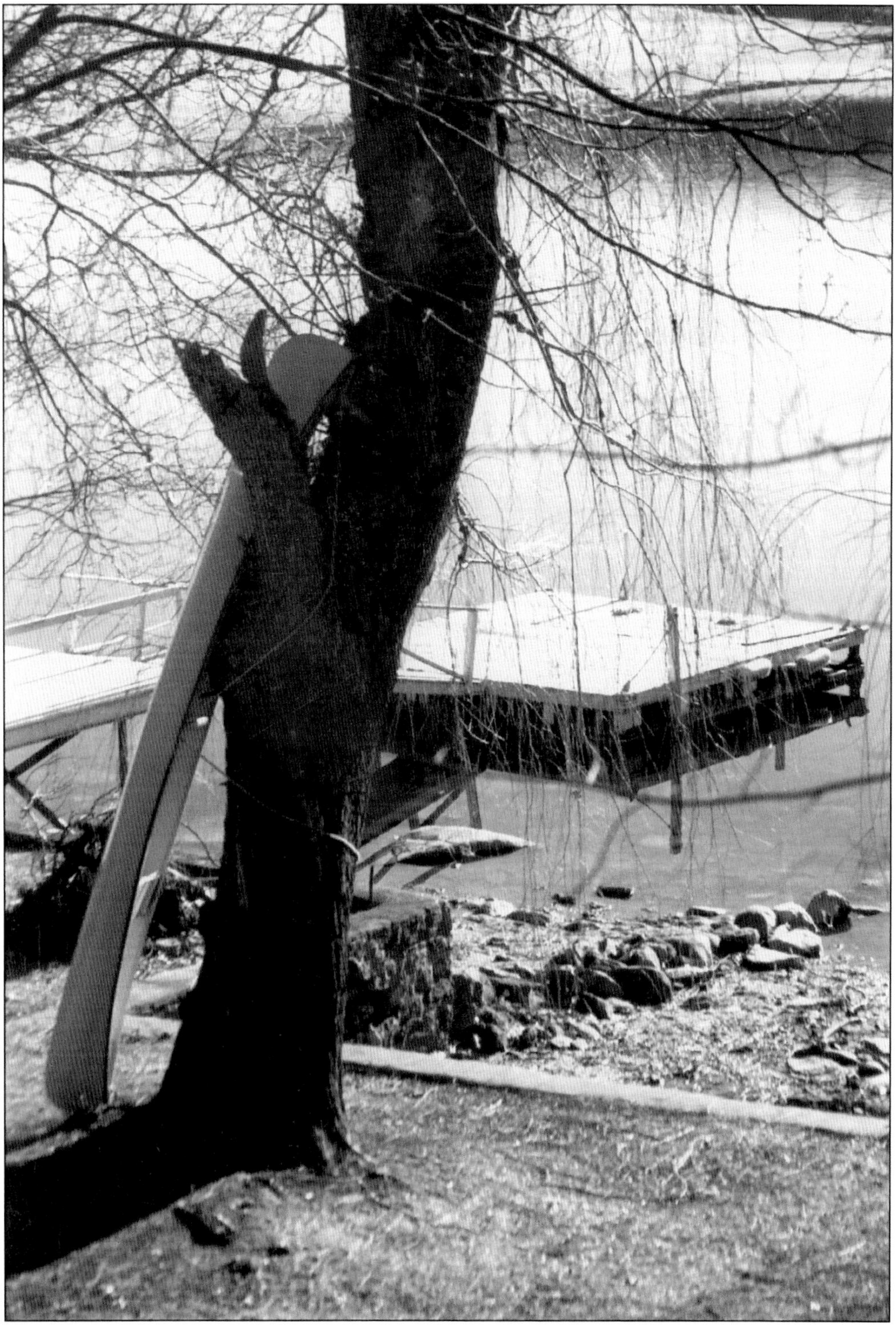

The Oak Point Club in New Milford is one of the many private communities found around Candlewood Lake.

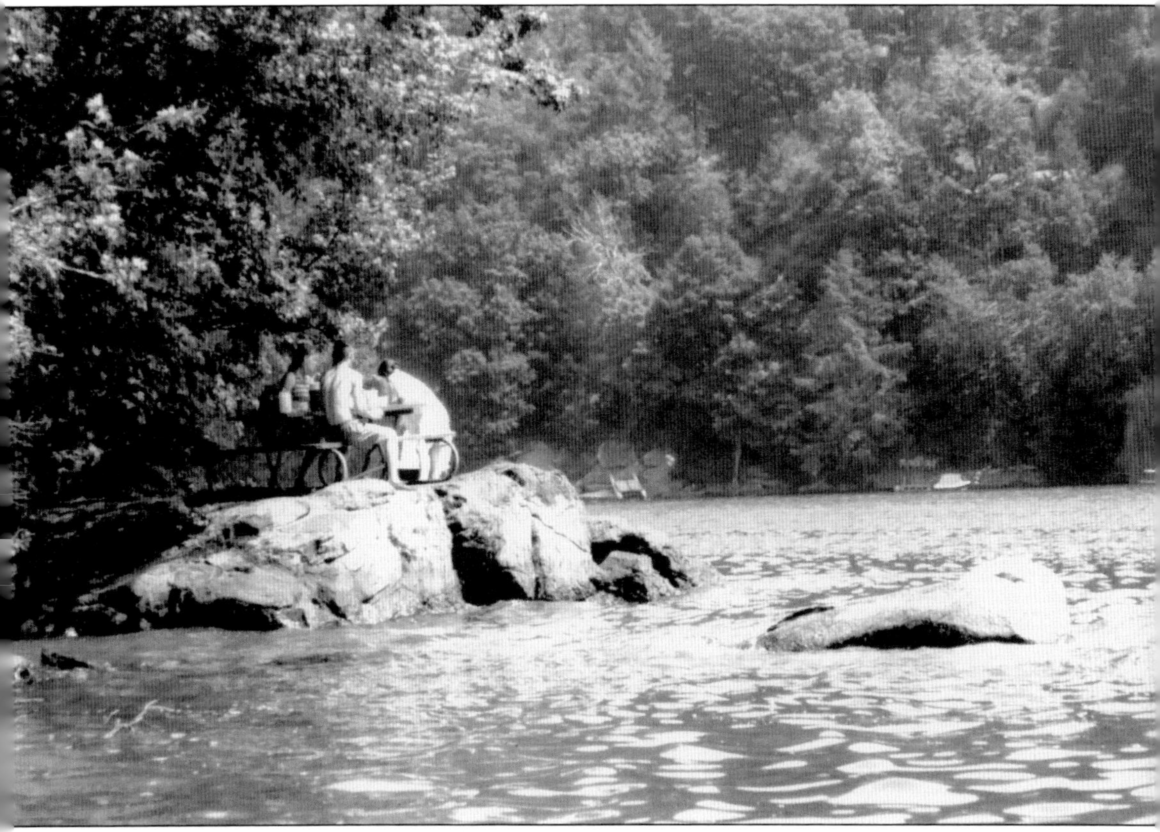

The lake provides many perfect spots for a picnic.

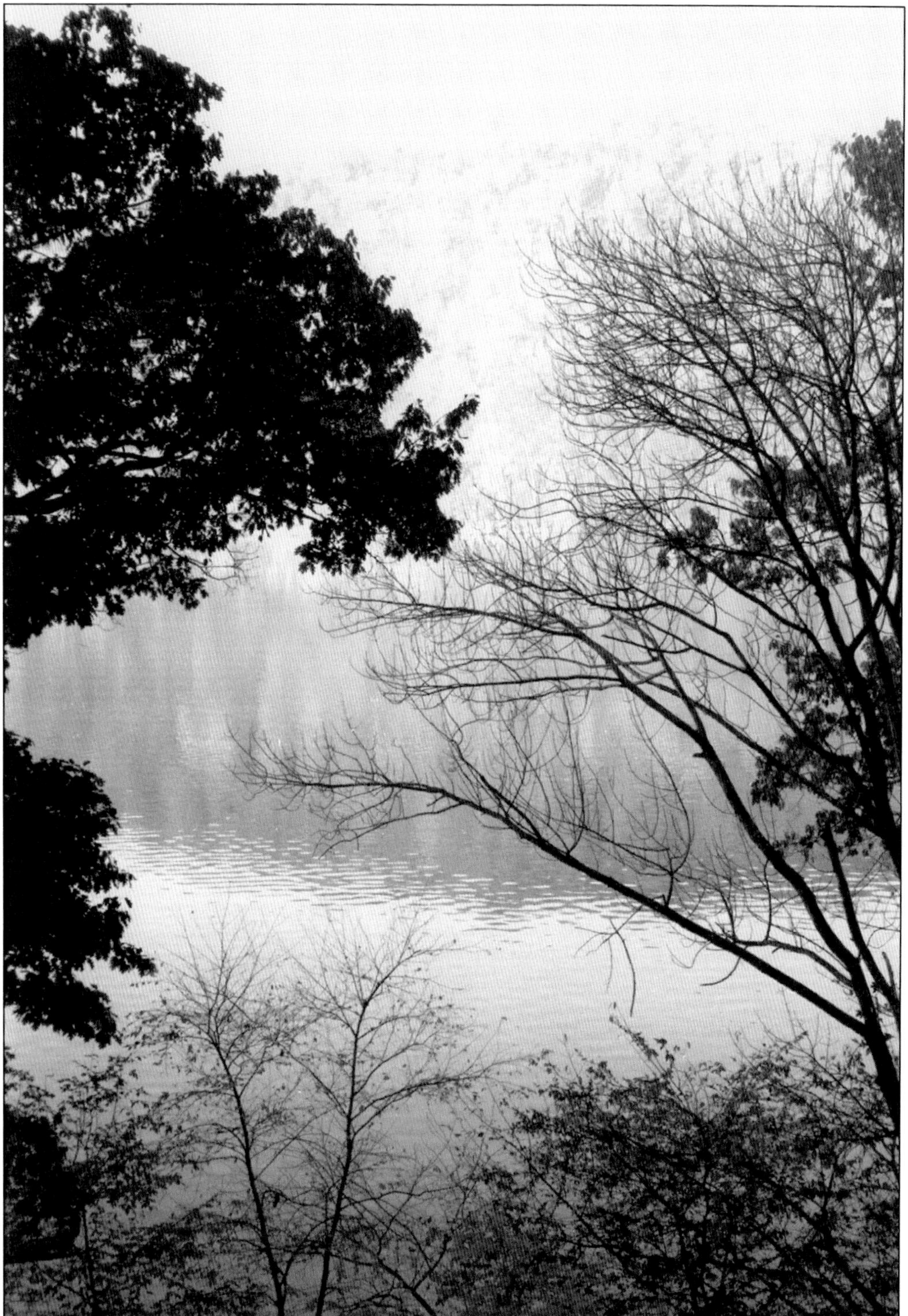

This view from the Pleasant Acres area of Candlewood Lake, located near the Danbury Town Park at the south end of the lake, looks west during an early fall day.

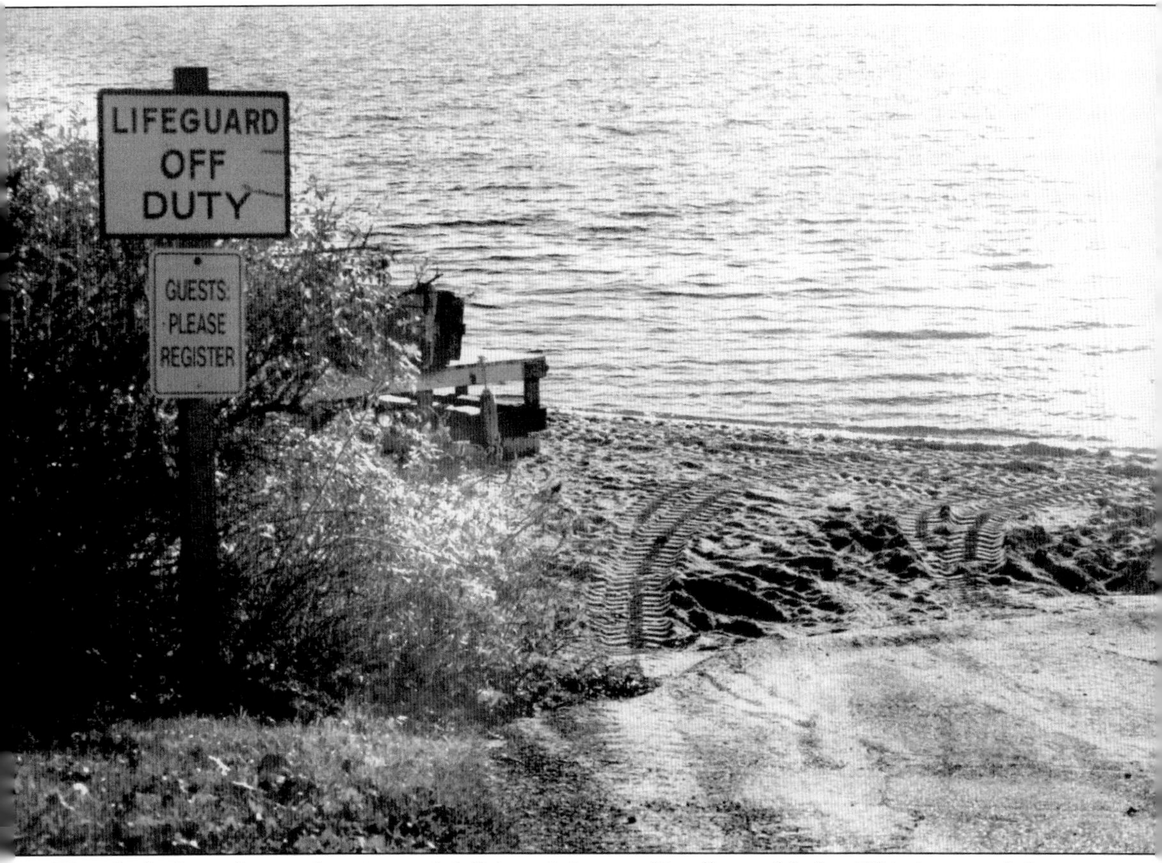

The docks have been taken in, and fall is arriving on Candlewood Lake. This is one of the many beaches around the lake. Since the building of the lake, many private communities have sprouted up around the perimeter of the lake. Where there were once only summer cottages, several of these communities now have year-round homes.

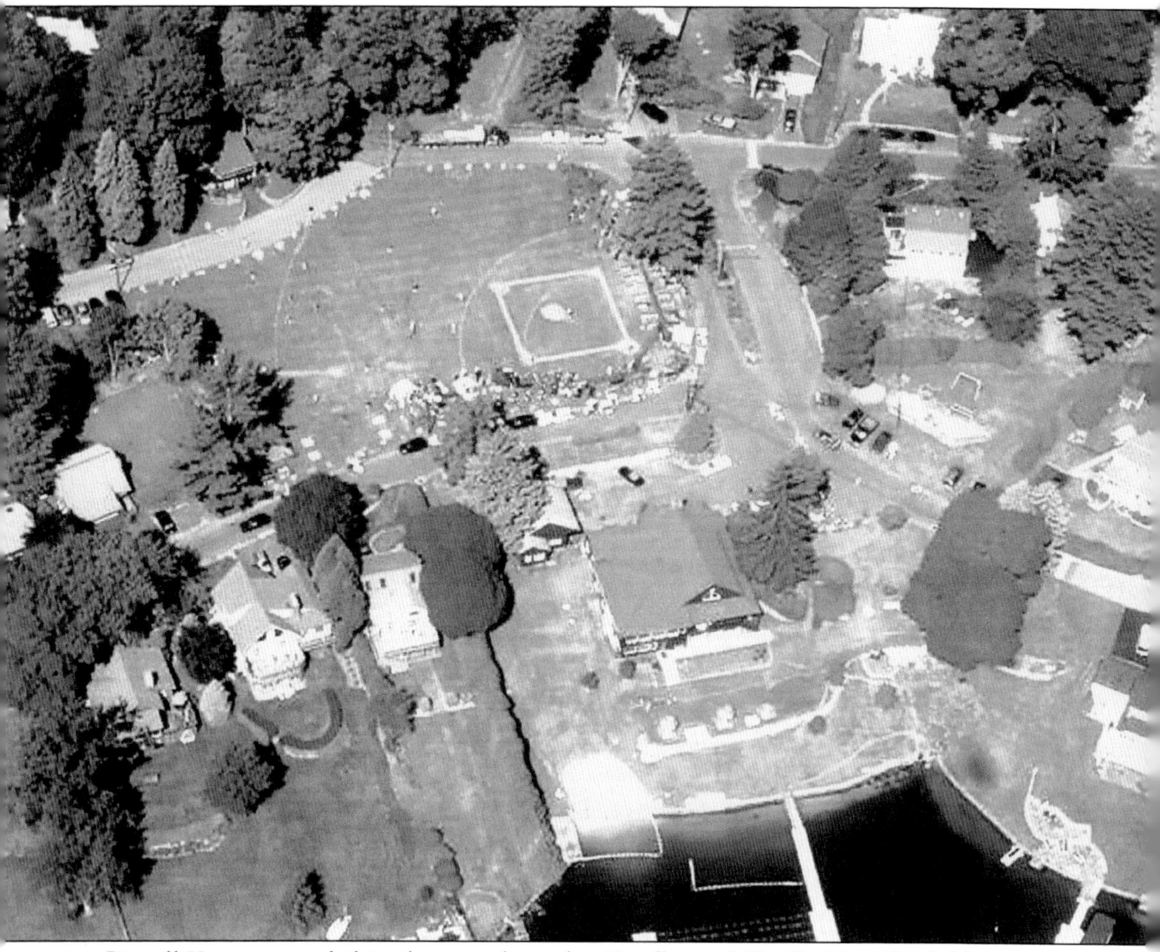

Russell Kaye snapped this photograph at the Candlewood Knolls-New Fairfield community picnic on July 17, 2004.

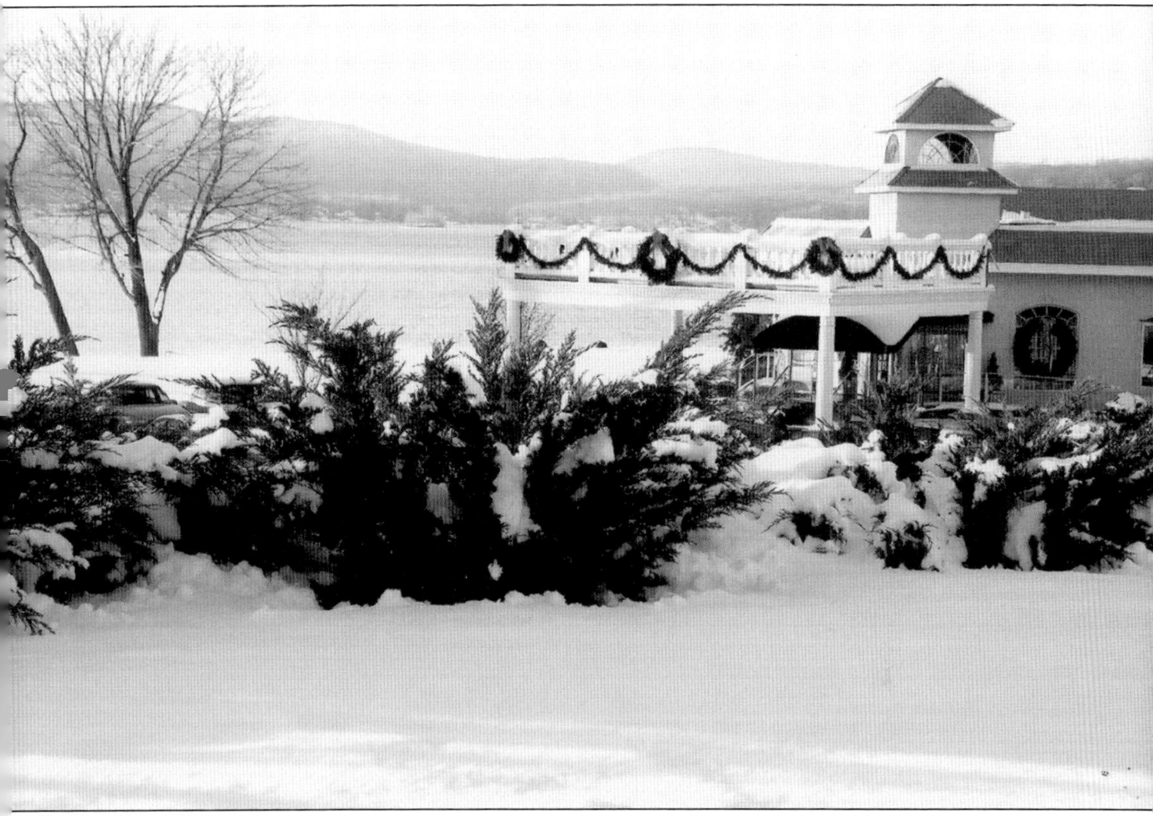

On a clear winter day one can look across the lake toward New Fairfield from the Candlewood Inn. This inn, which was built in the late 1950s as a motel and restaurant, has remained a popular entertainment spot on the lake.

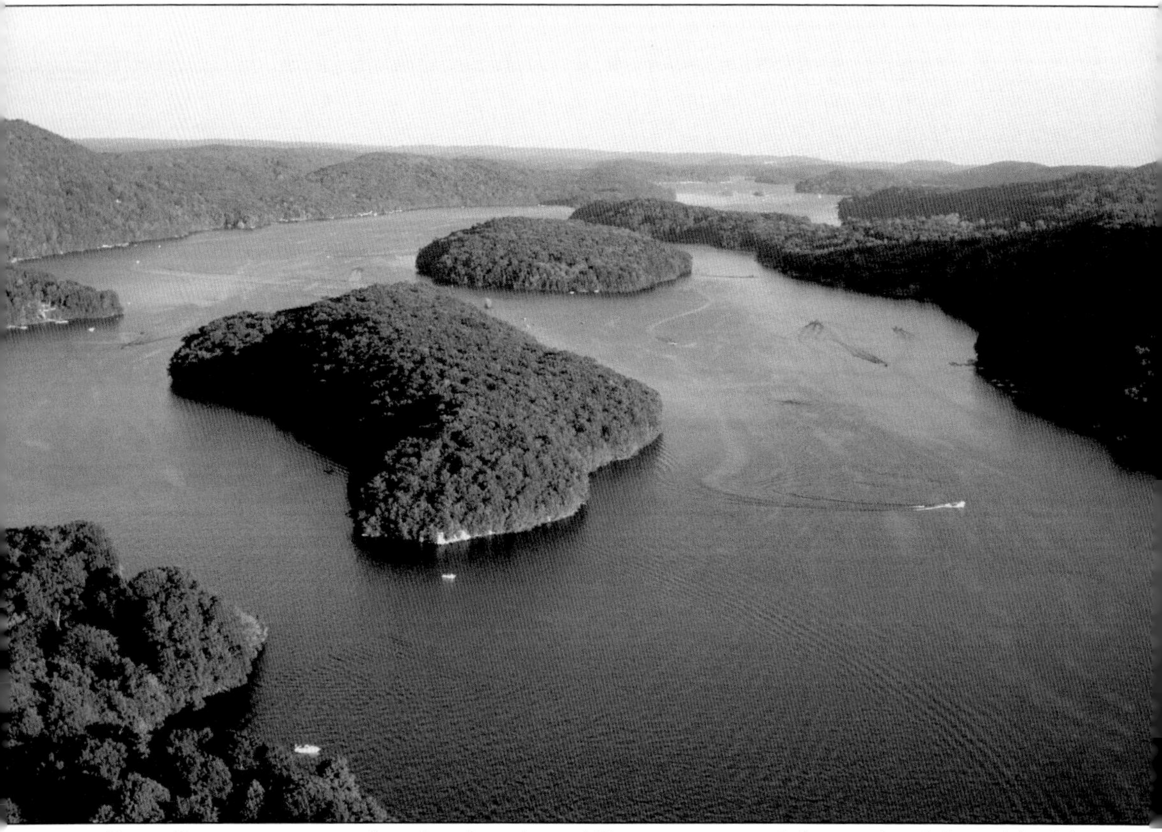

Bruce Byers, a summer and weekend resident of Sherman, captured this overhead shot of the lake.

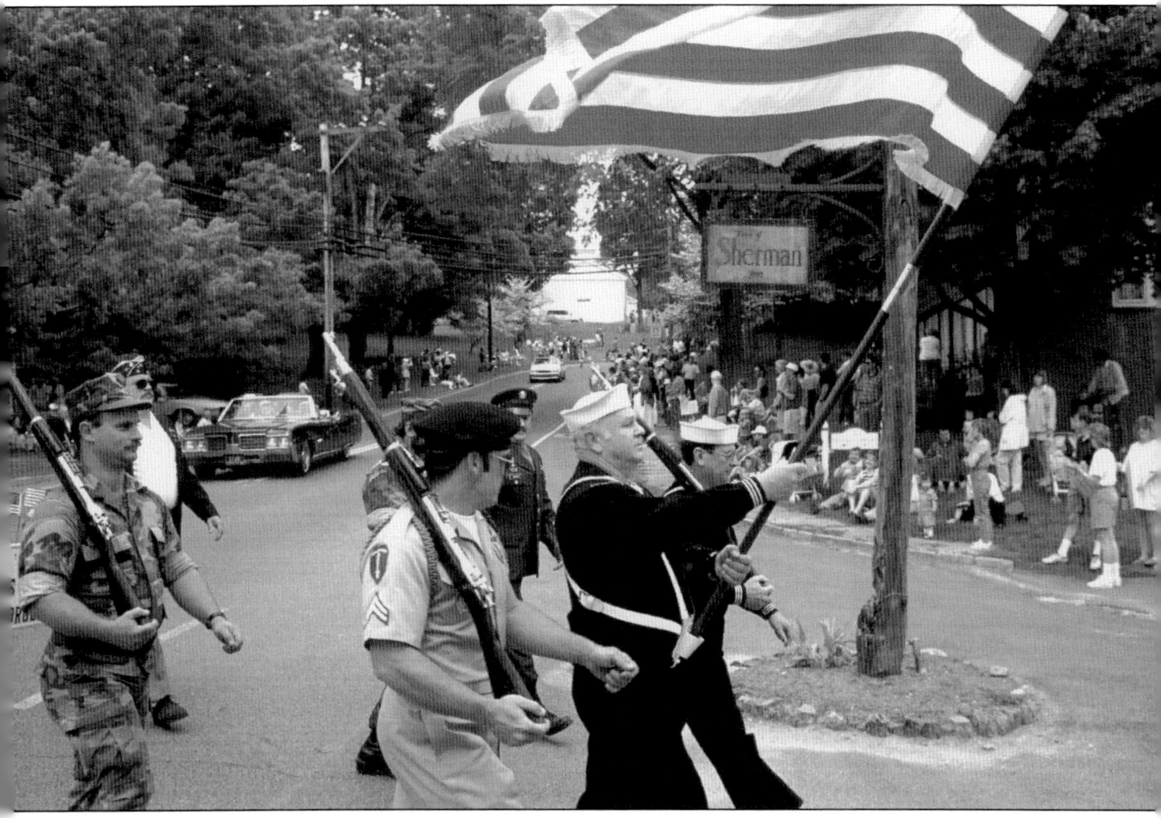

Military servicemen take part in the Sherman Memorial Day Parade in May 2004.

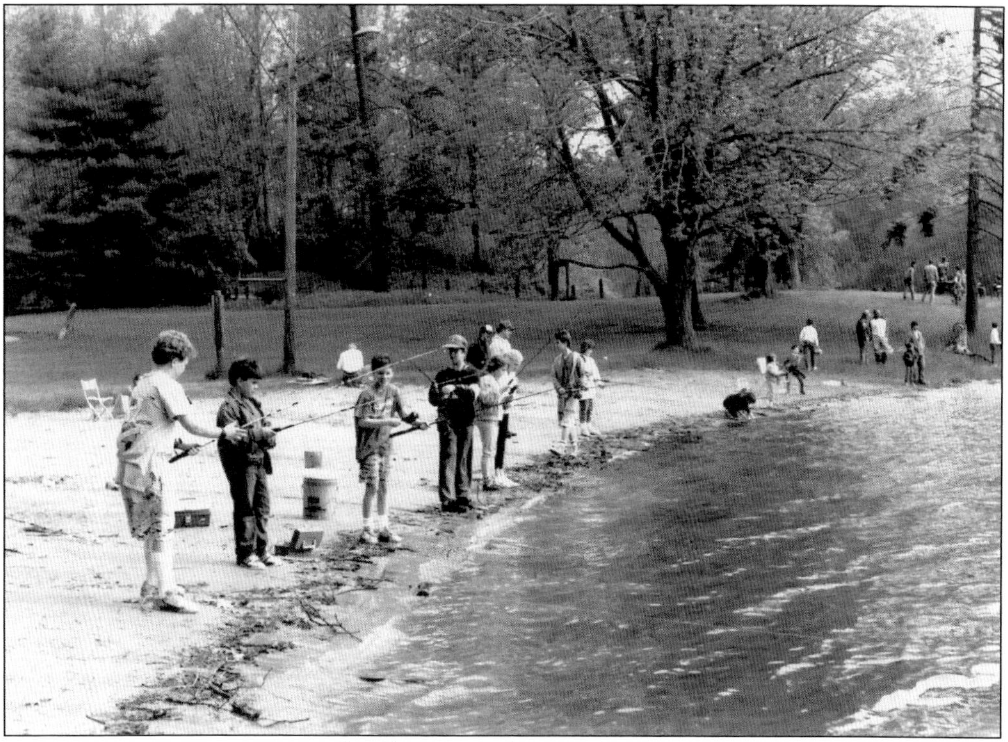

Here, youngsters participate in the Sherman Fishing Derby in May 1988.

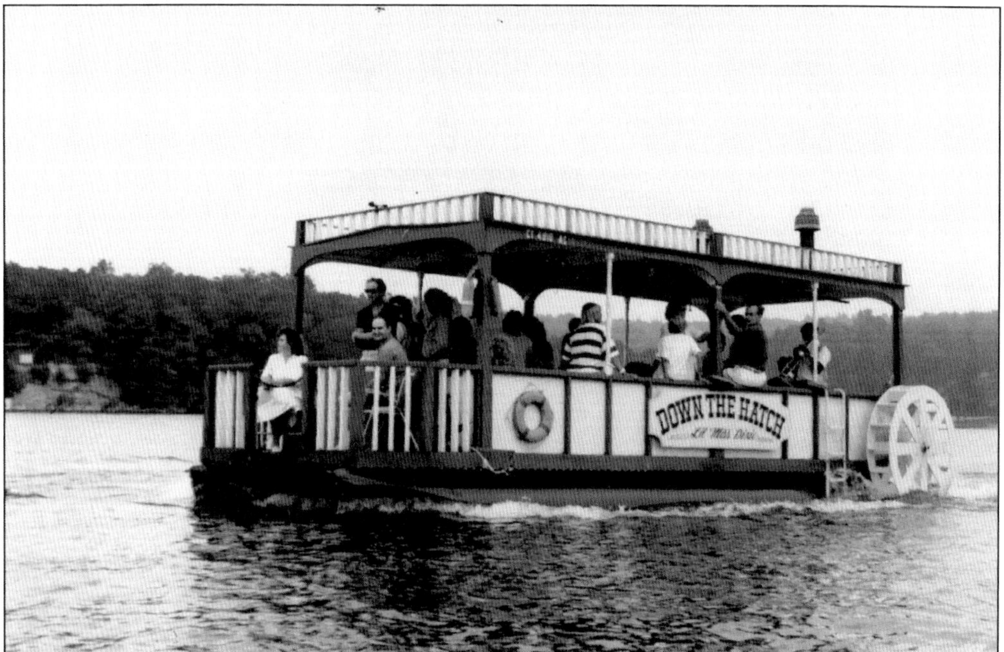

Dixieland jazz music entertained passengers aboard the old pontoon boat from Down the Hatch Restaurant as the boat cruised the lake a few years back. During the 1980s, this boat also took part in the boat parades that were held on the lake.

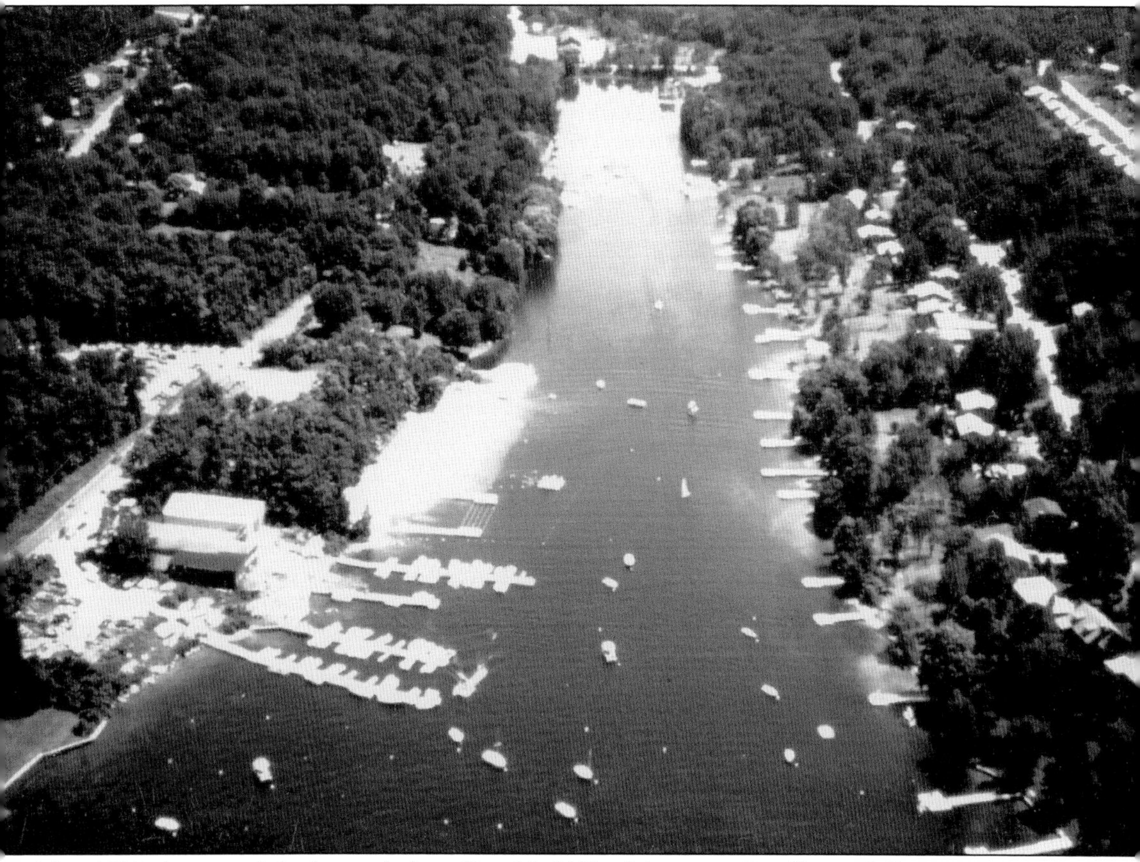

This 1988 photograph looks south from Brookfield Bay Marina to Candlewood Shores.

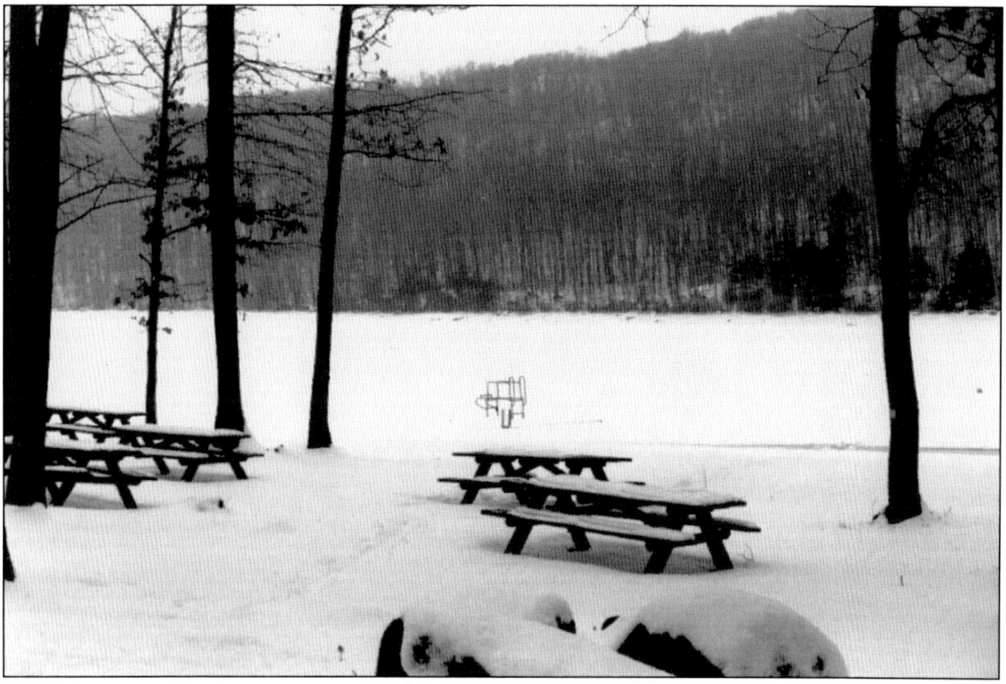

This is a tranquil winter scene on the lake.

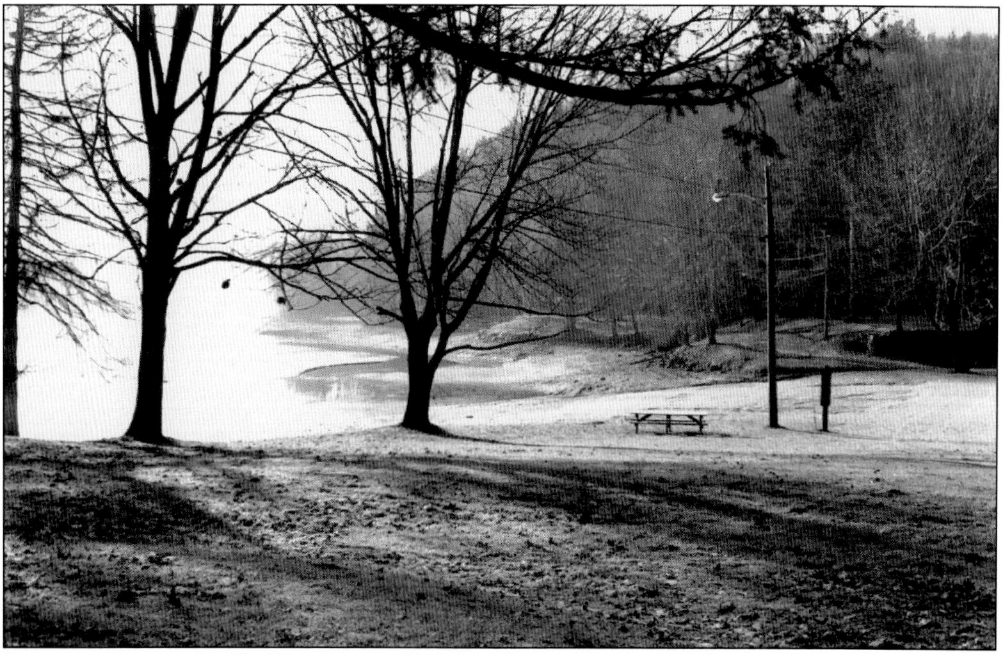

A non-native weed called Eurasian milfoil found its way into Candlewood Lake *c.* 1980, and it quickly became a major nuisance. In an effort to control the weed while not overly upsetting the lake environment, a protocol of alternating-depth winter drawdowns was embraced by the owning utility. This picture shows the drawdown at the Sherman Town Beach during the winter of 1984–1985.

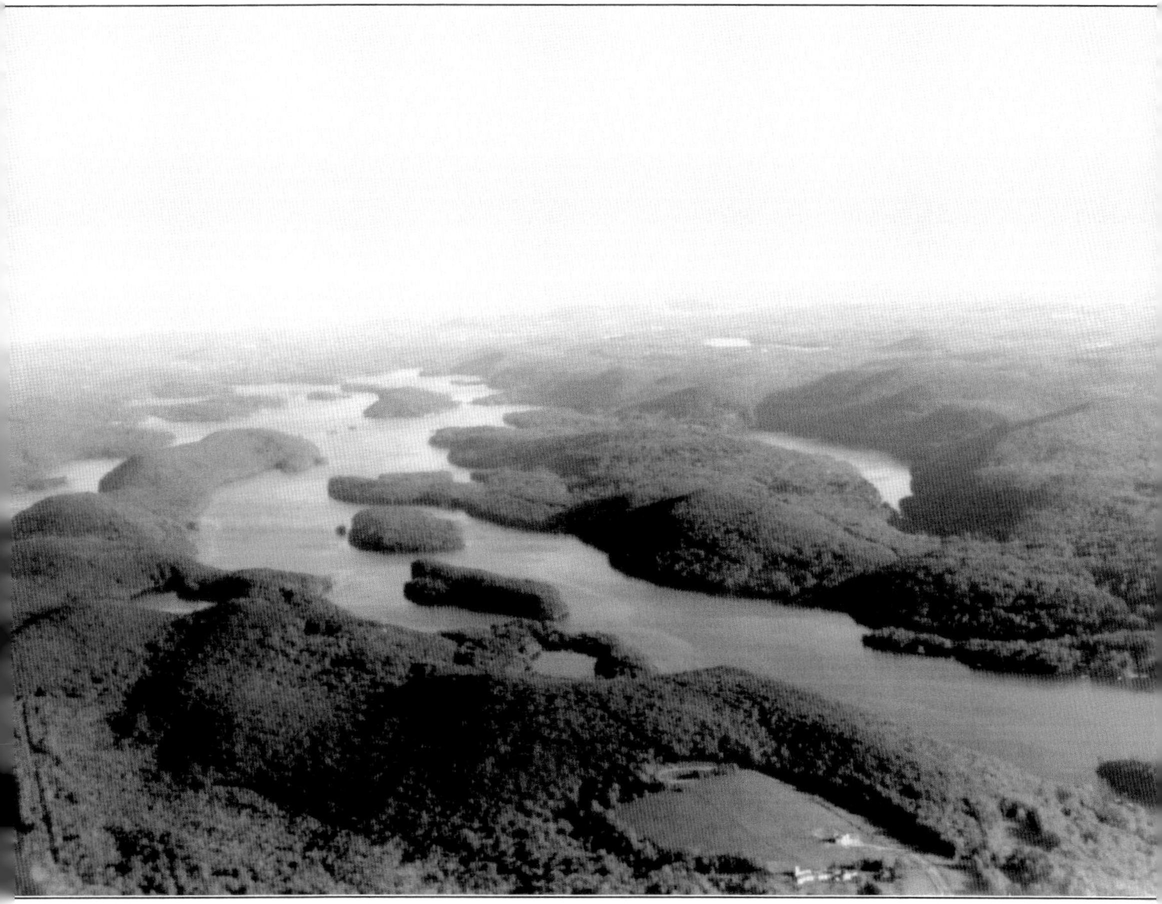

This view looks south from Sherman. Mill Pond is at the bottom center of the photograph and Squantz Pond is at the center right. Also seen are Vaughn's Neck and Candlewood Mountain, with the New Milford arm of the lake on the left.

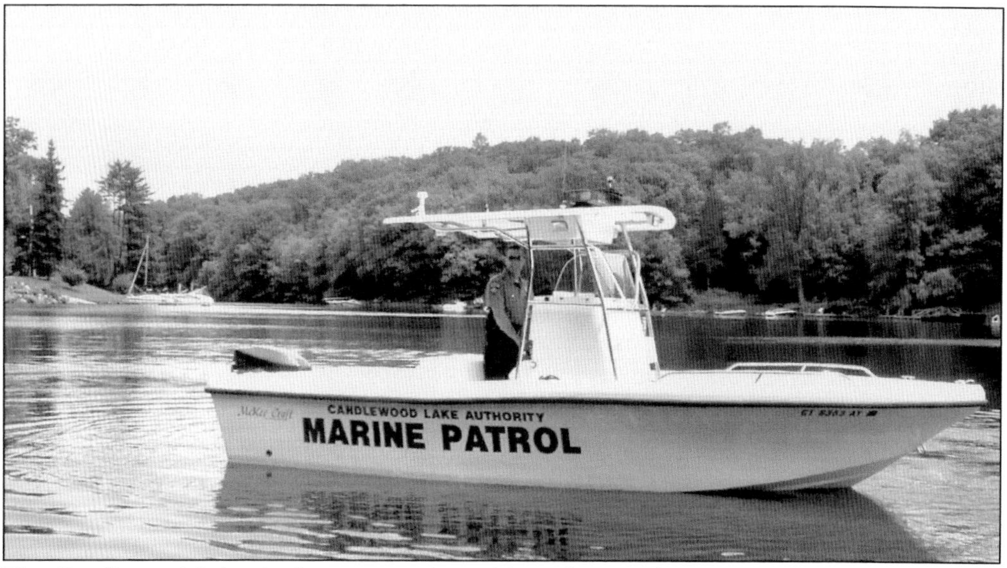

The Candlewood Lake Authority provides public safety on the water and protects the water quality of the lake. Here an officer patrols the lake.

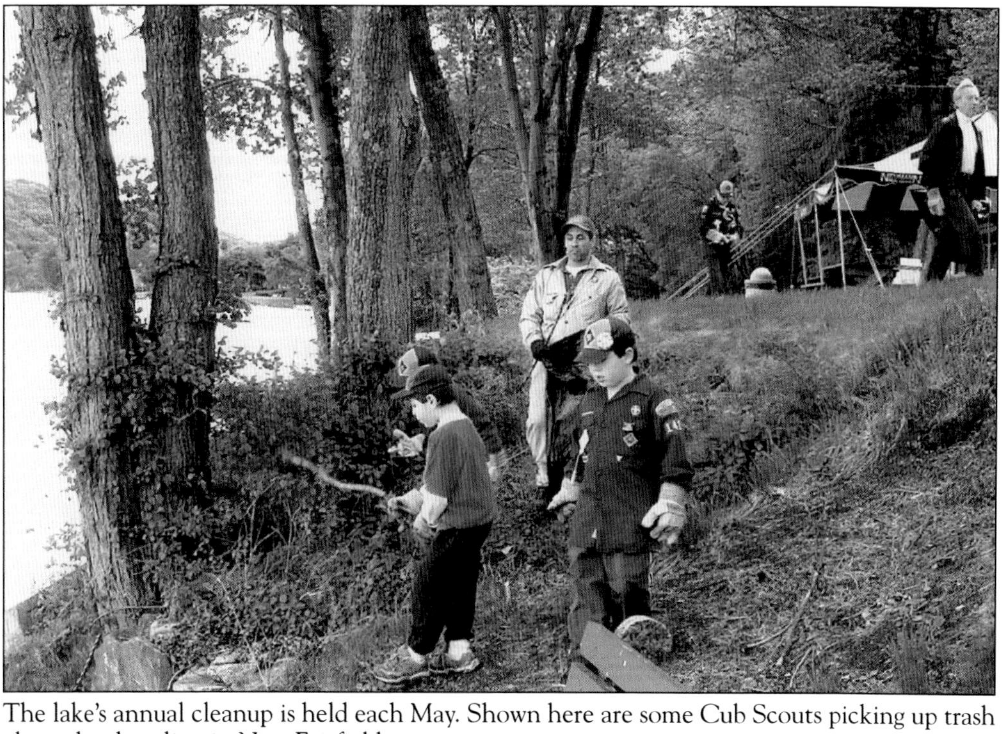
The lake's annual cleanup is held each May. Shown here are some Cub Scouts picking up trash along the shoreline in New Fairfield.

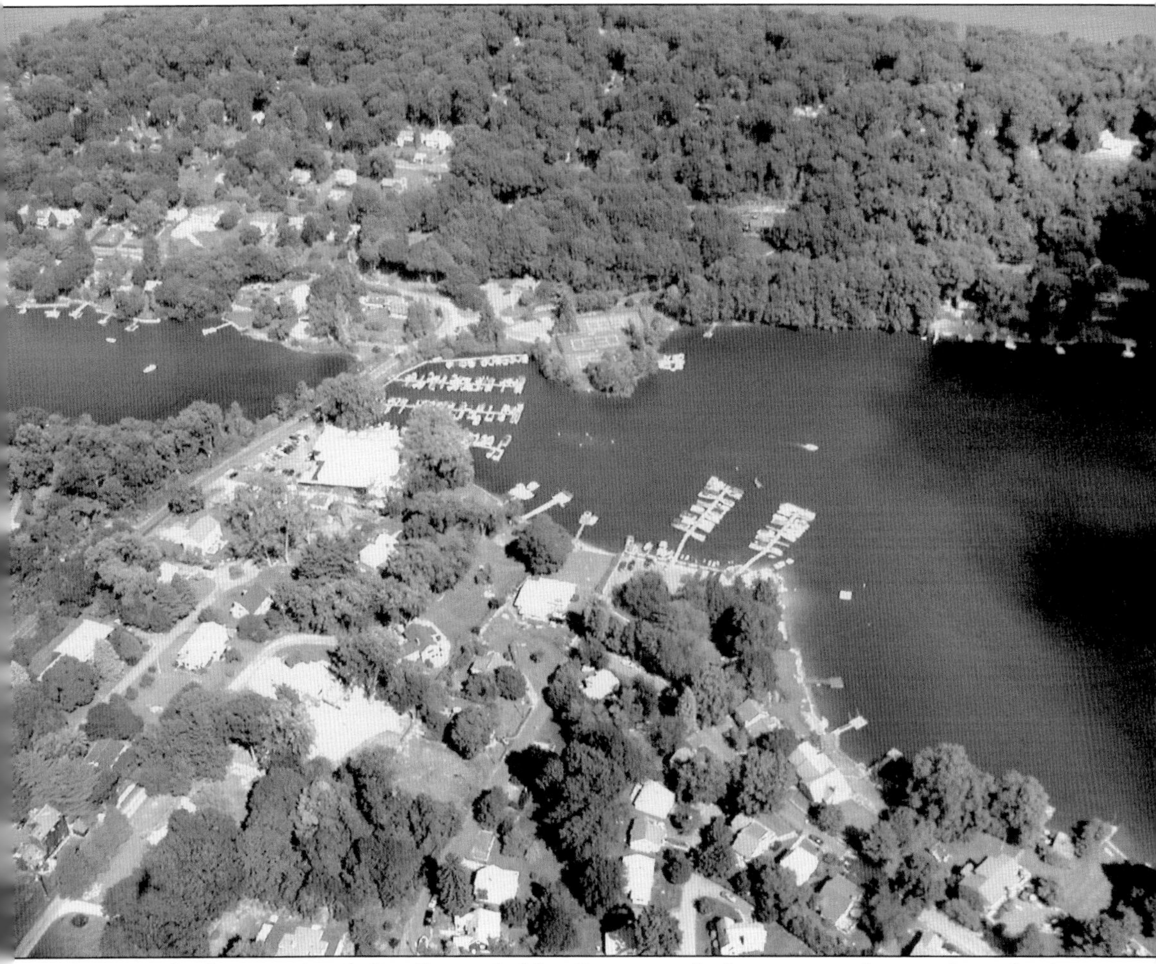

This aerial photograph of Candlewood Isle Causeway looks east at the north end of Candlewood Knolls.

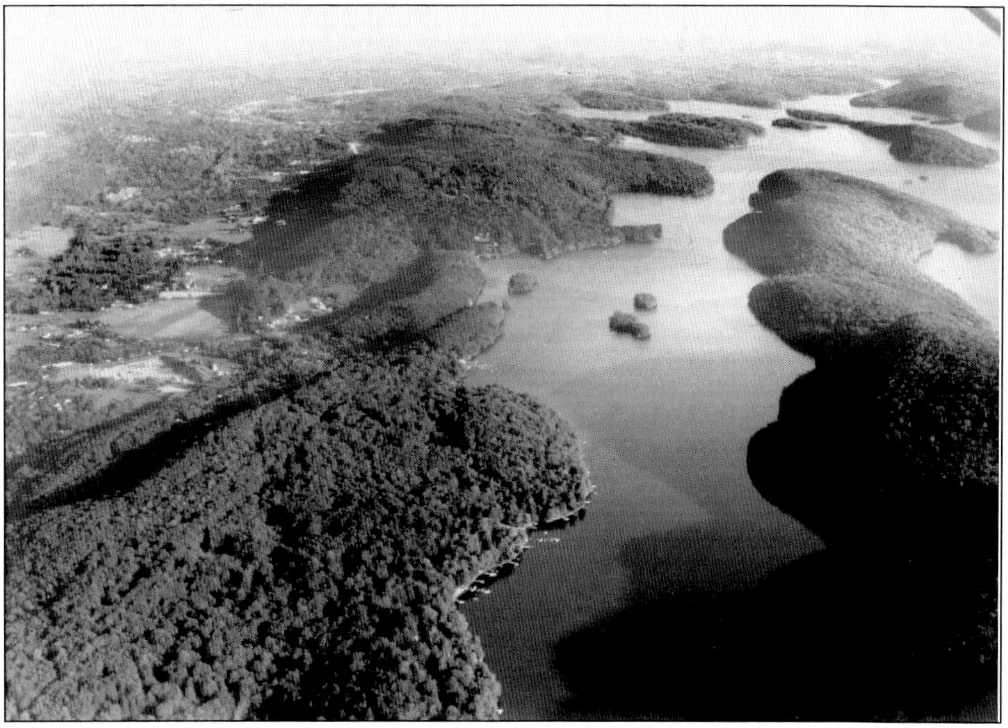

This overhead view shows the tip of Vaughn's Neck at the upper right of the photograph.

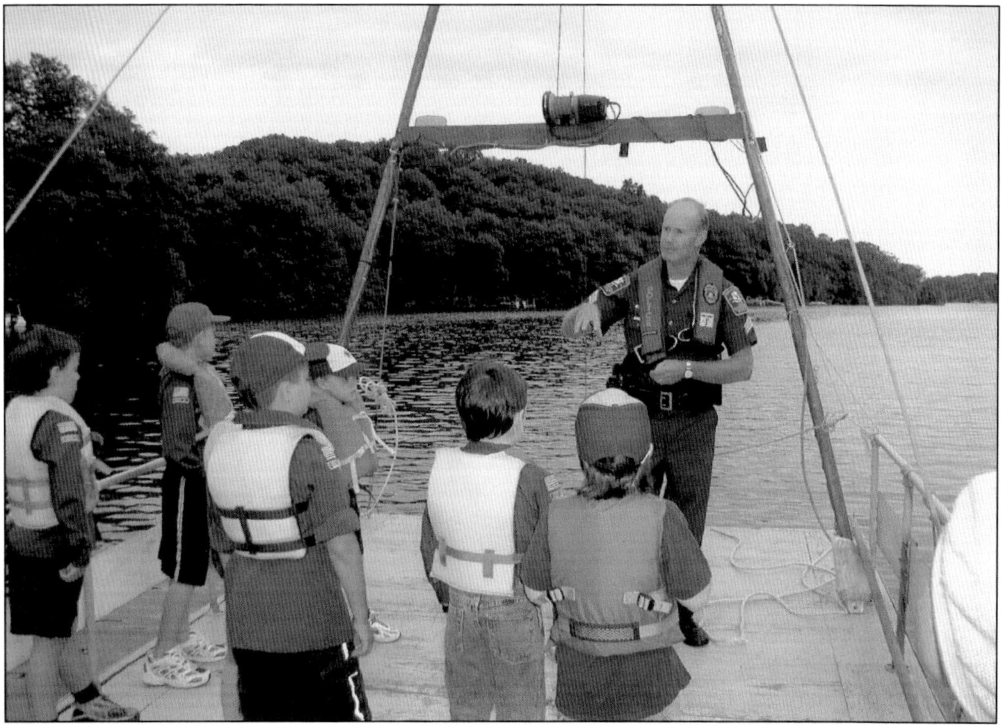

A Department of Environmental Protection officer educates Cub Scouts on boating and conservation issues around the lake.

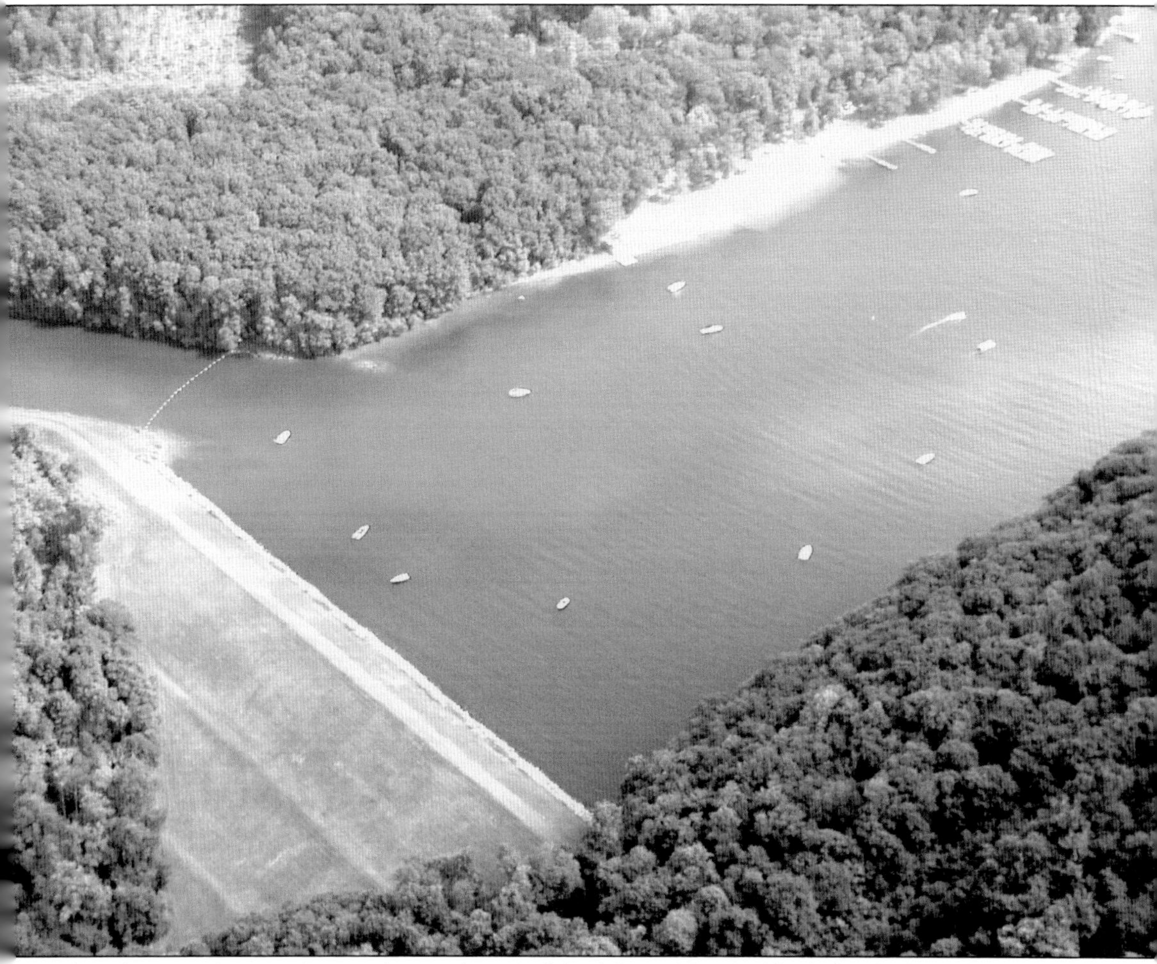

This photograph was taken at the north end of the lake in New Milford, overlooking the main dam. New Milford Town Beach can be seen at the top right of the image.

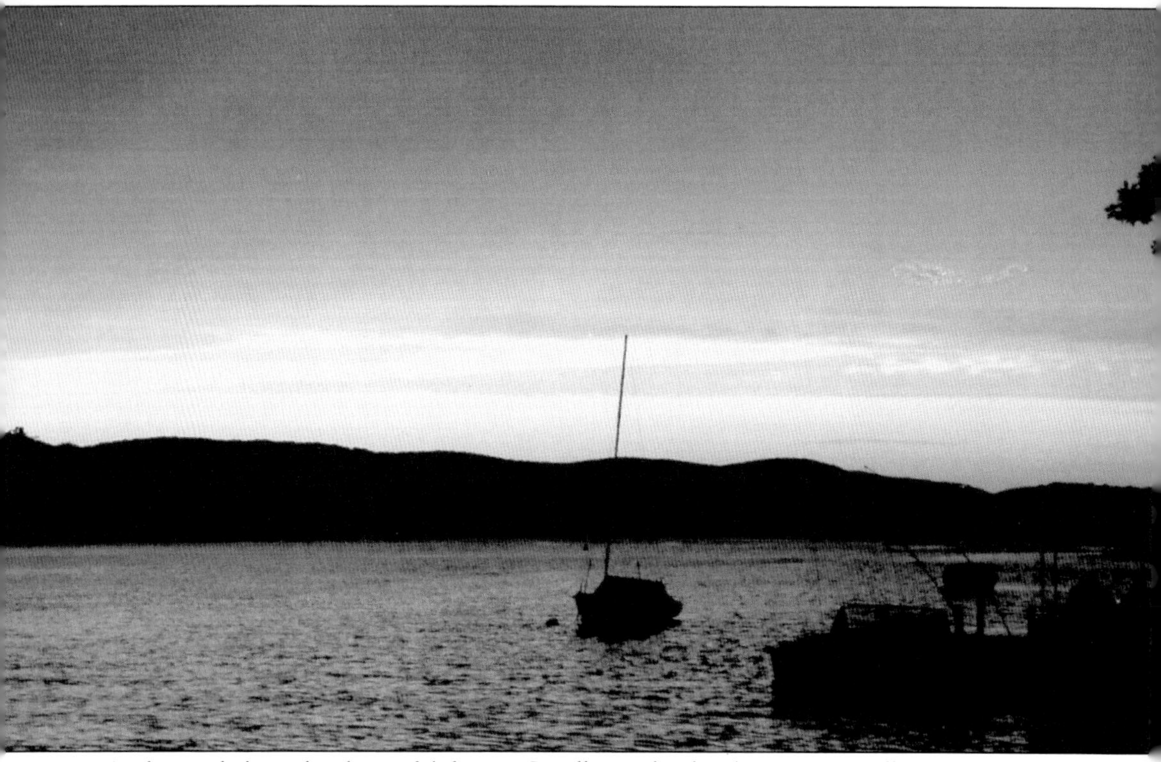

And so ended another beautiful day on Candlewood Lake. (Courtesy Bradley C. Fisher.)

About the Authors

Gary Smolen is presently a senior engineer with the Connecticut Hydro Group of Northeast Utilities in New Milford, Connecticut, and he has worked at NU for the past 24 years. He has a bachelor's degree in civil engineering from Worcester Polytechnic Institute, as well as a bachelor's degree in plant and soil science from the University of Massachusetts. In addition to various engineering assignments, he oversees the technical environmental challenges of the hydro plants, coordinates training, and oversees the recreation programs that complement the hydroelectric facilities. As an advocate of the multiple benefits of the renewable hydroelectric industry, he is also active in public-speaking engagements, plant tours, and media inquiries.

As a resident of Sherman, Connecticut, Gary can often be seen swimming in Candlewood Lake with his golden retriever, and he has participated in a cross–Candlewood Lake charity fund-raiser, swimming from the Sherman Town Beach to the Danbury Town Beach.

Susan Murphy is presently the executive director of the Greater New Milford Chamber of Commerce. She is a graduate of Iona College with a degree in business. Noted for her abundant community involvement, she volunteers and sits on the board of directors for numerous local organizations and charities. Of note for this book, one of her duties is to serve as the Brookfield delegate to the Candlewood Lake Authority, which oversees the water quality and safety of the lake. She is also on the board of directors of the Brookfield Historical Society and Museum. With her Navy family she has moved a total of 14 times around the country and abroad, and she finally moved to, and embraced, Candlewood Lake permanently in 1992. The Murphy family has been associated with Candlewood Lake since 1954.